'Brilliant, bold and beautifully written, Fe̶̶̶ infuriate – and inspire. Mary Harrington ̶̶ feminist vision for living together as the human beings we actually are.'

ERIKA BACHIOCHI, author of
The Rights of Women: Reclaiming a Lost Vision

'Mary Harrington has written a learned, witty, sometimes terrifying, but always hope-giving book. Recognising that modernity's "progress theology" has blinded us to the undeniable costs of an individualistic feminism and its relentless marriage to a dehumanising market, she calls for a new birth of care – between women and men, mothers and children, and humans to their humanity.'

PATRICK J. DENEEN, author of *Why Liberalism Failed*

'What a dazzling, radical, hope-filled book! With *Feminism Against Progress*, Mary Harrington launches herself to the front rank of public intellectuals of her generation. She takes us a great leap beyond the tired categories of liberal-vs-conservative, and gives us a powerful vision of social relations based on her lived experience, the gift of motherhood, and the truth that no man – and no woman – is an island. Part Julie Bindel, part Wendell Berry, the brave Mary Harrington is a true original, and the realistic, compassionate voice we have been waiting for.'

ROD DREHER, author of
Live Not by Lies and *The Benedict Option*

'Mary Harrington is one of the most courageous and compelling voices of our times. Never afraid to challenge orthodoxy; she is always thoughtful and thought-provoking. Those reading her had better be prepared to be shifted from their ideological comfort zone.'

PAUL EMBERY, author of *Despised:
Why the Modern Left Loathes the Working Class*

'Mary Harrington understands that human life is embodied and relational. She analyses the alliance between big tech, capitalism and progressive politics that is now dominant. It is essential reading for the left in particular, who are often unwittingly complicit in this cartel.'

LORD MAURICE GLASMAN, author of *Blue Labour:
The Politics of the Common Good*

'Mary Harrington is a brilliantly original thinker and a wonderfully engaging writer. Her handling of some of the most hotly contested debates of our time will, inevitably, spark controversy. But no one engaged with these questions can afford to ignore her penetrating insights and intellectual courage.'

MICHAEL GOVE, Secretary of State for
Levelling Up, Housing and Communities

'Original, fearless and profound, this beautifully written book will change the way you think about feminism, progress and, ultimately, what it means to be human: embodied, sexed and endowed by evolution with needs and desires that are an ever worse fit in an increasingly marketised world.'

HELEN JOYCE, author of
Trans: When Ideology Meets Reality

'Mary Harrington takes a flamethrower to our most cherished contemporary myths and it just might save our lives.'

ALEX KASCHUTA, host of the *Subversive* podcast

'A brilliant and necessary book by one of Britain's most important writers and thinkers. Every page offers a new way of seeing an old problem, or an introduction to a new one you might only have been dimly aware of. Any woman – or man – who is trying to negotiate the business of being human in the rising cyborg era needs to read it, and think hard about how to act on its arguments.'

PAUL KINGSNORTH, writer

'Sharp, funny, and occasionally shocking, reading *Feminism Against Progress* is like downing a packet of Tangfastics after a lifetime of gruel. Mary Harrington is a truly visionary thinker.'

LOUISE PERRY, author of
The Case Against the Sexual Revolution

'This is a bracingly provocative read from one of progressive feminism's most ingenious critics. You'll read nothing else quite like it.'

KATHLEEN STOCK, author of *Material Girls:
Why Reality Matters for Feminism*

Feminism Against Progress

MARY HARRINGTON

Regnery Publishing
WASHINGTON, D.C.

ISBN: 978-1-68451-526-4
eISBN: 978-1-68451-496-0

Published in the United States by
Regnery Publishing
A Division of Salem Media Group
Washington, D.C.
www.Regnery.com

Manufactured in the United States of America

10 9 8 7 6 5 4 3 2 1

Books are available in quantity for promotional or premium use. For information on discounts and terms, please visit our website: www.Regnery.com.

Contents

PART ONE: MEMES + MATERIAL CONDITIONS   1

1. Against Progress   3
2. Feminism, Aborted   24
3. Sex and the Market   52

PART TWO: CYBORG THEOCRACY   73

4. War on Relationships   81
5. The Devouring Mother   104
6. Meat Lego Gnosticism   133

Interlude: Detransition   163

PART THREE: REACTIONARY FEMINISM   175

7. Abolish Big Romance   177
8. Let Men Be   190
9. Rewilding Sex   207

Afterword: Ghost Books   217
Notes   225

PART ONE

Memes + Material Conditions

1

Against Progress

The arc of the moral universe is long, but it bends toward justice.

Martin Luther King

Losing my faith

WHAT STARTED ME DOWN the path towards writing this book was feeling like I wasn't a separate person from my baby.

Before I had a child, I had no idea how I'd feel once she was there, though I had a dim sense that pregnancy and birth usually does *something* far-reaching to the emotional landscapes of women who experience it. Even so, the starkness of the contrast between how I'd experienced the world previously, and how I experienced it once my daughter was in my life, still took me by surprise.

It first shocked me physically. Her birth was not straight-forward, we both nearly died, and I was bed-bound for a while afterwards. It shocked me emotionally as well. The hormonal aftermath of birth is well known for being an emotional time, but hearing that from someone else is different to riding the roller-coaster yourself. My midsection was held together with staples, while a tiny human I'd carried in my guts for months was now on the outside but still dependent on me for every need. It was, as they say, a lot.

But the story really begins at a point about ten years prior to becoming a mother: the moment I lost my faith.

I was raised to believe in Progress Theology – the more-or-less religious framework that governs much of modern culture in the West. This theology says there's a 'right side of history', and things can go on getting better forever. But one day, about 15 years ago, I realised I no longer believed.

What happened?

I was born the year Margaret Thatcher came to power, and politics turned against the postwar social-democratic consensus. My first political memory is the fall of the Berlin Wall. The reverberations of this event, which was fairly swiftly followed by *glasnost* and *perestroika*, marked the decade of my teens profoundly.

For an average middle-class girl, in 1990s Home Counties Britain, all the big battles seemed to have been won, and all the great disagreements of history settled. Progress Theology makes most sense seen against this backdrop, or one very like it, where relative material comfort and safety can be taken absolutely for granted. That then frees up time and mental energy for more rarefied topics such as identity and sexuality. My route into such reflections was via Simone de Beauvoir's *The Second Sex*, which I read in my early teens. Around the same point, I started to notice certain asymmetries in family life. Every day, for example, my mum would cook dinner and set the table, and after we'd all eaten my dad would get up and leave. It seemed to me a clear statement of status: 'I'm exempt from these petty chores.'

After a while, my two brothers began to follow his example, leaving my mum to clear the table again. This seemed unfair, to say the least. But it also left me with a dilemma. I felt a clear solidarity with my mum, the household's other female. But I also believed myself and my brothers to have equal status in the family. Should I then assert this equal status by declaring myself exempt from these petty chores, like they did? And if I did, what did that say about how we all saw my mum? In turn, as another female, what did this imply for me when I reached adulthood? That dilemma founded my lifelong interest in feminism.

I had reasons for optimism, though, as well as anger. For if feminism is a body of political theory dedicated to wrestling with just such thorny-yet-intimate questions of power, social order and the proper relations between the sexes, it was also widely treated as a central plank of the progressive story. How could I not believe its capacity to bring about positive change? After all, over the period between my grandmother's birth in 1914, and my own in 1979, women's lives changed immeasurably. And it was easy enough to connect that to the larger story of human progress and the fall of the Soviet Union: a fresh reminder that freedom and progress were marching ever on.

The evidence for progress was all around me, for all that my own home life suggested the balance was still not equal between men and women. But, as the D:Ream song declared in New Labour's 1997 party political broadcast, 'Things Can Only Get Better'.[1] Surely things could change – not just out there in the political world, but also in the intimate one of sexed roles in families. Ever greater freedom and equality was our destiny, if only we put our minds to it.

Meeting critical and queer theory as an English Literature undergraduate both confirmed and also radically scrambled my End of History faith in progress. I left school having received a fairly classical education, with a sense that societies and cultures evolve over time, but in a clear forward direction that we can grasp objectively. But at university, I met the postmodern insight that language itself helps to shape meaning – and, worse, that every 'sign' can only be defined in relation to other signs.

In other words, we have no way of experiencing truth directly or objectively. School told me I was learning about a stable realm of canonical human culture, built up over the ages. Now this new body of thought used language itself to attack the very foundations of that worldview. What had appeared, at school, to be a reliable framework for making sense of the world, was re-imagined by critical theory as an infrastructure of contingent memes, which is to say ideas aggregated over time. These, I was now told, serve to entrench covert hierarchies of class, sex, race and so on. How all this was meant to relate to the material world, the pressures of survival or the demands of physical life, was less clear. But these were generally treated as also shaped (if not wholly constructed) by the operations of power through memes.

This is all wildly over-simplified, but it's a fair summary of my takeaway from a whistle-stop introduction to critical theory as a young adult. And the mental shift from seeing the world in terms of stable meanings, to seeing it in terms of power, sent me (to say the least) a bit loopy. Overnight, the hallowed buildings of Oxford University stopped looking like an expression of ancient traditions within which I could find my place. Suddenly they were hostile incursions into my consciousness by something phallic, domineering and authoritarian. I remember describing to a friend how I experienced the 'dreaming spires' as 'barbed penises straining to fuck the sky'.

I wish I could say this paranoid state passed swiftly, but it didn't. After I graduated, I took this plus the feminism and the belief in progress into my adult life, in the form of a visceral aversion to hierarchies, a fierce defensiveness against anything that felt like someone trying to wield power over me, and an equally fierce determination to make the world a better place. Needless to say, all this made me a less than ideal employee. It also made me willing to experiment widely in how – and with whom – I wanted to live. So I drifted through low-paying jobs, wrote unreadable novels, tried my hand at intentional communities and anti-capitalism and the pursuit of a life freed from power, hierarchy and all limits.

Naturally, this extended to my views on women, which came out the other end of the encounter with critical theory heavily flavoured by it, and more focused than ever on ideology and representation. Perhaps the text along these lines that marked me most deeply was another End of History-era work, Judith Butler's immensely influential 1990 work *Gender Trouble*. Here, Butler argued that neither sex (our embodied, dimorphic, reproductive biology) nor 'gender' (our social roles, putatively rooted in sex dimorphism) exist pre-politically, but are instead both to an equal extent social constructs. It's not that biological processes don't exist, but how we make sense of them is inescapably social, meaning the supposedly clear distinction between 'natural' sex and 'cultural' gender is in truth muddier than we believe.

For Butler, we 'perform' both sex and gender, in a system that's imposed on us and that we re-impose on ourselves and others by participating in it. As such, while we're unable to escape it, we can embrace a revolutionary queer and feminist praxis of 'disrupting' the diktats of gender from the margins. The aim is to open up greater space for a wider range of gender expressions and roles, unmoored from the stifling impositions of the patriarchal heteronorm.[2]

From the point of view of a girl who'd spent her adolescence unhappily identifying both with my mother (who looked like me) and with my father (whose status I wanted), Butler's suggestion that we just set about subverting the whole ugly mess of sex roles, hierarchies and power relations was very appealing, to say the least. This goal also seemed possible, perhaps for the first time, thanks to something else that arrived in mainstream life during the End of History decade: the internet.

I fell instantly in love with the internet the moment we got dial-up, in the late 1990s, and was straight online looking for My People. That instant, deep attraction to the digital world has stayed with me, however ambivalent I've since become about the widespread impact of the internet on our culture and society. Online, the intoxicating escape Butler imagined from a 'gender binary' freighted with millennia of oppressive hierarchy felt, for the first time, tantalisingly within reach.

After university, in the heady early years of social media, I mutinied against every form of 'normal'. Thanks to the internet, it was suddenly relatively easy to find others with similar interests; I experimented with drugs, with kink, with non-monogamous relationships. And I experimented with selfhood. Online, I could be anyone. Whiling away the days at the slacker jobs I took to make rent, I hung out among the 'genderqueer' cliques in early-2000s messageboards, meeting up with those groups offline too.

Drenched in queer theory and adrift in the endless possibilities of digital culture, it suddenly felt possible to re-imagine our genders in bespoke terms, and to create supportive enough communities to somehow realise our inner lives in the world. We found others of our 'tribe' via suddenly proliferating social networking sites, where we crafted elaborate imaginary identities for ourselves while congregating offline at regular meets. Everyone politely ignored the slippage between the two. Online, someone who in reality was a pudgy, moon-faced woman with a buzz cut could be a sleek, suave, debonair Oscar Wilde figure, and everyone joyfully played along. I changed my name to Sebastian for a while. I pondered whether I really was female. It all felt thrilling, liberating, revolutionary and unambiguously like the 'progress' I'd always dreamed of.

In my working life, I also found a way of bringing together my conflicting desires for achievement and optionality, ambition and egalitarianism, money and ideals. With friends, I founded a 'social enterprise' web start-up that aimed to 'disrupt' education the way eBay had disrupted auctions. All of us were Thatcher's babies: progressive in outlook, but drenched from our earliest memories in the world she created, where ingenuity, entrepreneurship and markets were to deliver the solution to all the world's ills. We hoped to extend those markets to education, and somehow in the process both make the world a better place *and* make ourselves a whole lot richer.

Our team was heavy on ideas and ideals, and relatively light on commercial experience, but we still made it to first-round funding. We were even briefly celebrated, in the age of 'Third Way' social enterprises, noughties Web 2.0 tech-optimism and boundless progressive conviction, as a Next Big Thing in East London's febrile 'Silicon Roundabout' community.

Like many kinds of revolution, losing my faith happened slowly, then all at once. Every egalitarian commune I drifted through turned out to be full of interpersonal power-games. With hindsight, one likely common factor was me; maybe real egalitarian utopia might have been possible, just without me and my issues. But I don't think it was *just* me. Historically, egalitarian utopias have a tendency to disintegrate after a while because they turn out, inevitably, to be not very egalitarian. The postmodern worldview I'd learned at university encodes a deep pessimism about how inseparable power is from human relations at both the large and small scale. My experiences seemed to underline this hypothesis.

I found myself wondering: if this really is inescapable, whether as our cultural legacy or a fact of the human condition, does it really make sense to treat power relations as bad? Why not just accept that they're a fact of life?

Increasingly, too, I found loose, shifting, postmodern constellations of romantic entanglements unsatisfying, and began to long for a more enduring partnership. I'd been sceptical up to that point of the prospect of sustaining such relations over the long term – and indeed of the political ramifications of doing so with a man. Would that not just represent selling out to The Man? And yet, as I inched towards the end of my twenties, a settled home life started to seem more and more appealing.

Then two things happened simultaneously. The start-up imploded (much as in the communes, I was a major contributing factor in said implosion), and at the same moment, so did the global economy, in the Great Crash of 2008. The latter wasn't my fault, but it punctured my fantasies about reconciling political idealism with an economic 'Third Way', in which (as Gordon Brown famously put it) there'd be 'not stop go and boom bust but economic stability',[3] and about how social challenges could be solved through the creativity and dynamism of markets.

In the course of that simultaneous macro- and micro-crash, I lost my social circle, my career, most of my convictions and the majority of my identity. I'll spare you the recovery story, except to say it took years to reassemble something like a workable worldview from the smoking ruins of my queer-theory-inflected, double-liberal, anti-hierarchical idealism. By the time I emerged at the other end, I was married, not living in London, had qualified as a psychotherapist and had comprehensively questioned more or less everything I had thought up to that point. And I no longer believed in progress.

People sometimes look a bit shocked when I say this. But why? It's not self-evident that humans have progressed, in some absolute sense. That doesn't mean everything was perfect once and we're all going to hell in a handbasket. But pick a subject, and you'll find some things are better, while other things have become worse.

If you're going to believe in progress, you have to define what you mean by 'progress'. More stuff? More freedom? Less disease?

Pick any subject, and you'll find that what looks from one vantage point like 'progress' mostly seems that way because you're ignoring the costs. We've grown immeasurably richer and more comfortable in the last 300 years, for example. But we did so on the backs of plundered, colonised and enslaved peoples, and at the cost of incalculable environmental degradation. Meanwhile, torture in warfare hasn't gone away. Warfare hasn't gone away. Nor has hunger, misery, want or human degradation.

Is this progress in some absolute sense? It's beyond the scope of this book to try to answer this question; I'll only point out here that, in order to settle it, you have to define your terms and exclude some costs as irrelevant to progress. And as soon as you do that, you have (as the lawyers say) begged the question. That is, you've rigged the game by assuming the truth of what you set out to prove.

Regardless, the world is full of people who really, fervently *believe* in progress. Martin Luther King famously claimed 'The arc of the moral universe is long, but it bends toward justice', a statement that captures the religious origins of the belief in progress: the sense that we can and must go on getting better, forever. Barack Obama loved the quote so much he had it woven into a White House rug.

In 2018, Steven Pinker wrote a 576-page book that piled up statistics to support his version of progress, which is to say in the terms set out by Enlightenment rationalism.[4] (He dismisses economic inequality as irrelevant to progress.) More recently, queer activist Jeffrey Marsh expressed the same sense of an ineluctable onward march. 'Let me tell you about LGBTQ rights,' Marsh declares in a 2021 TikTok video. 'This is only going in one direction. You will respect us.' Like Pinker, Marsh sees some costs as irrelevant, declaring: 'You can be upset. You can be angry. You can feel like we're stealing something from you, but it's still only going in one direction.'

For our purposes here, the key is to notice the underlying *structure* of belief: that there exists a kind of axis along which progress can be measured, and that we're inexorably moving along that axis, from 'more bad' to 'less bad'. Confusingly, this is often accompanied by the sense that even though the movement from 'more bad' to 'less bad' is supposedly unstoppable, it also demands constant life-or-death defence against the forces of reaction. My starting premise for this book is that this structure is a belief, not a fact.

This isn't an original point. Back in 1991, social critic Christopher Lasch was already asking how progressivism continued to assert such a grip, when infinite economic and moral progress was certain to hit social and environmental buffers in the end.[5] More recently, legal scholar Adrian Vermeule has dissected what he calls 'sacramental liberalism', a 'lived and very concrete type of political-theological order' representing 'an imperfectly secularized offshoot of Christianity'. This quasi-theological regime, he argues, takes as its central sacrament the disruption of existing norms, in the pursuit of an ever-receding goal of greater freedom, transformation and progress towards some undefined future goal of absolute human perfection – that we somehow never attain, and whose externalities are never counted, save as further evidence of how far progress still has to go.[6] This is the core of Progress Theology.

I am not a believer in Progress Theology.

Feminism without progress?

If you've been wondering why this book has, so far, taken the form of a slightly odd *Bildungsroman*, it's because I want to invert the claim made by the feminists of the second wave that 'the personal is political', and share something of how, for me, the political is also personal.

For while I've lost my faith in progress, I haven't discarded everything. I still love the internet. And I'm still a feminist, in the sense that I care about women's interests and think these are often sidelined. Also, crucially, though I have some questions about the direction critical theory has taken since my university days, I'm deeply shaped by some of its insights.

It's clear enough to me that language does shape meaning, and more broadly, that memes really do help to structure reality. That is, those ideas and meanings that succeed in replicating themselves within culture, over time, really do serve as vectors for power. And we're all implicated in that system. When earnest academics recite a litany of their 'privileges', what's being gestured at, however clumsily, is a related truth: that we're all shaped by our particular place in the world. I'm a bourgeois, white, Anglophone woman, living in the developed world, and this structures what I see, and what I consider important – as well as my blind spots. Given all this, it's not really possible to avoid being roped into the push and pull of power, privilege and violence. Nor is it possible to be wholly objective.

The argument that follows is the intimate result of that personal story. On the face of it, if feminism is inseparable from the progressive story, it would seem impossible to lose faith in progress without also losing faith in feminism. The solution to this thorny problem, as I'll explain, is that it depends what you mean by 'feminism'. And my path to this conclusion started some years after my world fell apart in the year of the Great Crash, when I became a mother.

Up to the point where I got pregnant, I'd taken for granted the notion that men and women are substantially the same apart from our dangly bits, and 'progress' meant broadly the same thing for both sexes: the equal right to self-realisation, shorn of culturally imposed obligations, expectations, stereotypes or constraints. The experience of being pregnant, and then a new mother, blew this out of the water. I'd bought uncritically into the idea that individual freedom is the highest good, that bonds or obligations are only acceptable inasmuch as they're optional, and that men and women can and should pursue this equally. Then I went through the wonderful and disorienting experience of finding my sense of self partly merged with a dependent infant.

The kind of absolute freedom I'd accepted as an unalloyed good, pre-baby, was suddenly a great deal less appealing to me than it had been, because I actively enjoyed belonging to my daughter. It was also, obviously, not in her interests to go on insisting that my obligations to her were always optional. Where, pre-baby, I could do more or less what I liked, as a mother I couldn't very well refuse to get up and feed my crying newborn at 3:30 a.m. just because I didn't feel like it.

Her interests mattered more to me than anything else in the world, including my once-treasured autonomy. Chewing this mental shift over led me, in time, to read more deeply into the often-conflicted relationship between motherhood and women's liberation: a debate I discovered goes all the way back to the dawn of the women's movement in the 18th century. In turn, this led me to wonder: why did we start having these arguments at all? From the progressive point of view, it's because human society is moving from 'more bad' to 'less bad', as evidenced by our transition from women occupying subordinate social roles to enjoying relatively equal opportunity in the workplace and in public life. If you take off the Progress Theology goggles, though, does the picture change?

I concluded that what's usually narrated as a story of progress towards feminist freedom and equality can be better understood as a story of economic transitions: in particular, of the transition into industrial society, and the transformative effect that shift had on every aspect of how men and women live – whether apart or together – including how we organise family life.

I should note that when I talk about this story, I'm talking mainly about the story of bourgeois white women in the developed world. And talking about how men and women meet and form families by definition means my discussion focuses on those bourgeois white developed-world women who are heterosexual. Many feminists from outside this demographic have rightly pointed out that the political and class interests of this group were often (and still are) framed as a universal women's struggle, when they were nothing of the sort and in fact sometimes outright inimical to the interests of women in other demographics. If I'm choosing this focus, it's *because* it's still routinely framed as the story of feminism, and because (in terms of what feminism achieved in concrete political terms) those class interests still dominate. Those class interests are still being advanced under the banner of 'feminism' – to the growing detriment of a number of other groups. None of this, however, should be taken to imply that there are no other available, useful or important lenses on this story.

The inception of feminism is the story of men and women adjusting to market society, and particularly of women's response to the asymmetrical impact of that society on areas of our life in common that have historically been women's domain: that of care and the household. From the earliest days of feminist debate, a clear tension is visible between efforts to escape the domain of care, for an equal share of individual autonomy – Team Freedom, if you will – and efforts to defend and valorise that domain of care – Team Interdependence.

Women's response to industrial modernity negotiated a tension between individual freedom from the ways we're shaped by our biology, and woman-centred accommodation by both sexes *of* our embodiment. But the more recent history of the women's movement is also the story of coming out the other end of industrial modernity. The hinge moment for this transition was the emergence from the industrial era of still newer material shifts, with equally transformative effects: reliable birth control and digital technology. And this debate ended in the 1960s with a conclusive victory for Team Freedom, thanks to the mastery granted to women over our bodies via reproductive technology.

Since then, mainstream feminism has morphed from a movement with both communitarian and libertarian strands, to one focused almost entirely on individual freedom, imagined as the property of functionally interchangeable 'humans'. The pursuit of ever more complete freedom from the constraints of biology has extended to viewing as feminist an individual's right to adopt the stereotypical 'gender presentation' of either sex, according to personal preference, and for all purposes to be treated as his or her chosen sex – or as neither sex. That is, an effort to extend 'equality' and 'freedom' to the fundamental fact of sex dimorphism itself.

For Team Freedom, this is a logically consistent feminist stance. You've probably guessed by now, though, that I'm not on Team Freedom, or at least I have questions about how indisputably pro-women the effort to transcend our sexed bodies in favour of a genderless 'human' state really is. (Reflecting my position, in what follows I will wherever possible use 'men and women' rather than 'people' for the simple reason that, as Norma Swenson pointed out,[7] no one has ever seen such a thing as a 'human' body. Just male and female bodies.)

We're increasingly uncertain about what it means to be dimorphic in this way. But when we socialise in disembodied ways online, even as biotech promises total mastery of the bodies we're trying to leave behind, these efforts to abolish sex dimorphism in the name of the 'human' will end up abolishing what makes us human men and women, leaving something profoundly post-human in its place. In this vision, our bodies cease to be interdependent, sexed and sentient, and are instead re-imagined as a kind of Meat Lego, built of parts that can be reassembled at will. And this vision in turn legitimises a view of men and women alike as raw resource for commodification, by a market that wears women's political interests as a skin suit but is ever more inimical to those interests in practice.

What we call 'feminism' today is for the most part this worldview, the Team Freedom one, which should more accurately be called 'bio-libertarianism': the doctrine that legitimises the vision of men and woman as Meat Lego, and which is taking on increasingly pseudo-religious overtones. This doctrine focuses on extending individual freedom and self-fashioning as far as possible, into the realm of the body, stripped alike of physical, cultural or reproductive dimorphism in favour of a self-created 'human' autonomy. This protean condition is pursued ostensibly in the name of progress. But its realisation is radically at odds with the political interests of all but the wealthiest women – and especially those women who are mothers.

In turn, this pursuit of technologically enabled liberation, underwritten by a medical guarantee of freedom from motherhood, has formed the centrepiece of a war on relationships of all kinds that has accelerated radically since the digital revolution. This has, since the 1960s, compounded an advancing process of social atomisation under liberalism whose endgame will have far-reaching consequences – particularly for women, but more broadly for our ability to survive as functioning polities. And the replacement of relationships by individual desires has everywhere been mediated, encouraged and glorified by digital media that have moved swiftly to colonise and monetise our every individual longing – even (or perhaps especially) at the expense of interpersonal connection.

This whittling-away of every relational understanding of identity has, in conjunction with new biomedical technologies, reopened the question of what it means to be a person. Are we, as Hollywood has long told us, whatever we dream ourselves to be? Online, you can be; today, new branches of elective surgery are springing up filled with the promise that you can re-skin not just your digital avatar but also your meat avatar.

Some feminists have embraced this as a positive opportunity. But if liberation for everyone means the radical separation of selfhood from embodiment, what does that mean for those who have to stay embodied? Who cleans the toilets? Who births the babies? Recalling the dilemma of my adolescence, who does the dishes? Team Freedom is galloping us at full speed towards a putatively liberatory cyborg future; but while trying to mitigate our natural limits seemed to be – and perhaps was – in women's interests during the industrial era, as we enter the cyborg era it is increasingly obvious that this is no longer the case.

The endpoint of a three-century struggle for 'progress', understood as individual separateness, has culminated in a political effort to eliminate all meaningful sex differences through technology. Though conceived of as an idealistic project, in practice this largely serves corporate interests. And it dresses in feminist garb a commercially driven effort to deregulate all of human nature, which will enslave our minds in digital fantasies even as it monetises our bodies via biotech. And notwithstanding the hopes of 'radical' progressives and cyborg feminism, a howlingly dystopian scenario can't in fact be transformed into a dream future just by looking at it differently.

Another way

So what might it look like to pursue women's political interests in practice, when we stop squinting desperately at dystopia through Progress Theology goggles, and ask instead what those interests might be in terms of where we actually are now? We've inherited a set of memes from the long 20th century that connect feminism firmly with freedom. And we're taking those memes into a set of material conditions in which technology is rapidly expanding the scope of what we have the 'freedom' to attempt. The product of that is a fusion of once-emancipatory ideas with new technologies and commercial interests that calls on us to pursue the fantasy of an abstract 'human' body all the way into a post-human social order.

Resisting this means pursuing not untrammelled freedom,

mindless hedonism or the final victory of one sex over the other, but a broader project of staying human together, as men and women in the cyborg era. To this end, we'll need to reckon with some of feminism's unpaid debts, and to take more of a realist stance on where the limits to individual freedom really are. We are all, perhaps, liberated enough. It's not just women who need a freedom haircut; it's everyone. And it's my hope that we may be able to mitigate some of the negative side effects that may otherwise accrue from our effort to scrape the barrel of freedom long after its best fruits have been exhausted. We can do this by taking the initiative on where and how we set about constraining ourselves, in ways that are overall in the common interests of both sexes.

The first of these must be reinstating single-sex spaces. And this isn't just to protect women from predatory men; men, too, need social spaces where they can do whatever it is men do when women aren't around. More broadly, we need more realism than is even found among 'gender-critical' feminists, concerning how and why we place limits on making social settings 'gender neutral'.

Women can further shape how we live together in the rubble of absolute freedom by challenging the centrality of abortion and birth control to our sexual culture. This isn't so we can make some absurd pretence that women are all high-minded virgins who never get horny, but because there are well-documented asymmetries in how men and women view sexual desire, and sexual access, along with the obvious asymmetries in the male and female reproductive roles. Medical technologies which eliminate those asymmetries physically haven't also done so emotionally, and many women suffer at present less due to constraints on their ability to say 'yes' to sex, than for lack of a reason to say 'no'.

But it doesn't have to be like that. Our assent to this regime, and these medical interventions, is voluntary. The most powerful weapon at women's disposal for defending ourselves against the undercounted cost of supposedly 'empowering' hook-up culture is making sex properly consequential again. And I suspect many men would prefer a robust 'no' from a self-possessed young woman un-neutered by progesterone and in command of her own reproductive cycle, to being resentfully #MeToo'd or hectored on TikTok about toxic masculinity. By thus reclaiming human sexuality as something that men and women govern together as part of our common life, we can begin to claw the power of sexuality back from its current jaded, affectless role as low-consequence leisure activity or mere marketing tool. And we can reclaim it instead as one of the most profound and beautiful mysteries of our common humanity.

The third plank in a reactionary feminist programme is the post-romantic case for marriage, as against the industrial-era vision of that institution as a vector for self-fulfilment. The cyborg era calls on us to re-imagine marriage as the enabling condition for radical solidarity between the sexes, and as the smallest possible unit of resistance to overwhelming economic, cultural and political pressure to be lone atoms in a market. Households formed on this model can work together both economically and socially on the common business of living, whether that's agricultural, artisanal, knowledge-based or a mix of all these. And this is an infinitely better setting in which to be a mother than trying to 'have it all' on the 20th-century model, even as the 21st is busy dismantling your family for parts. In other words: it's an essential precondition for the sustainable survival of human societies — and will become more so if the world continues on its present trajectory away from the kind of 1990s-style End of History stability towards something more volatile.

Our biggest obstacle is an obsolete mindset that deprecates all duties beyond personal fulfilment, and views intimate relationships in instrumental terms, as means for self-development or ego gratification, rather than enabling conditions for solidarity. This radical reordering of women's politics, women's priorities and even our bodies to the interests of the market, in the name of 'freedom', has racked up a growing mountain of uncounted costs and unpaid debts. As the mother of a young daughter, I look at that growing mountain of deferred repayment, and the growing chorus of resentment from groups that gather outside feminist filter bubbles, and I worry about her future should we face the ideological equivalent of a subprime crisis.

My aim in writing this book isn't to stuff feminism back into its box, as if such a thing were even possible. I've no wish to be banned from voting or working, any more than I want my political agency to be subsumed into that of my husband. In any case, those policies make no sense today. But sex continues to be politically salient, even if you take off the Progress Theology goggles. We're shaped in part by memes: our culture and habits concerning how to live. And we're also shaped by material conditions: our economic circumstances, the wider political world, and also our sexed nature as evolved animals. But *contra* the Prophets of Progress, neither memes nor material conditions necessarily evolve, as Jeffrey Marsh claims, 'only in one direction'.

Even if, as I suspect, we're past Peak Progress, men and women will continue to exist, and certain basic facts about us will remain true. Most of us want children; most want a life lived in common, usually with a member of the opposite sex; same-sex-attracted men and women exist, of course, but heterosexuality is still the default. Humans can't change sex. The shape of our bodies still matters, despite everything the modern world has done to minimise those disparities. And even as the industrial era recedes in the rear-view mirror, we're not powerless. We don't have to stumble blindly into an age of technological upheaval with a worldview shaped by a set of industrial-era memes that are now making everything worse. Other futures are possible, as well as the cyborg one. But just as we have in the past, we can and must once again re-evaluate how men and women can be human together.

2

Feminism, Aborted

*The endeavour to keep alive any hoary establishment beyond its
natural date is often pernicious and always useless.*

Mary Wollstonecraft

Interdependence Day

AFTER I HAD A BABY, I fell off the edge of the working world. It
probably helped that my grip on that world was never very strong,
so I wasn't massively motivated to claw my way back into it again.
But the core reason was simply that I didn't want to be away from
my baby for any length of time. I was (unusually, today) fortunate
in that we could manage without my income. So for some years
after my daughter was born, I was a small-town stay-at-home mum.

Contrary to what I'd assumed from seeing my own mum chafe
in that role, I was surprised to discover that being a stay-at-home
mum can be a pleasant life, provided you have a good relationship
with your spouse and enough funds to get by. Its main downside,
in fact, is loneliness – and that's less a by-product of the role than
of the fact that it's been waning in popularity for half a century
now. Between 1975 and 2015 the proportion of UK households
with only one working parent almost halved, from 47 percent

to 27 percent.[1] In 2019, the Office for National Statistics (ONS) reported that over three-quarters of mothers with dependent children now work. I felt this acutely, as women who'd given birth around the same time as I did began returning to work, and the number of other mothers around for daytime meet-ups in parks and so on dwindled.

The usual story we hear about this is the Progress Theology one. It's a celebratory story, in which the second-wave feminist movement fought off stifling stereotypes to secure an equal right for women to work and enter public life. But beyond my personal loneliness, I found myself wondering whether there was a wider societal story there as well. For one thing, a rise in the number of working adults implies a fall in the number volunteering: for example, figures from the United States indicate that, while volunteering has increased in absolute terms since the 1970s, nearly all of this increase is accounted for by volunteers over the age of 60.[2] And based on what I saw around me in our small town, this felt true: I discovered that everything that made small-town life feel like a community, rather than a dormitory with some shops attached, was powered almost exclusively by retirees. The church groups, the charities, the children's clubs and so on – in a word, the institutions of public life that aren't either official organs of the state, or else commercial ventures oriented towards making money.

As Christopher Lasch documents, female voluntarism was the powerhouse behind much of 19th-century civil society. Bourgeois domestic women didn't sit at home all day: they organised libraries and museums, improving works and 'benevolent societies, female reform societies, and foreign missions', along with 'a vast network of temperance societies' and 'charities and philanthropies of all kinds', to name but a few.[3]

25

When we tell the story about women entering the workplace only in terms of progress and equality, implicitly we're saying that all such non-market activity – whether in private domestic life or non-commercial civic associations – is less important. So, too, are the forms of human association that happen in those settings: all those aspects of artistic, aesthetic, caring and relational work that are not visible to the market. And this hierarchy dates back to the dawn of the Enlightenment. In *Emile*, his 1762 treatise on education, the philosopher Jean-Jacques Rousseau set out his vision for the proper education to form young men into ideal liberal subjects. Young women, meanwhile, should be raised as charming, compliant support humans:

> The whole education of women ought to be relative to men.
> To please them, to be useful to them, to make themselves
> loved and honoured by them, to educate them when young.[4]

The job of women was to 'delight' men, and to birth and care for a man's babies. In other words: the domain of care is a necessary backdrop to the more important business of full personhood – but still just that: a backdrop.

The hierarchy Rousseau set out is alive and well. Caring has largely been, traditionally speaking, 'women's work' – and to a great extent it still is: the Organisation for Economic Co-operation and Development (OECD) reports that, worldwide, women do between two and ten times as much unpaid caring work as men.[5] It's routinely treated as *infra dig*: anyone who has been a stay-at-home mum knows the moment when someone at a party asks what you do, and then politely moves on from talking to you when you tell them. If you're a working-age adult in this position, chances are you're used to being unreflectingly written off as boring, inadequate and probably a bit dim.

And this hierarchy of values – economic work good, caring work taken for granted – is everywhere, whether in the ways we underpay workers in caring roles or characterise a loss of earnings due to taking a family career break as a 'motherhood penalty'[6] that punishes women, even as it harms the economy by keeping skilled women away from the workplace.[7]

Stay-at-home parents turn up in the statistics under the dismissive term 'economically inactive', as though the defining trait of someone caring for dependent others is their lack of measurable contribution to GDP.[8] At best, caring is 'unpaid work': a poor relation of the economically productive type that happens in workplaces and contributes to GDP. Women carry out the lion's share of this work: 60 percent, according to the ONS.[9]

US President Joe Biden expressed this perception of caring work as impediment, loss or punishment when he tweeted in November 2021 that 'Nearly 2 million women in our country have been locked out of the workforce because they have to care for a child or an elderly relative at home'. The solution, Biden said, was to 'make caregiving accessible and affordable and help them get back to work'.[10]

There have long been feminist voices who criticise this dismissal of care.[11] But the history of feminism is also synonymous with women challenging the long-standing social norm that care should be 'women's work' at all. And it's this challenge, and women's ensuing entry into the workplace, which we generally hear narrated today as evidence of progress. Meanwhile, the loneliness I felt, trundling a baby buggy around the depopulated working-hours streets of my small town, and my invisibility as a person mainly

27

engaged in caring for a dependent baby, felt no less real for being side effects of that progress.

This conflation of women's autonomy with feminism and progress, and associated denigration of care, today forms the core of a well-worn conservative accusation: that the hollowing of civil society, denigration of the family and numerous associated problems can be laid squarely at the door of the women's movement. The conservative American televangelist Pat Robertson famously declared, in a 1992 campaign letter opposing the Equal Rights Amendment, that the feminist agenda 'encourages women to leave their husbands, kill their children, practice witchcraft, destroy capitalism and become lesbians'.[12]

More recently, the American anti-feminist academic Scott Yenor argues that the abolition of marriage and the family is a central plank of the feminist pursuit of absolute female autonomy.[13] And if (as Yenor does) you review second-wave feminist writing, you can find plenty of arguments that support this.

Germaine Greer, for example, in 1970 depicted women who embraced 'feminine' domesticity as 'eunuchs', 'castrated' and cut off from their own authentic desires by malign patriarchal stereotypes.[14] 'Childbearing was never intended by biology as a compensation for neglecting all other forms of fulfilment and achievement,' she argued.[15] And when contemporary feminists such as Jill Filipovic declare cheerfully that the birth rate is collapsing today because women have more choices,[16] we might wonder: do the conservatives who blame feminism for a thinning social fabric, hollowed-out families and collapsing birth rate have a point?

Yes, and no. As I went down the real-world rabbit hole of stay-at-home motherhood, and followed my research nose down the historical rabbit hole of its origins, several things became clear. The story of feminism is one of economic transitions – and particularly of the Industrial Revolution. In seeking to navigate that transition, women wrestled with reproductive asymmetries and the competing calls of individualism and relational bonds. And seen from this perspective, the version of women's 'liberation' that has become dominant emerges less as another step up some endless ladder of moral advancement and more as a campaign to enter the market on the same terms as men.

Contra the heartless and antisocial terms in which this campaign is characterised by conservatives, though, there's nothing monolithic about the association between the women's movement and a rejection of familial ties or social norms. Rather, the tension between interdependence and freedom has occasioned rich and internally fractious debates among women, complicated too by differences such as class and race. For much of feminist history, women sought a settlement that valued maternity, care and interdependence *alongside* a just measure of economic and political agency and individual freedom. And as we'll see, women were right to seek this – for the pre-industrial cultural legacy combined with industrial-era material conditions together placed women in an invidious position.

For many, then, the aim has historically been a recognition of men and women as physiologically distinct but equal in dignity, interdependent and capable of excellence. But over the 20th century, the movement has taken a decisive turn against care, and in favour of individual autonomy. This happened via another material transition: the arrival into this picture of reproductive technologies that seemed to level previously irreducible differences between the sexes.

For with fertility under control, it became possible to imagine that the central asymmetry between the sexes could be eradicated – and with it many of the injustices associated with sex dimorphism.

But in embracing this dream, the feminist movement adopted a vision of personhood defined in opposition to interdependence – and thus settled the feminist debate decisively against care, and in favour of autonomy. I'll discuss the implications of that shift in Part 2. First, though, we need to sketch the contours of how we got there.

Domestic disembedding

The idea that material conditions help to shape culture and ideas is not new. In the preface to his 1859 *Critique of Political Economy*, Karl Marx argued that moral and cultural changes are less a cause of social transformation than their effect: 'It is not the consciousness of men that determines their being, but, on the contrary, their social being that determines their consciousness.'[17] I'll return later to Marxist thinking on women and family, and just hold for now to the simple insight that human lifeways emerge not in a vacuum, but in a dialogic relationship between cultural norms and material incentives, constraints and pressures, such as prevailing climate, topography and so on.

The political economist Karl Polanyi makes a similar argument when he challenges the now-orthodox belief, originating in theorists such as Adam Smith and Ludwig von Mises, that there's anything eternal or self-evident about the bartering, self-interested *Homo economicus* of free-market lore. Rather, Polanyi suggests, while some measure of exchange characterises most societies, there has never before existed one prior to ours 'even approximately controlled and regulated by markets'.[18] Rather than being controlled by markets, Polanyi argues, the division of labour springs from 'differences inherent in the facts of sex, geography, and individual endowment' – material conditions – while the consistent feature of pre-industrial economies was that 'man's economy, as a rule, is submerged in his social relationships' (in other words, the broader matrix of shared meaning, or memes). Polanyi argues that this can be straightforwardly explained by the fact that in a low-tech society, strong social bonds have much more to offer in survival terms than material possessions.[19]

In such relatively low-tech societies – such as that of medieval England – it was normal for all women save the uppermost aristocracy to work. For most economic activity took place within households, as part of the activities we'd understand as 'work' but which Polanyi characterises as 'embedded' within social relationships. Looking after children and getting on with the everyday tasks of subsistence agriculture and cottage industry all happened in the home, with children also expected to pitch in with work as soon as they were old enough. In such homes, women might tend a smallholding, make food or craft products for sale, make the household's clothes and perform countless other tasks – along with the care of children – that were every bit as vital to the household as earning money.

Historian Elizabeth Wayland Barber argues that a number of these jobs became 'women's work' precisely *because* they were compatible with keeping half an eye on small children. Textile production, for example, was a largely female occupation for some 20,000 years, until the Industrial Revolution. Wayland Barber argues that this worked because a loom can be kept off the ground away from toddlers, the work is somewhat interruptible, and it's communal.[20]

Such women were practical, multi-skilled and extremely busy. So much so that it appears men and women argued about whose work was the most arduous, to a sufficient degree for medieval

31

poems on the theme to emerge. Historian Toni Mount cites one 14th-century poem, in which a ploughman is depicted accusing his wife of sitting around all day. At this she retorts that after a broken night with the baby she's fed the animals, taken the cow to pasture, prepared food for the house, made butter and cheese, brewed, baked and prepared flax for weaving – all while keeping an eye on the children.[21]

> The goodman [husband] and his lad to the plough are gone,
> The goodwife had much to do, and servant had she none,
> Many small children to look after beside herself alone,
> She did more than she could inside her own house.

How did pre-modern women think about their own relations to their children, husbands or communities? The philosopher Ivan Illich argues that the 'embedded' relations of pre-modern societies were irreducibly dual not just in material terms – the work men and women did – but also in roles, gestures and so on: every facet of each person's way of being. For Illich, this 'vernacular gender' was concerned not with the subordination of one sex to the other, but in 'ambiguous complementarity' in which each depended on the other, just as the ploughman and his wife together perform the vital tasks of a subsistence household.[22]

In pre-modern English writing, it's common to find this 'ambiguous complementarity' framed hierarchically, with husbands set over their wives. Chaucer expresses this in 'The Parson's Tale', where he declares that a married couple should love one another, but at the same time the husband should be set hierarchically over the wife – though not too high: she should be a fellow, not an underling.[23] The idea of mutual love coexisting with hierarchy is alien to a modern perspective, in which all such asymmetries are treated as exploitative by definition. But it was a familiar idea in the medieval world, where thinkers such as Giles of Rome described the world as a set of nested hierarchies in which God governed mankind as the king governed his subjects and a *paterfamilias* governed his household.[24] Within that worldview, Christian teaching held that higher rank implied not simply a relation of domination and control, but one of service and sacrifice.[25]

In practice, of course, the ideal and reality often diverge: there were no doubt many household tyrants. Feminist histories of the pre-modern world are fond of pointing to devices such as the 'scold's bridle' – a punitive, muzzle-like contraption placed on women who were thought by their community to be too vociferous in criticising others – as evidence of women's pervasive oppression at that time. But in communities where men and women genuinely depend on one another to perform work that's indispensable for the survival of the community, the idea that one sex could be uniformly 'exploited' by the other makes little sense. It's clear from the dialogue between the ploughman and his wife that she more than holds her own. The ethnologist Susan Carol Rogers supports this view, in her study of power dynamics between men and women in agrarian communities. Subsistence work in such societies tends to be divided clearly into 'men's work' and 'women's work', and in most cases men monopolise formal types of power. But Rogers shows that in practice women in such communities wield considerable informal power, via channels such as control of information or the ability to inflict public loss of face. In such agrarian settings women are in any case as indispensable as men to the overall functioning of the household.[26] So while this is not to dismiss historical evidence of male violence against women, in an agrarian context male supremacy in theory must be set against interdependence of the sexes in practice.

As the world industrialised, from the 17th century onwards, everything changed. I can offer only the broadest outline of that change; it happened throughout the West, began a century earlier in Britain than in America, and evoked distinct local responses depending on prevailing cultural and material conditions. But this change has some general features. An explosion of legal, philosophical and technological innovation, from the 17th century onwards, began a cascade of changes, including (in England) the enclosure of common land and associated displacement of peasant communities, the centralisation of formerly home-based artisan work in factories, greater abundance of material goods and ever more extractive means of producing them. As Polanyi argues, economic life in this world was increasingly conducted not within a web of relationships but between supposedly atomised trading individuals.

To grasp the effect within individual households of the transition into market society, let us revisit textile-making: a craft that for some 20,000 years of 'vernacular gender' had been 'women's work'. As textile-making technologies advanced, women went on contributing, under the 'putting-out' system. Here, manufacturers handed raw materials to women who would spin yarn in their own homes: the origin of the term 'cottage industry'.

But James Hargreaves' spinning jenny (1764), Richard Arkwright's 'throstle' or 'water frame' (1769) and Samuel Crompton's spinning mule (1779) all made spinning more efficient – and centralised the work outside the home. The 'putting-out' system that had enabled women to do this work within the household gave way to factories filled with large, dangerous machines. The same went for weaving. As the production of basic goods drained away from households towards centralised factories, so family life also needed to adjust. It's one thing doing a bit of spinning at home, to your own schedule, with half an eye on your kids. But now imagine you have to clock in for a 12-hour shift, in a location some distance away from home, and you can't bring your breastfed baby with you. What do you do?

Illich characterises this as a transition from a social regime of 'vernacular gender' to one of 'economic sex', which he characterises as 'the duality that stretches toward the illusory goal of economic, political, legal, or social equality between women and men'. Illich argues that in practice 'economic sex' is not less but *more* discriminatory towards women.[27] In 1845, Friedrich Engels described the appalling working conditions faced by women in factories, whether working through pregnancy or even on occasions giving birth on the factory floor.[28] Within a system of 'economics' premised on treating men and women as 'people', which is to say fungible, interchangeable work units, women who are mothers will always be more encumbered and thus, in a sense, disadvantaged.

Karl Marx documents the grim downstream effects on babies of making their mothers fungible: in industrialised areas, new causes of infant death emerged, 'principally due to the employment of the mothers away from their homes, and to the neglect and maltreatment arising from their absence, which consists in such things as insufficient nourishment, unsuitable food and dosing with opiates'. This was made worse, Marx observes, by 'an unnatural estrangement' between mothers and children that resulted in 'intentional starving and poisoning of the children'. This bleak predicament held, too, for those rural areas where farming moved to an industrialised model, with a contract workforce that required women to be highly mobile, and absent from children for long periods of time.[29]

In response to this shift, wherever families could afford to do so the formerly embedded, gendered household regime of work and family life began to stratify and separate into a 'public' one of economic productivity and a now consumption-oriented 'private' one.[30] It's commonplace from the perspective of contemporary liberal feminism to argue that women's 20th-century accession to the workplace represented a gain in economic agency. This is true, relative to how women began the industrial era. But relative to life prior to this era, industrialisation in practice *reduced* women's economic agency: as work became more centralised, more mechanised and less agrarian, the resulting split between 'work' and 'home' drove women increasingly into a domestic-only role. Illich describes the role that became women's domain there as 'shadow work'. From a distinct but equal contribution to the overall economy of a productive household, women's principal task became operating the products that poured forth from consumer society. As Illich puts it: 'The unpaid upgrading of what wage labor produced now became women's work.'[31]

In turn, this transformed the social meaning of women's activities. The ploughman's wife could point to yarn spun, cheeses made, animals well-tended and so on: material output every bit as indispensable to the household as her husband's muddy toil in the field. But under the new regime 'women's work' was, as Illich puts it, 'not only unreported but also impenetrable by the economic searchlight'.[32] Women's responses to this challenge followed two characteristic patterns.

Some women sought to make the new kind of 'women's work' in the home more visible and valued. This considerable body of 19th-century writing across Britain and America has since been characterised by feminist historiographers as the 'Cult of Domesticity'.[33] Here, women were newly framed as more delicate, nurturing and morally superior, in charge of education and creating a haven from the brutal, competitive ravages of the market society in which men were forced to compete. Publications such as the 19th-century American magazine *Godey's Lady's Book* extolled these rarefied feminine domestic virtues in stories, advice columns and illustrations. As one female writer put it in 1838, the father's role was 'acquisition of wealth, the advancement of his children in worldly honor'. To the wife, on the other hand, fell the solemn task of shaping 'the infant mind as yet untainted by contact with evil [...] like wax beneath the plastic hand of the mother'.[34]

Much of 20th-century feminist historiography was influenced by the Marxist view that, as Engels put it in 1884, women's oppression began with the transition to agriculture and with it to patrilineal families, a shift that he characterised as 'the world historical defeat of the female sex'.[35] From this vantage point, the 'Cult of Domesticity' has generally been read as the effort of women in the grip of false consciousness to propagandise a new evolution of patriarchal subordination.[36]

More recently, though, scholars have argued that women who celebrated the newly private domestic sphere were seeking rather to elevate public appreciation of a realm of social activity sharply curtailed by industrialisation.[37] If the 19th-century equivalent of the ploughman challenged his wife to justify what she did all day, she could throw *Godey's Lady's Book* at him. This was also to acknowledge the necessity of the private home as a space of respite from market society. As the historian Nancy Cott argues, women's positive rationalisations of their new, separate 'sphere' constructed that role as a site of resistance to an often-exploitative and cruel public world. 'The literature of domesticity', she suggests, 'enlisted women in their domestic roles to absorb, palliate, and even to redeem the strain of social and economic transformation.'[38]

I ended up as a stay-at-home mum because I felt a powerful *need* to stay close to my baby. It was difficult to explain in terms of my then averagely liberal beliefs about women's right to unfettered autonomy; but something like it is reported near-universally by mothers,[39] and is also evident in the way many non-human species care for their young.[40] I'll say more about this bond of 'attachment' in Part 2, but for now simply point out that this need to be close to one's children is the most plausible explanation for women's effort to valorise care under the industrial regime of 'economic sex'. Work happened 'out there'; but meanwhile loved dependents still needed care. Many articulate mothers wanted the world to see what they saw, about how much that mattered.

Far from acting as malignant agents of internalised patriarchy, then, the women who extolled domestic life sought to defend an 'embedded' pre-industrial domain of relational human activity, centred around the care of vulnerable children, that was difficult to valorise in market terms but still intuitively understood as being of great importance. Particularly in urban contexts, as Christopher Lasch notes, these social forms persisted until the great 20th-century migration to the suburbs, with women's lives remaining considerably more 'embedded' – that is, bound up in social relations – than those of men.

Things fall apart

That visceral wish to be close to our babies is still powerful enough to induce many Western women every year to opt for life as stay-at-home mums, temporarily or permanently, despite near-universal public messaging that valorises more or less any other life choice you care to name. But I also gave two provisos at the start of this chapter, for my surprise discovery that being a stay-at-home mum is quite a nice life: enough funds and a good relationship with your spouse. These, or rather what happens when they're missing, form a crucial background to the other pole in women's response to the 'disembedding' of family life: the campaign for female freedom.

Memes often take longer to change than material conditions, and this can have far-reaching effects. Women entered the industrial era with family life governed by a social and legal order still structured in accordance with the pre-modern, interdependent subsistence household, in which households – not individuals – were treated as the constitutive units of society. In this pre-modern order, women didn't lack legal personhood exactly; single and widowed women in medieval England were able to buy and sell property. But once married, women's legal personhood was subsumed into that of her husband, as they were deemed 'one flesh' as part of a single household.

This rendered women subordinate, in a sense – but it also shielded them from legal and economic exigencies. Under medieval English law, for example, landowners had military obligations to their lord; landowning women had to hire or persuade proxies to perform this service on their behalf, but married women had no such obligations.[41] And, as historian Linda Kerber has noted, the pre-capitalist system of property relations imposed restrictions on women, but also served to keep women's property out of the marketplace – for example, when dower property was shielded from debt seizure.[42]

As the world industrialised, though, and the 'ambiguous complementarity' of subsistence work in the productive household was replaced by 'separate spheres', women were to a far greater extent at the mercy of their legally and financially all-powerful husbands. And it's one thing extolling the private virtues of domesticity and the proper care of children in a household where your husband likes and respects you and supports the whole family responsibly. It's another altogether if your husband is abusive, neglectful or violent.

Women trapped in this absolute dependence by marriage to cruel or tyrannical men could suffer immensely. The American writer Mary Gove Nichols, a lifelong campaigner against marriage, drew on her own abusive first marriage to describe that unhappy predicament:

> When she is owned by a man who can maintain her, though he is loathsome almost as death to her; when her health is utterly lost in bearing his children, and in being the legal victim of his lust; when her children are not hers, but his, according to inexorable law; when she has no power to work, and no means of sustenance but from this owner; when public opinion will brand her with shame, most probably, if she leaves her husband [...] what is such a woman to do but to live a false and unholy life?[43]

While an updated version of the 'household' model could still work – as described by the so-called 'Cult of Domesticity' – a society that now measured 'work' in waged terms rendered women acutely vulnerable to their husband's goodwill and good behaviour. Early women's rights campaigners sought not to destroy family life, but to secure greater recognition for what Illich calls the 'shadow work' of the home. As legal historian Reva Siegel shows, early American women's rights campaigns sought to challenge the unequal value accorded to domestic and workplace contributions, updating the law of marriage and inheritance in line with the suddenly invisible interdependence of working husband and 'non-working' wife. But as the 19th century wore on, bourgeois women in particular chafed increasingly vocally against the legally entrenched regime of difference. And while arguments for joint property ownership were, as Siegel puts it, often 'rooted in values of community and sharing', other feminist voices argued from more Lockean, individualist premises of 'self-ownership'.[44]

The 19th-century English writer and feminist Harriet Taylor Mill, for example, explicitly linked full personhood to participation in market society, arguing that women's economic dependence was the root of our subordination.[45] In her view, confining women to economic dependency was to treat women in a 'contemptuously tyrannical manner', in that 'however she may toil as a domestic drudge, [she] is a dependent on the man for subsistence'.[46] Enfranchisement meant 'admission, in law and in fact, to equality in all rights, political, civil, and social'.[47] Taylor Mill rejected the attempts by some women to construct women's 'sphere' as a site of resistance to the competitive, individualist market society. Any obstacle to women participating in that society on the same terms as men was merely evidence of male animus: '[W]hen [...] we ask why the existence of one-half of the species should be merely ancillary to that of the other [...] the only reason that can be given is that men like it.'[48] For Taylor Mill, then, women were fundamentally the same as men and, like men, gain happiness from self-determination and developing their capacities. To that end, Taylor Mill rejected what she saw as a regime of compulsory male-imposed difference, arguing that women should be free to compete with men on a level playing field:

We deny the right of any portion of the species to decide for another portion [...] what is and what is not their 'proper sphere'. The proper sphere for all human beings is the largest and highest which they are able to attain to. What this is, cannot be ascertained, without complete liberty of choice.[49]

41

It's clear that for Taylor Mill, the emancipation of women meant the right to enter the market on the same terms as men – and to succeed or fail on those terms, too: she argued for 'every occupation' to be 'open to all', suggesting that then 'employments will fall into the hands of those men or women who are found by experience to be most capable of worthily exercising them'.[50]

But from this perspective, women's distinct reproductive role rapidly emerges as a handicap to competition with men on equal terms. Ensuring a level playing field between the sexes thus implies social infrastructure. The 19th-century American writer Charlotte Perkins Gilman recognised this, arguing in her 1898 work *Women and Economics* that, for women to have access to professional self-development on the same terms as men, the work of family life – which Perkins Gilman calls a 'clumsy tangle of rudimentary industries' – should as far as possible be professionalised. Cleaning, education and childcare ought to be subcontracted, while food could be prepared in common kitchens by professional cooks.[51]

Long before women's suffrage was attained in either Britain or America, then, the core tension in the women's movement was well established. On one side stood a pro-women defence of care and the importance of the domestic realm, and on the other a pro-women dismissal of care as an unjust impediment to women's capacity for self-realisation on the atomised template of liberal personhood.

Both these stances had merit. The 19th-century effort to update 'vernacular gender' as women's 'sphere' was rooted in a realistic assessment of reproductive asymmetry, and the deep caregiving attachment experienced by most mothers. In effect, it represented an attempt to defend a still relatively 'embedded' social domain from the liquefying and alienating forces of market society, in

42

which caring activities both essential to human life but invisible to the market society could still be pursued and valued.

But the demand by Taylor Mill, Perkins Gilman and other individualist feminists for women's entry into the market on the same terms as men was also justified. For one thing, it made a realistic assessment of the dismissively secondary status accorded to caregiving commitments within the emerging market regime of 'economic sex'. For another, it recognised the invidious ways that this secondary status meshed with patriarchal social structures inherited from an earlier, more interdependent and complementary order of 'vernacular gender'.

For these liberal feminists, the claim that there existed anything fundamentally distinct between the normative roles of men and women could only ever institutionalise women's ancillary status. And where reproductive biology seemed to imply anything thus fundamentally distinct, these feminists called for social and political remedies. As the industrial age advanced, these social and legal efforts to level the playing field in service of gender-less common 'personhood' were increasingly supplemented by technological remedies, oriented at levelling the most stubborn source of difference: fertility itself.

The tech fix

You may have noticed by now that I haven't yet addressed the feminists of the 20th century. I'll have more to say about this era in the next chapter. My aim in this one is to make the case that those challenges addressed by feminism are less evidence of eternal male animus than effects of material changes. As such, disputes between women and men over how to resolve these challenges, and also among women about the best approach, date all the way back to the beginning of that era. Central to those disputes is the tension I've outlined above, between on the one hand the acknowledged persistence of dependency and importance of care, and on the other the privileged value accorded to freedom and autonomy within the wider paradigm of market society.

If Perkins Gilman's call for communal nurseries and domestic infrastructure foreshadows contemporary feminist themes such as the so-called 'motherhood penalty', or calls for universal childcare, so too critics of the individualistic current within 19th-century feminism discerned the oncoming form of another, profoundly divisive feminist issue: abortion. Presciently, one American critic of *Women and Economics* linked Perkins Gilman's conflation of liberation and paid work with a tacit denigration of all unpaid forms of activity. This anonymous commentator pointed out the logical endpoint of arguing that 'all work becomes oppressive that is not remunerative', namely that women's liberation was thus predicated on being able to escape any obligation that isn't paid – including (or perhaps especially) reproductive ones:

> [T]he prejudice against bearing children [...] has become so ingrafted upon the minds of married women, that tens of thousands annually commit ante-natal murder.[52]

For if all unpaid work is oppressive, then the work of relationships and caring is intrinsically oppressive, except to the extent that it can be re-imagined as paid work. And if this is so, having babies itself is oppressive – unless, as we'll see, it's the 'work' of surrogacy. And once this premise is accepted, anti-natalism becomes a feminist position, as does the right to abortion.

As we'll see, we're some distance further down this path today. But its foundations were laid in the 19th century, in arguments that – not without justification – rejected 'embedded' forms of social life as second-best, and conflated personhood with freedom and self-realisation. These core premises aligned the nascent women's movement with that overall drive for individual self-realisation which formed the moral justification for market society.

As Polanyi shows, the core enabling condition for the 'liberation' of industrial-era societies from an embedded economic order was the replacement of interdependent social relations with abstract economic and technological ones. And in time, applying an equivalent set of interventions to the 'sphere' of women and family life came to seem not just plausible but indistinguishable from 'progress' – and not just within homes, but in women's very bodies. In seeking to adapt market individualism to women's reproductive physiology, the liberal strand within feminism opened the space for disembedding women via not just social and legal means, but also technological ones.

The legal scholar Erika Bachiochi traces these competing philosophical currents in the American women's movement, showing how most 19th-century advocates of women's rights regarded abortion as indistinguishable from infanticide.[53] As Bachiochi argues, 19th-century feminists called for 'voluntary motherhood' (or the right to say 'no' to sex even when married) as a remedy for the risks and burdens of women's fertility.[54] But her account traces how, as technology developed, 20th-century science replaced this social and cultural remedy with a simpler and (notably, especially for men) less demanding solution: medical contraception.

The contraceptive pill was approved by the US Food and Drug Administration (FDA) in 1960 and made available on the

NHS in Britain in 1961. And, as Bachiochi points out, the legalisation of contraception created a ratchet towards the legalisation of abortion. The original aim of birth control advocates was to enable married women to control their fertility. But the existence of reliable contraception radically changed social behaviour, as casual or extra-marital sex no longer had the same potentially grave consequences and rapidly became less taboo. Thus, while contraception may, as its advocates argued, have reduced the rate of accidental pregnancy as a total proportion of sexual encounters, the existence of contraception so radically changed social norms that many more casual sexual encounters took place. And contraception was only *mostly* effective – so the absolute number of accidental pregnancies went up.

This in turn lent vigour to demands for legal abortion, which originated first with progressive advocates of eugenics and population control, as Bachiochi notes.[55] And this movement set about courting the then-nascent feminist movement in support of legal abortion via an influential 1966 monograph, *Abortion*, in which this was described as 'the one just and inevitable answer to the quest for feminine freedom'.[56] And as this argument gained traction, feminist arguments turned chiefly on personal autonomy. Betty Friedan wrote in her 2000 memoir that a woman's 'right to control her reproductive process' was core to the 'personhood and dignity of woman'.[57] She saw motherhood as important, but 'choice' as central: 'Motherhood is a value to me [but] [y]ou couldn't have women's equality without her own control of the reproductive process.'

And despite Friedan's qualification, this inevitably subordinates motherhood to equality. As Bachiochi points out, if your concept of personhood is based on market participation, mothers don't really show up as 'people'.[58] Mothers are only visible within this market society to the extent that we detach ourselves from care-giving, which is seen largely as an obstacle to that participation, and therefore to self-realisation. The American feminist jurist Ruth Bader Ginsburg expressed this in a 1978 paper, in which she echoed Friedan's insistence on 'a woman's autonomous control of her full life's course' and characterised that as essential to 'her ability to stand in relation to man, society, and the state as an independent, self-sustaining, equal citizen'.[59]

Since the dawn of the Industrial Revolution, then, the women's movement has sought to navigate between legacy social and cultural norms, changing material conditions and the bonds and obligations of family life. Many protofeminist and feminist voices spoke in defence of those human bonds — especially between a mother and baby — that need protection from the market. The 'housewife' role I inhabited for some years, now sparsely adopted and seemingly a relic of past ages, was itself an effect of that defence.

Second-wave writers such as Greer and Friedan railed against this vestigial form of 'embedded' social life available to bourgeois mothers within advanced industrial society. To them, it was a shrunken, alienating role, in which productive activity and thus meaningful agency was near zero, the wider culture rendered one's entire mode of being invisible, and much everyday activity consisted of 'shadow work', which is to say operating consumer products. In 1970, Germaine Greer argued that there are no differences between the brains of men and women, and that women have simply been 'castrated' by male stereotypes that force them into a subordinate role. As Greer puts it:

Children live their lives most fully at school, fathers at work. Mother is the dead heart of the family, spending father's earnings on consumer goods to enhance the environment in which he eats, sleeps and watches television.[60]

Instead of what she sees as a 'castrated' and diminished womanhood, Greer called for revolution, in the name of 'freedom to be a person, with the dignity, integrity, nobility, passion, pride that constitute personhood. Freedom to run, shout, to talk loudly and sit with your knees apart. Freedom to know and love the earth and all that swims, lies and crawls upon it.'[61]

Greer's left-libertarianism and Friedan's differ in many respects, and Greer was dismissive of Friedan's careful, policy-oriented campaigning. But they share the same basic template for personhood: the autonomous one, who becomes a person in the manner envisaged by Rousseau: that is to say, in a world where some unspecified other does all the dull, sticky drudgery that keeps the world of freedom and selfhood turning. Second-wave feminism definitively rejected women's obligation to bear the publicly unrecognised persistence of dependence and burden of care, within a market society predicated on disavowing these features of our common social life even as it eagerly extracts value from the subjects nurtured by that care.

Women who defended bourgeois domesticity sought, under new conditions, to carve out a space relatively free from that market, within which dependency and care could be prized and nurtured. But the logic of these arguments propelled us towards the opposite pole: a strand of feminism that embraced the individualist market logic, and sought women's entry into that market on the same terms as men. In her essay 'Are Women Human?', the writer Dorothy Sayers observed tartly:

It is perfectly idiotic to take away women's traditional occupations and then complain because she looks for new ones.

> Every woman is a human being – one cannot repeat that too
> often – and a human being *must* have occupation, if he or she
> is not to become a nuisance to the world.[62]

Women thus sought the opportunity to be 'human' on the same terms as men. And for women, increasingly, this template came inescapably to be identified with its corollary: the 'right' of women to medical interventions that would 'liberate' us from unchosen embodied obligations. But, as Bachiochi shows, the price for doing so was accepting as the default paradigm for what 'human' means a now supposedly gender-neutral template person shorn of female-specific reproductive vulnerabilities, potential or obligations.

And the feminist campaign to grant women the 'right' to this form of personhood, and thus prioritise autonomy even to the extent of killing an unborn child, settled the century-and-a-half of back-and-forth between the feminism of care and the feminism of freedom, decisively in favour of freedom. As the pro-life feminist Daphne Clair de Jong put it in 1978, 'Accepting the "necessity" of abortion is accepting that pregnant women and mothers are unable to function as persons in this society.'[63]

When conservatives blame feminism for all the ills of the world, they're usually enumerating the many social trade-offs that accompanied women's move, in the 20th century, to claim for themselves the same ideal of personhood as had already been established for men since the days of Rousseau. For women, this ideal of personhood took definitive legal form in the legalisation of abortion, and broader form in the rejection of 'care' as in any sense a female domain or obligation. But the net impact of women rejecting a sexist obligation to shoulder the burden of care hasn't yet been men taking on an equal part of that burden. Rather, it's been an awkward mixture of poorer people – usually women – being deputised as paid substitute carers, and those most in need of care often going without.

Side effects of this generalised desertion of interdependence in favour of freedom include widespread loneliness; abuse of the elderly and disabled in care homes; substandard childcare;[64] family breakdown; and the well-documented disadvantage experienced by children in one-parent families, such as greater risk of poverty,[65] reduced life chances,[66] and adolescent mental health issues.[67] The American social critic Mary Eberstadt has argued that the very fixation on selfhood within contemporary identity politics is driven by the relentless attenuation of family life.[68]

But where the conservative analysis often falls short is in looking no further back than the mid-20th century, rather than tracing the logic of care's defeat by freedom all the way back to its inception in the material conditions of market society as such. When conservatives call for a return to 'traditional' family life, but mean by this a return to some variant of 'separate spheres', whether in its 19th- or 20th-century forms, this misses the fact that such forms of family life are not 'traditional' at all, but distinctively modern.

The twin poles of dependency and freedom, then, have served as systole and diastole of feminist thinking since feminism emerged with the modern era. But in the mid-20th century the women's movement, long balanced in ambivalent tension between resisting and embracing the market society, came down unambiguously in favour of that society – and of the technological interventions without which that society's dream of radical equality would be inconceivable. In Part 2, I'll draw out some implications of this convergence. For after this inflection point, feminism largely abandoned the question of how men and women can best live together, and embraced instead a tech-enabled drive to liberate humans altogether from the confines of biology.

First, though, we must unmoor another core preoccupation of feminism from the story of 'progress', and re-examine it through the lens of memes and material conditions: the thorny questions of how and why men and women come together, and stay together. That is, the question of how sex relates to the market.

3

Sex and the Market

It is a truth universally acknowledged, that a single man in possession of a good fortune, must be in want of a wife.

Jane Austen, *Pride and Prejudice*

The pleasure of your company

WHEN I WAS A TEENAGER, I remember my mum giving me the same advice about boys as her parents had given her: 'Remember, if someone takes you out, you don't owe them anything. They've had the pleasure of your company.' It's a fine enough sentiment, but I recall being baffled. It was the 1990s; things didn't really work like that. Between the 1960s, when my mum reached adolescence, and the 1990s, when I did, the sexual revolution, and an accelerating digital one, radically reordered how, why and when we come (pun intended) together.

But this story starts much earlier. For if industrial civilisation reordered families, these changes also affected *how* families formed. And as the feminism of freedom consolidated its victory, the rules governing this most intimate and consequential side of our common lives transformed in the wake of that victory. Fundamentally, this part of the story is about babies. But it's not just about babies. Millennia of great works of art make it clear that sex is rarely *only* about babies – but until relatively recently, if you were having sex, you were on track to conceive one.

As such, no matter how ethereal the transports of passion, desire was forced to remain rooted in the material. It's commonplace within feminist historiography to note that questions of genetic legacy, and economic wealth, also converge on those of female sexuality. At the top of the scale, marriageable young women have throughout history been treated as bargaining chips in political power-broking; marriages had little to do with affection and a great deal to do with dynastic and political planning: uniting families, preserving peace, consolidating holdings and ensuring legacies.

Further down the scale, controlling women's fertility took on a more pragmatic complexion. In a world without institutional childcare or a welfare state, single motherhood posed a range of thorny social difficulties. So, considerable social effort went into yoking sexual desire to long-term unions, where children could be raised with the support of both parents. Accordingly, along with heavily stigmatising extra-marital sex, in medieval England marriages were easy to form and extremely difficult to sever. Unions were considered binding and permanent after an exchange of vows between the couple, followed by sexual consummation. Sex outside marriage was heavily discouraged, and divorce all but impossible. But, as the historian Christopher Lasch notes, as England industrialised through the 18th and 19th centuries, something like the dynastic approach to marriage once common only in the aristocracy began to spread down the social scale.

This triggered several related changes in the everyday relations of men and women: first and foremost, a growing commodification of women. As homes grew less productive and women less economically active, individual women were increasingly treated

as resources to be laboriously cultivated in the hopes of achieving –
as in the world fictionalised by Jane Austen – an advantageous
match.[1] The process of securing a spouse came to be seen as a kind
of marketplace: the popular London venue Almack's Assembly
Rooms was explicitly referred to as a 'marriage mart'.[2] In tandem,
as interdependence *with* men gave way to greater dependence *on*
men, this also changed behavioural norms for women in relation
to men. As women were increasingly raised to be commodities in
the 'marriage mart', and their agency in selecting a spouse accordingly subject to ever more elaborate regulation and constraint,
the practical, multi-skilled women of the pre-modern agrarian
age lost status.

This shift was already well advanced in 18th-century England,
as evidenced by Daniel Defoe's 1726 observation that middle-class
women increasingly aspired to be 'gay delicate ladies' who acted
'as if they were ashamed of being tradesmen's wives'.[3] And women
themselves were educated more for charm and 'accomplishments'
than practical skills, in keeping with the new orientation towards
bagging a man with good prospects. This new, sentimental style
of female education prompted intense criticism, as in this letter
to Addison and Steele's *Spectator* in 1711:

> The general mistake we make in educating our children is, that
> in our daughters we take care of their persons, and neglect
> their minds. [...] To make her an agreeable person is the main
> purpose of her parents; [...] to that all their care [is] directed,
> and from this general folly of parents we owe all our present
> numerous race of coquettes.

Over the same period, the ways in which men and women
themselves conceptualised marriage changed. The easily formed

marriages of medieval tradition were now fraught with risk, for cultivating a daughter to marry 'well' was an enterprise that took immense preparation and investment. All could be lost should she have her head turned by a charming ne'er-do-well. In turn, this drove calls to introduce greater parental and state regulation of marriage contracts. In 1753, after heated debate, Parliament passed the Marriage Act, intended to prevent 'clandestine' marriages. 'How often', declaimed the Attorney General, Sir Dudley Ryder, 'have we known a rich heiress carried off by a man of low birth, or perhaps by an infamous sharper?'[4]

Even as new educational ideas shaped young women as marketable commodities, while imposing ever tighter regulation on their access to the opposite sex, both feminists and anti-feminists of the period wrote critically of the individual and social downsides of this new class of bourgeois women. Both Mary Wollstonecraft and her most vocal antagonist, Hannah More, agreed on the pernicious social impact of what More in 1799 called 'the showy education of women', which 'tends chiefly to qualify them for the glare of public assemblies' rather than to make a lifelong contribution to everyday life.[5]

For Wollstonecraft, this approach harmed not only the women in question, but the marriages into which they entered – and wider society too. 'It would be an endless task', she lamented, 'to trace the variety of meannesses, cares, and sorrows, into which women are plunged by the prevailing opinion, that they were created rather to feel than reason, and that all the power they obtain, must be obtained by their charms and weakness.' For Wollstonecraft, rather than being 'sweet flowers that smile in the walk of man', women should aim to become 'more respectable members of society' able to 'discharge the important duties of life by the light of their own reason'.[6]

A similar tension between 'marriage mart' incentives that nudged women towards an emotionally labile 'sensibility', and the moral and practical benefits of retaining a measure of 'sense', provides the title to one of Jane Austen's best-loved novels. And in *Pride and Prejudice* the relationship between Elizabeth Bennet and the man she eventually marries, Mr Darcy, has since become perhaps the definitive fictional template for women's best-case scenario under these socioeconomic conditions: a 'companionate marriage'[7] to a well-off man, based on mutual respect. As Austen describes this relationship:

> It was an union that must have been to the advantage of both: by her ease and liveliness, his mind might have been softened, his manners improved; and from his judgement, information, and knowledge of the world, she must have received benefit of greater importance.[8]

The negative foil for this template is Lydia Bennet, whose union with the feckless Wickham comes about 'because their passions were stronger than their virtue'.[9] And this growing emphasis on mutual regard had, as *Pride and Prejudice* obliquely signals, a pragmatic as well as an idealistic justification. As Austen recounts, Wickham's attraction to Lydia 'soon sunk into indifference'. Between this and Wickham's weak economic prospects and general improvidence, Austen indicates in the book's closing chapter that Lydia is shielded from loveless penury only by regular bailouts courtesy of her more affectionately (and wealthily) connected sisters. What Austen never needs to spell out is the extent to which under the new regime of economic dependence, mutual affection in marriage took on new significance for women. An aspiration to companionate marriage – Big Romance – was one means of protecting women from tyranny, in a married condition where they had relatively little material or legal leverage, and few avenues of escape.

Sentiment for sale

'Sentiment' thus took on new significance from the 18th century onwards, as a means of maximising appeal to a man with good economic prospects. For women themselves, the pursuit of emotional intimacy in marriage offered some consolation for the loss of pre-modern economic agency, and also a shield against the potential negative consequences of that loss. Big Romance was also big business: Austen's work is one outstanding exemplar of an industry that boomed over the same period, and whose product was content aimed at women: novel-writing. This industry, many of whose narratives turn on that central sentimental concern of 'happy ever after' within companionate marriages, in turn triggered the first modern moral panic.[10] As a letter to the *Monthly Mirror* thundered in 1797, 'Without this poison instilled, as it were, into the blood, females in ordinary life would never have been so much the slaves of vice.'[11]

This degradation came about, it was argued, because of the sentimental diversion it offered from women's practical duties.[12] But we might equally understand the new universe of feminine sentiment in terms framed by Adam Smith's other work: *The Theory of Moral Sentiments*. This text, written in 1759, sets out to answer the question: Why are humans not wholly callous in their self-interest? Smith argues that in fact humans have a basic instinct to feel, as closely as we can, the emotions of others, a natural projective instinct that's formed in the course of trading interaction, and which forms the foundation of our capacity to live with one

another: the domain of 'sympathy'. And viewed in this more positive light, as the mirror of self-interest, 'sentiment' appears less
as something frivolous than as a protected and highly feminised
cultural space, outside the cut-and-thrust of trade – one that Smith
argued was every bit as crucial to the good life as the market.

This sentimental domain became women's terrain, whether
cultivated to charm men into marriage, or nurtured by married
women on behalf of their economically active husbands under the
Cult of Domesticity. What emerged from these roiling disputes
about sentiment, romance and mutual marital regard was a new
understanding of marriage and the market, as domains constructed
in relation to one another. Ideals of romance and companionate
marriage sought new grounds for a partnership based not on
mutual economic interdependence but mutual regard and affection.
The high ideal of romance and 'happy ever after' served as a kind
of emulsifier, chiefly for women but in practice for both sexes,
to bind the unruly forces of desire and affection to the pragmatic
and sometimes cruel exigencies of material subsistence. But in
the parallel construction of 'sympathy' within marriage, and
competition beyond it, the institution of marriage also became
a key part of that market society. And the stage was thus set for
the ongoing unravelling of that opposition over the course of the
industrial era, and the steady shrinking of those domains of men
and women's common life that still remained relatively shielded
from the market.

Abolish the family

A key force in that unravelling was the Marxist critique of the
nuclear family as complicit *with* the market. This began with

Engels' argument in 1884 that the bourgeois family forms a key mechanism whereby capitalism subordinates women and women's reproductive labour, in order to reproduce itself.[13] Following this line of reasoning, writing in 1909, the Marxist feminist Alexandra Kollontai argued that the withering-away of marriage was essential for women's liberation. For 'feminism', she claimed, had hitherto focused only on the interests of bourgeois women, who had the most to gain from greater access to political and economic agency within the existing social order. But this did little for proletarian women: 'For the majority of women of the proletariat, equal rights with men would mean only an equal share in inequality.'

For proletarian women, Kollontai argued, transforming family structures was as critical to women's fight for equality as that among bourgeois women for representation and access to cultural power: 'To become really free woman has to throw off the heavy chains of the current forms of the family, which are outmoded and oppressive.' The only equitable solution was full abolition of family bonds, state care of children and the liberation of men and women to love as they saw fit, freed from the material obligations of the family as bourgeois survival unit. And this liberation of women required the root-and-branch socialist transformation of society, for 'women can become truly free and equal only in a world organised along new social and productive lines'.

So, if Harriet Taylor Mill argued for a radical emancipation of women from the legal and cultural structures of marriage and family, on behalf of her educated bourgeois female milieu, 60 years later Kollontai made a similar case on behalf of proletarian women. But where Taylor Mill viewed this emancipation through an individualist lens, Kollontai pointed out, correctly, that proletarian mothers don't generally have the economic or cultural capital to survive in such a competitive environment. For women in this situation, she asserted, emancipation must necessarily be underwritten by state support, to replace those social activities traditionally performed by women – especially childcare. Only state responsibility for subsistence and the care of children would truly liberate women to live and love freely.[14]

Taylor Mill and Kollontai disagree over how far state infrastructure should underwrite women in their pursuit of emancipation from family life. Both, though, share the same core assumption: that the older understanding of marriage as a covenant was (variously) a constraint on women's freedom, or a constraint and also (as Engels argued) a vector for the reproduction of bourgeois capitalism. As such, both argued that marriage should be undermined, loosened or even outright abolished. This follows as a logical consequence of efforts to challenge what Kollontai called 'the bourgeois ideal that recognises woman as a female rather than a person'.[15] Here, again, the earliest Marxist feminism reveals the implicit hierarchy first set out by Rousseau in the 18th century, which views 'female' as a lesser category than the theoretical neuter 'person'. For this strand of feminist thought, the aim was to re-class women as 'human': a class of sentient primates whose important features are wholly unrelated to the sexed features of their bodies.

In 1920, Kollontai envisaged communism as resolving the tension between motherhood and personhood, by socialising the burden of material obligation that having a baby entails. Under communism, she argued, women would be free to love without fear or economic pressure:

It is not in her husband but in her capacity for work that she will find support. She need have no anxiety about her children. The workers' state will assume responsibility for them. Marriage will lose all the elements of material calculation which cripple family life. Marriage will be a union of two persons who love and trust each other.[16]

It was an entrancing vision, especially for those women who chafed at men's far less ambivalent capacity to taste the fruits of liberal modernity. One such, the philosopher Simone de Beauvoir, envisaged in her groundbreaking 1949 feminist classic *The Second Sex* the same parity of working personhood for both sexes, under communism. To Kollontai's vision of equal access to work, de Beauvoir added that in liberating women from the material consequences of sex, i.e. child-rearing, communism would also grant us equal sexual freedom. In her vision, 'erotic freedom would be accepted by custom [...] marriage would be based on a free engagement that the spouses could break when they wanted to; motherhood would be freely chosen – that is, birth control and abortion would be allowed – and in return all mothers and their children would be given the same rights'.[17] In the end, though, it wasn't communism but technology that delivered.

Tech to the rescue

There have been multiple attempts at sexual revolution in Britain, as in America, but none gained widespread traction before reliable birth control became widely available. It's not as though an unplanned pregnancy can be shared equally by both parties, and historically the parent left holding the baby was most often the woman.

Under those conditions, societies maintained elaborate social codes to manage contact between horny young men and women – and to channel sexual desire towards commitment and

61

child-rearing. But the material incentive to maintain sexual constraints on women fell away abruptly with the arrival of the birth control pill in the 1960s. In turn, women celebrated their new freedom to enjoy sex. *Cosmopolitan* editor Helen Gurley Brown's influential *Sex and the Single Girl* (1962) argued that women have as much right to sexual pleasure as men, and encouraged women to become financially independent and enjoy an active sex life before marriage.[18] The book sold two million copies in its first three weeks, and was eventually sold in 35 countries.[19]

Also animated by these shifts, those inspired by the Marxist feminist trail blazed by Kollontai and de Beauvoir in turn embraced new technologies, to imagine a still more complete emancipation for women. Like de Beauvoir, the radical feminist Shulamith Firestone envisioned mechanical wombs enabling 'the freeing of women from the tyranny of reproduction by every means possible'. In turn, she thought, this would enable the sexuality of men and women to flourish in its unconstrained, joyful and natural form, meaning 'humanity could finally revert to its natural polymorphous sexuality' where 'all forms of sexuality would be allowed and indulged'.[20]

The downstream social impact of these changes is evident in how differently my mum's dating advice landed between her teenage years in the 1960s, and my own in the 1990s. Perhaps the central difference between my mum's generation and mine is that her relationship-forming years were still ordered by a structured and socially controlled set of romance norms that were a distant descendant of the 18th-century 'marriage mart'. These norms had obtained to a significant extent since the era of Wollstonecraft and Austen, and for the same reasons.

As my mum reached adolescence, the material incentives for shielding sexual intimacy from the market were still clear. The grave consequences of unplanned and unsupported pregnancy provided an overwhelming individual and social incentive to insist on reserving sexual access only for men who were at minimum willing to provide economic support, and ideally – as in the Elizabeth Bennet template – the emotional kind as well. In that context, it was wholly reasonable to frame a right to deny sexual access to men as a pro-women stance.

But as my mum reached adulthood, the material risk of pregnancy was already being undermined by reproductive technology, and by growing postwar female access to paid work. In her youth it was normal and unquestioned outside avant-garde circles for encounters between men and women to be structured by courtship: a ritual that assumed the presence of a female monopoly on sexual access, and male monopoly on economic resources. These two monopolies were tacitly understood to merge under the sign of romance, implicitly ordered to marriage and children. But by the time I was a teenager, sexual encounters happened not within this controlled infrastructure but at largely unsupervised house parties or music nights. I don't think I ever went on a formal date until my late twenties, when I began looking more intentionally for a long-term partner.

In the process, the tension that marriage upheld, between the material facets of men and women's life in common and the sexual and emotional ones, also began coming apart. I don't recall ever taking any clear message from the culture I grew up in that sexual contact need involve anything more than the most minimal risk of accidental pregnancy. Correspondingly, there was little to suggest I had any right to assume that sexual contact – now reframed as a fun and relatively trivial activity – need imply emotional closeness. And while many remained relatively conventional in their approach to love and marriage for some decades following the

1960s, for those at the cutting edge this change had immediate impact. As described by one veteran of the sexual revolution, the British journalist Virginia Ironside, the Pill had an immediate impact on women's ability to say no:

> With every man knowing you were armed with the pill, pregnancy was no longer a reason to say 'no' to sex [...] I mainly remember the 60s as an endless round of miserable promiscuity, a time when often it seemed easier and, believe it or not, more polite, to sleep with a man than to chuck him out of your flat.[21]

And this 'disembedding' of sexuality – its unmooring from material limits and implication in social relations – didn't exactly bring about a new universe of boundless, polymorphous pleasure, as Firestone imagined. Much as industrialisation enabled the deregulation, enclosure and commodification of productive work, so reproductive technologies enabled the deregulation, enclosure and commodification of sex – and with it, the extension of market society to sexuality, in the creation of a so-called 'sexual marketplace'.

In 1960, the FDA licensed the Pill. The same year, Hugh Hefner opened the first Playboy club in Chicago. By the end of 1961, Hefner's Chicago club was the busiest nightclub in the world – and the role of 'Playboy bunny' was marketed to young women as a glamorous and high-earning occupation. Though feminists celebrated women's escape from patriarchal constraints towards a utopia of erotic freedom, they also protested against the ineluctable parallel marketisation of sex. In 1963, Gloria Steinem went undercover as a Playboy bunny, in a groundbreaking work of investigative journalism that exposed the squalid, penny-pinching reality behind the supposedly glamorous facade of life as a paid Playboy hottie.[22] By 1976, radical feminists were mobilising against the booming empire of pornography. Andrea Dworkin organised protests against the film *Snuff* in 1976. Two years later, the first Women Against Violence Against Women anti-pornography conference took place in San Francisco.[23]

But much like the Cult of Domesticity in the 19th century, women's efforts to defend a space free of market penetration proved unequal to the power of the market. Even as women mobilised in San Francisco against the brutal consequences – especially for vulnerable or impoverished women – of marketised sexual desire in pornography, Austrian economist Friedrich Hayek was arguing elsewhere that markets achieve a 'spontaneous order', delivering a better 'allocation of societal resources than any design could achieve'.[24] Hayek wasn't addressing the question of sex and the market directly; but those two domains were on a collision course. It wasn't Dworkin who won the so-called 'sex wars' in 1980s feminism. And however much she and other radical feminists protested at the mismatch between the Hayekian idea of 'spontaneous order' and the reality of women's sexual experiences, that paradigm has nonetheless come to shape how we understand the interactions between men and women.

For Adam Smith, the 'marketplace' was relatively narrowly defined. 'Moral sentiments' merited a whole other book, just as in the culture he inhabited and shaped, the domain of 'sympathy' was ring-fenced as that of women, marriage and family and celebrated in the popular novel. Two centuries on, though, the incentives to maintain that separation dissolved with the arrival of technologies able (fairly) reliably to separate sex from reproduction.

Spontaneous order

By the time I was a teenager in the 1990s, the feminist field had been comprehensively conceded to the 'sex-positive' faction: women who took into new, sexual territory Harriet Taylor Mill's 19th-century utilitarian individualist arguments for women's entry into the market. And even as ever greater swathes of sexual intimacy were commodified, cheered on by this outlook, the 'spontaneous order' itself took on newly visible form in the emerging digital space. In Hayek's vision, markets seem not driven by individual humans – so-called '*Homo economicus*' – but to be something increasingly smooth, self-organising – and best left as free as possible, in order to maximise their ability to deliver what every individual actor desires.

As reproductive technology has collapsed the boundary between sex and the market, so too has digital technology progressively virtualised that market – which in turn has enabled it to penetrate those domains of 'moral sentiment' that, in Smith's time, were treated as off limits. While I was reading de Beauvoir as a teenager, that purportedly spontaneous market order took large-scale digital form for the first time, with the founding of Amazon in 1994 and, the following year, eBay – and, importantly, the first dating website: Match.com.

My mum's dating advice to me contained the unspoken understanding that women have a relative monopoly on sexual resources and men on economic ones, and that romance serves as the harmonising medium in which these resources are exchanged without becoming crudely transactional (in other words, degrading into prostitution). Also understood in that advice was an acknowledgement that this must remain tacit, or the spell is broken. But by the time I began working life, academics were writing papers on 'Sexual Economics', arguing that 'A heterosexual community can be analyzed as a marketplace in which men seek to acquire sex from women by offering other resources in exchange. Societies will therefore define gender roles as if women are sellers and men buyers of sex.'[25]

The year this paper was published, 2004, the 'spontaneous order' envisaged by Hayek was made still more visible, via a new website that extended the self-organising, peer-to-peer 'marketplace' principle to human sociality itself: Facebook. By the end of the decade this marketplace of human selves had been joined by Twitter, LinkedIn and Instagram. All these platforms, in different ways, visualised and accelerated our desire to connect and exchange things, whether products for money on eBay or Amazon, or ideas on social media platforms – or each other. Suddenly we could see all those desires, combining to (say) drive up the price of a collectible on eBay, or connect two passionate fans of some obscure subculture via Facebook or one of the many other social media sites that sprang up to offer their services to those eager to find 'their people'.

In my start-up years, I was entranced by the apparent promise of this new internet of people: that digital platforms could render visible and traceable all those existing and potential movements of desire, interest, curiosity or connection between individuals, in myriad directions. Networked, decentralised dynamic systems at scale! All built of code, and brought to life by countless millions of tiny interactions of individuals all doing their own thing! It felt liberating, subversive and almost mystical: a powerful new way to be together, in perfect individual freedom.

But as the communication theorist Marshall McLuhan put it in 1964, at the dawn of the information age, 'The medium is the message.' That is, in McLuhan's formulation, '[T]he personal and social consequences of any medium – that is, of any extension of ourselves – result from the new scale that is introduced into our affairs by any extension of ourselves, or by any new technology.'[26] And the message delivered by the internet of 'online marketplaces' and social media platforms that emerged in my early adulthood is as follows: everything is a marketplace, including – thanks to social media – those 'moral sentiments' Adam Smith ring-fenced as distinct from the marketplace. Inasmuch as we 'connect' with others, we do so while reserving the right to disconnect again: metaphorically speaking, to log off again or leave the platform if it's not working for us. The 'marketplace of everything' invites us to be together, at scale, but to do so without obligation: always in perfect individual freedom. And this includes – or perhaps especially concerns – sex and relationships.

At the start of the noughties, the decade the internet went mainstream, there were already several online dating platforms. But social norms tend to lag behind technological changes, and at that point men and women mostly still stuck to something like the Big Romance norms that had obtained prior to online dating, and treated the platforms simply as a means of meeting someone new. Couples who'd met online were rare in the 2000s, and those who had were often faintly embarrassed to admit it.

It's now the norm. According to one 2019 Stanford study, 39 percent of couples today met online, compared with only 22 percent doing so via friends.[27] And with the arrival in 2009 of Grindr and in 2012 of Tinder, what happens *after* you meet online changed radically. Unlike early dating sites, which assumed a desire to meet someone for a long-term relationship, these two smartphone apps were geared towards quick judgement of potential partners and seemingly optimised for transient hook-ups: a new, throwaway form of sexual consumerism. And just like more overt e-commerce platforms, the profiles their users are invited to create incentivise self-commodification. Just as on eBay, you create your listing with an image and product description. Just as with eBay, one can browse idly or with serious intent.

Online shopping and online dating diverge at the 'check-out' process: the latter (theoretically at least) doesn't involve the exchange of money. But in the act of digitising human intimacy as options that can be keyword-searched, browsed, selected and consumed, dating apps and websites invite us to consider the search for love as just another online marketplace. And with sex thus subject to market logic, the main consideration in arranging it – as in any other transaction – is that both parties agree to the deal. But the relationship between sex and 'consent' has long been ambiguous. Half a century after Ironside 'consented' out of politeness to sexual encounters that she neither wanted nor enjoyed, women consent to considerably more. And while this is framed as freedom and empowerment, often accompanied by a celebratory embrace of self-commodification via online or in-person 'sex work', the collapse of sentiment into the market has come with a range of undercounted costs.

Limbic limbo

The visionaries of the love revolution dreamed of a post-capitalist future of boundless pleasure, shorn of stigma, constraint or regret. And we got it: we live, in fact, in the world Shulamith Firestone envisaged – with the caveat that it's not, as she imagined, a world also liberated from the exigencies of the market. Rather, it's one where the market's power to liquefy, to commodify and to alienate has mobilised the ubiquity of digital communications to effect a final dissolution of the barrier Adam Smith carefully erected, between 'sympathy' and the market. What we have in its stead is what the historian David Courtwright calls 'limbic capitalism', in which commerce hacks pre-rational pleasure and reward systems and re-orients them to commercial ends.[28]

The industrial era raised new questions about how the economics of life in common could and should mesh with sexuality and the asymmetric material realities of child-rearing. Over the first two centuries of industrial-era life, men and women re-negotiated those parameters, co-constructing twin spheres of emotional sensibility and market competition: spheres that articulated via the axis of romance. But with the advent of the sexual revolution those spheres began to dissolve into one another. And as we'll see, the romantic vision of marriage has shed the crucial role it played in balancing relations between the sexes, becoming instead an active impediment to those relations.

Underwritten by economic and technological changes that freed wives from financial dependence, and sexual intercourse from pregnancy risk, feminist advocates for that dissolution envisaged a utopia of joy and pleasure. Liberated from the burden of social constraint heaped for millennia on women, as a means of discouraging unplanned pregnancy, women could at last explore their sexuality untrammelled. They succeeded.

Accelerated by the pervasive metaphor of the virtual 'marketplace', in which individual men and women are packaged as products to browse, select and enjoy, casual sexual encounters are normalised today. Now, in a world where romance has lost its function as the connective tissue between desire and material reality, and the Hayekian marketplace serves as governing metaphor even for our most intimate encounters, the prospect of making, or trusting another to make, a binding promise of mutual commitment seems ever more remote. Instead, the 'human' dream of radically malleable sexual and reproductive identities envisioned variously by Kollontai, de Beauvoir and Firestone has set the stage for a new, nominally feminist vision, foundationally premised on the power of reproductive technologies to eliminate or at least de-nature every embodied limit experienced by men and women.

Under the sign of this bio-libertarianism, governed by the 'spontaneous order' of digital markets, relationships are formed and dissolved in an unbounded space marked by what one millennial man of my acquaintance describes as a 'general film of impermanence'. And the radical pursuit of unattached individual freedom this both presumes and legitimises comes at considerable, if asymmetrical, cost to both men and women.

For the price of transition first into an industrial-era marriage marketplace, and now from that into a cyborg-era sexual marketplace, has been the steady dwindling of any space for solidarity – not just between men and women, but between individuals of any kind. As I'll show, it has instead set off an all-out war on relationships.

PART TWO

Cyborg Theocracy

Naturam expellas furca, tamen usque recurret
You may drive Nature out with a pitchfork,
but she keeps on coming back.

Horace, *Epistles*

THE STORY SO FAR, THEN: over the course of industrialisation workers were disembedded – or, if you prefer, 'liberated' – from agrarian life by enclosure and industrialisation. This process radically reordered how bourgeois women understood family life: marriage became a vector for social aspiration, even as the home was framed as a space for respite from the rigours of market competition.

This ambivalent relation was kept more or less together by Big Romance: an ideal of lifelong partnership founded on personal affinity and mutual respect that could then serve as the basis for all the more material and practical work undertaken within a family. This ideal served to fuse the material economic and reproductive asymmetries of men and women. But that balance began to fall apart after contraception eliminated (or nearly enough so) the central asymmetry. This so-called 'sexual revolution' was less a moral change than a technological one, with ramifications as far-reaching as those of the industrial factory technologies of preceding centuries. And like those innovations, reproductive technologies have been in many ways genuinely emancipatory. But they also serve to illustrate the dual face of progress: freedom, and trade.

What travels under the term 'progress' is revolutionary destruction of previously immutable-seeming limits. This is usually framed as moral advancement, but in practice follows a two-step ratchet. This first is a shining picture of the utopia that will follow when all the old norms are dissolved and new, improved ones are free to form in the space thus cleared. Then, whatever has been smashed in pursuit of progress ends up reordered to the atomised laws of the market.

Since the days of Adam Smith, freedom and trade have functioned as two sides of the same coin, or two coins of the same side. Smith himself would never have imagined that his theories might be applied to sex. The moral traditions he took for granted were, he emphasised, an essential framework for ensuring markets functioned properly. More recent conservative enthusiasts of the market, such as the UK's Margaret Thatcher and Ronald Reagan in the United States, also shared this view. But why apply the solvent of freedom to some social norms and not others? As the political theorist Patrick Deneen has observed, liberalisation doesn't halt at the barriers of those social norms conservatives would prefer to retain.[1] Instead, it serves as the solvent for norms across the board, and trade — the logic of individual profit — moves into the space.

Where this process takes place in the intimate sphere of human relations, it's common among Western conservatives to argue that its negative externalities are the fault of feminism. Some suggest it could be cured by eradicating feminism. It's more accurate to view feminism, and commerce underwritten by technology, as facets of the same phenomenon. To illustrate, we can compare this process in two distinct geopolitical entities: the West and China. In the West, the liquefaction of family structures seemed to happen organically, or perhaps as a consequence of feminism. In China, though, it was imposed from the top down with the aim of creating a modern urban labour force. Social scientists were already reporting in 1984 on the concerted effort by the Chinese government to disrupt traditional family bonds in the interests of mass urbanisation and modernisation.[2] The disruption worked: according to World Bank data, between 1980 and 2020 the proportion of China's population living in urban areas went from 19 percent to 61 percent.[3] Meanwhile, between 1982 and 2010, multigenerational households have plummeted and single-couple and single-person households have seen rapid growth.[4] All these are changes that we see reflexively attributed to feminism, by conservatives in the West.

Similarly, if Western conservatives often point the finger at feminism for social atomisation and the decline of the family, in China feminism has emerged as a by-product of the social atomisation and decline in family size resulting from top-down interventions aimed at transitioning to a market society. One such intervention was the 'one-child policy' imposed by the Chinese state from 1978 to 2015. Along with spiking rates of female infan-ticide,[5] this policy also *produced* a number of 'feminist' changes to the social expectations placed upon those Chinese girl-children who did survive to adulthood. In traditional Chinese society, for example, women were expected to become mothers and wives. But women born under the one-child policy were now their parents' only offspring, and as such obliged to take on the trad-itional Chinese burden of 'filial piety' that includes supporting their parents in old age. This has, in turn, weakened patrilineal inheritance conventions, driven female careerism, and fanned Chinese women's frustration with a persistent male expectation that they should continue to perform traditional female domestic roles alongside these new aspirations.[6]

In both China and the West, then, feminist viewpoints emerge in tandem with technological advancement and social atomisation, and direct their efforts at mitigating the sex-specific impacts of a high-tech market society on women. But if the causal relationship between feminism and atomisation is complex, what's indisputable is its deep implication in what it seeks to remedy. And thus many of the solutions proposed by feminism in response to women's specific challenges under market society serve in practice to worsen women's alienation and subordination to that market. As we move further into the transition from the industrial to the cyborg age that began with the contraceptive and digital revolutions, the resulting liquefaction is reaching an endgame – and the negative effect of these ideas on women's concrete interests is growing more difficult even for feminists to deny.

What, if any, limitations are there to this ongoing process? How you answer this turns on a fundamental question: whether or not men and women have a nature as such. This metaphysical theme has filled whole books written by writers far more erudite than me. For the purposes of this volume, I'll just say that in my view we do. What specifically our 'nature' looks like is to some degree relational and context-bound, and this book addresses some of those relational and context-bound evolutions over time. But it's not infinitely malleable.

This, though, is an affront to the dream of freedom pursued by Progress Theology. It suggests that we can't, in fact, be 'whoever we want to be' and that constraints exist on what our 'true selves' may realistically become. The counter-argument might be as follows: if we can defy 'nature' by using pumps to make water run uphill, or defy a local climate by creating air-conditioning to keep homes cool, why should we not defy 'nature' in our own bodies and societies, in the name of imposing our will on ourselves as well as our natural environment as well? And why shouldn't we make a profit while we're at it, if we want to?

78

But this triumph over nature hasn't been as complete as its 20th-century visionaries might have wished. Whether at the small or large scale, human nature refuses to be entirely liquefied. And this resistance prompts increasingly frenzied efforts by the proponents of liquefaction-as-progress to stamp out the last traces of resistance. This can be seen across countless areas, but I'll discuss three in particular: the drive to liquefy sexual intimacy, the effort to interrupt the bond between women and children, and the push for medical victory by a disembodied 'self' over the flesh that 'self' inhabits.

In each case, liquefaction doesn't free us from normative, embodied patterns of behaviour or inclination. Rather, it dissolves social codes developed over millennia to manage such patterns, and reorders the still-existing patterns to the logic of the market. And while the result may sometimes benefit a subset of wealthy, high-status women in the West, the class interests of this group are increasingly at odds with those of not just many men but also the young, women with fewer resources, and women who are mothers.

4

War on Relationships

Now get your boots and your coat for this wet-ass pussy
He bought a phone just for pictures of this wet-ass pussy
Pay my tuition just to kiss me on this wet-ass pussy
Now make it rain if you wanna see some wet-ass pussy

Cardi B and Megan Thee Stallion[1]

The zipless marketplace

HOW COUPLES MEET is the subject of endless romantic books, songs and movies – as is what happens after you meet. How do we govern desire? What, if any, are the rules? What's the *point*?

Throughout history, the answers to these questions have been shaped by the fact that only one sex gets pregnant, and the risks of an unchosen pregnancy don't fall equally on the man and woman who caused it. But by the time I was an adult, birth control could be had from clinics and GPs, no questions asked. And with free, pervasive tech in place to manage the sexual risk, the rules of courtship felt genuinely arbitrary, archaic and puzzling: quaint traditions at best.

I spent my single years alternately longing for the orderly and heavily gendered dance those rules implied, and also aware at a fundamental level of their weightlessness. When individuals of both sexes really can just fuck, with no material consequences, what is even the point of going out for dinner first? As I was reaching adolescence, the sociologist Anthony Giddens argued that, with women now equal to men, for the first time ever the 'pure relationship' was possible, and with it a 'plastic sexuality'; that is to say, a 'decentred sexuality, freed from the needs of reproduction' and oriented not towards wider social goals but personal identity and the rewards of another's company.[2] In the context of my own intimate life, I conducted many experiments in just this 'plastic sexuality'.

The passionate life I wanted was the authentic, liberated and libidinal one imagined by Germaine Greer in *The Female Eunuch*: emancipation not just politically but for women's passionate lives too. In her view, even if our bodies differed, purported differences between the characters of men and women were imposed by stereotype. And these malign stereotypes had induced women to internalise a stunted image of our own desires, due largely to sexual shame. This served, she thought, to 'castrate' women, dimming a fully engaged and emancipated female libidinal energy to 'femininity', indistinguishable from the attributes of 'the castrate': that is, 'timidity, plumpness, languor, delicacy and preciosity'.[3]

Greer called for feminists to move beyond what she saw as the conservative political demands of first-wave feminism, and of campaigners such as Betty Friedan. These merely represented accommodations to bourgeois domesticity: different shades of the same self-imposed prison. For Greer, then, passionate emancipation was the foundation of revolution. Women 'are not by nature monogamous'[4] and ought to reject domesticity as 'an attitude of impotence and hatred masquerading as tranquillity and love',[5] instead opting to be 'deliberately promiscuous'.[6] For Greer, 'revolution' meant the 'freedom to be a person, with the dignity, integrity, nobility, passion, pride that constitute personhood'.[7]

And she saw men, too, as crippled by these norms – in particular by shame, which she viewed as a key driver of men's hatred of women. 'As long as man is at odds with his own sexuality', she argued, he will regard women 'as a receptacle into which he has emptied his sperm, a kind of human spittoon'. For such men, every instance of sexual intimacy creates not love or bonding but 'violent hatred'. And the more repressed we are, the more violent men will become: 'The more hysterical the hatred of sex, the more extravagant the expression of loathing.'[8]

Three years after *The Female Eunuch*, Erica Jong published *Fear of Flying*, a hugely successful novel depicting the extra-marital sexual exploits of a frustrated young female writer. Jong's book is remembered for one catchy phrase, which encapsulated women's longing for consequence-free sexual jouissance – the 'zipless fuck':

> The zipless fuck is absolutely pure. It is free of ulterior motives. There is no power game. The man is not 'taking' and the woman is not 'giving'. No one is attempting to cuckold a husband or humiliate a wife. No one is trying to prove anything or get anything out of anyone. The zipless fuck is the purest thing there is. And it is rarer than the unicorn.[9]

Greer's and Jong's books were bestsellers. Women raised to go on respectable dates and resign from their jobs upon marriage thrilled at the idea of launching from dull domesticity into a higher, wilder, more authentic and passionate sexual world. It also promised to extend to women a liberatory zeitgeist that already animated many men.

When *The Female Eunuch* rocketed Greer to international fame, the West was already a decade into the 'counterculture', which began with the Beat Generation. Of the literary figures lionised by this era, one of the most famous is Dean Moriarty, the central figure in Jack Kerouac's 1957 *On the Road*. Moriarty is a fictionalised account of the drifter, petty criminal and serial bigamist Neal Cassady. He lives seemingly conscience-free in every liberated moment, floating from place to place and leaving chaos in his wake. He's also a prolific and faithless shagger, taking up with lover after lover before abandoning them – in one case with a newborn baby.

When Greer demanded that women's response to underwhelming marriages should be to 'run away', she was claiming the same countercultural liberation from ingrained social norms for women as the Beat Generation had already claimed for men. Contraception promised to level the reproductive asymmetry gestured at in Kerouac's story, by the baby Dean Moriarty leaves behind, when he walks out on its mother – a change that should, in theory, have liberated women to be as free as Moriarty. But this assumes that such a liberation would actually be possible. And what's transpired since suggests it's more complicated than this.

Above the neck

Half a century on from the contraceptive technology transition, and Greer's call for women to emancipate desire from family formation, some 40 percent of Americans now meet their partners via the frictionless, boundary-less, disembodied free-for-all of online dating. And what this delivered wasn't the blossoming of sexuality Firestone imagined: it was the modern 'sexual marketplace'. In this 'marketplace', age-old sexed asymmetries have returned in cartoon form – without social codes to govern their action.

Greer's passionate erotic individualism is now the default, rather than the emancipatory exception – for the logic of this 'sexual marketplace' is obviously inimical to marriage. This is visible in the numbers: the average age of first marriage grows later and later: one survey puts this at 33 for women and 35 for men in the United States in 2021,[10] while in the UK in 2019, for opposite-sex couples, it was 32 for women and 34 for men. This is when they marry at all, a rate that's been trending steadily downwards since 1972.[11] This decline is usually attributed to unfavourable economic conditions for forming new households. But material conditions can't be the whole story; after all, men and women have continued forming families through more extreme social and economic hardship than the challenges we currently face. The rest of the story lies in the memes we've inherited from the sexual revolution.

It's now widely understood that women and men who marry young are impeding their own individual personal growth. Marriage is no longer a foundation and starting point for growth within interdependent family life, but tacitly treated as an obstacle to individual flourishing. This is especially the case for bourgeois women, who face sometimes intense social pressure not to marry young.

Anecdotally, young women I've spoken to corroborate this. Charlotte, 23, was raised in a well-off, liberal New York family, but rebelled against the imperative to pursue only freedom as an adult. When she got to college it was, as she put it, 'all about empowerment' which seemed to mean claiming 'I don't have feelings, I'm all about money and my own stuff'. And this mindset delivers, in her view, 'an incredibly miserable existence'. Charlotte met her now-husband aged 20, and when she got engaged in her senior year of college, 'people looked at me like I was crazy'. In the UK, meanwhile, I hear the same story from Lucy, now 30, who married her university boyfriend when she was 24. In bourgeois circles, she tells me, getting married in your early twenties is widely viewed as eccentric, low-status or just outright 'crazy'.

While the culture looks askance at women like Charlotte and Lucy, it energetically lionises those who reject marriage altogether. Liberal pop-feminism of the kind found in consumer magazines abounds with celebration of single life for women, with titles such as 'This New Year's Eve, Celebrate the Women Who Choose to Stay Single'[12] or '5 Reasons Why So Many Women Love Living Alone'.[13] The business press joins the chorus, with articles celebrating the fact that single, childless women now out-earn single, childless men.[14]

This dynamic raises a fair question. If everyone is economically independent, and sex needn't result in babies, and none of us *needs* to rely on anyone else at all, why would any young, heterosexual woman get married? Some simply argue that we shouldn't: a stance held today across both feminist and anti-feminist sides, where solidarity between the sexes is routinely treated as a bad-faith cover for exploitation and reframed in transactional terms. In 2008, for example, the feminist Sheila Jeffreys argued that marriage is a form of prostitution.[15] It's a view shared by the pro-porn, anti-feminist activist Jerry Barnett, who characterises graduate women who marry high-earning men as 'switching some of their corporate earnings for sex trade earnings'.[16]

It's expressed, too, by many in the 'incel' (involuntary celibate) subculture, in which men gather online to bemoan their sexual deprivation – and among 'Men Going Their Own Way' (MGTOW), for whom a core precondition for male well-being is rejecting relationships with women altogether. One 'incel' website defines marriage as 'a system of legalized prostitution'[17] – a cynicism made tragic by evidence that male sexlessness is principally an effect of rising marriage age.[18] At the same time, these subcultures dismiss marriage as part of the problem, exacerbated by the ease with which such commitments may be dissolved under no-fault divorce law.

In other words: feminist and male-separatist views differ mainly in what advantage they claim the opposite sex is covertly pursuing via marriage. For feminist critics, it's a bait-and-switch designed to trap women into low-status drudgery and sexual subordination. For male-separatists, it's a bait-and-switch designed to trap men into a permanent 'provider' status.[19] With the material constraints on desire grown weightless, and marriage treated as suspect by separatists of both sexes, the mutual respect and affection of the Austen-era 'companionate marriage' ideal has come to seem implausible. Perhaps in response, the purview of marriage has shrunk from a social to an individualistic one.

As we've seen, prior to the contraceptive revolution sex asymmetries were managed via social codes that negotiated between a relative male monopoly on resources, and a relative female monopoly on sexual access. These converged under what I've called Big Romance: an ideal of lifelong partnership that centres not on practical cooperation but on sexual and romantic affinity. In Jane Austen's day, this found expression as the ideal of companionate marriage: a vision with real-world practical benefits for women within a context where they could be very vulnerable.

But as companionate marriage has grown materially less necessary, it's become less a matter of survival than an optional enhancement, evolving into what psychologist Eli Finkel calls the 'self-expressive marriage': coupledom as a vector for self-actualisation.[20] For this ideal, the purpose of a marriage – or indeed any relationship – is to enable each partner to become more fully themselves, while retaining peak emotional fulfilment and romantic and sexual spark.

The positive form of this ideal is evident in those boundless narratives about finding The One, where the emphasis tends to be on the intensity of the bond, and rarely on what life looks like once you've found them. It appears more clearly, though, in shadow form, in the justifications offered for severing a bond with someone whose status as The One has been withdrawn.

The central justification given by 19th-century feminist campaigners against marriage was freeing women from abusive relationships. And there's no doubt such relationships exist, and being trapped indissolubly in such a situation must surely be a kind of living hell, as it was for Mary Gove Nichols. But if the feminist case for divorce travels under the banner of protecting women from abuse, the liberal demand is far broader: for the right to sever long-term commitments at will, for any reason.

At the extremes, this could simply be a desire to shake off the dull constraints of everyday life, and live more completely (like Dean Moriarty) in the moment. The writer Honor Jones gives such an account, describing in the *Atlantic* how she ended her marriage simply because it stood in the way of her individual self-actualisation: 'I loved my husband; it's not that I didn't,' she says. 'But I felt that he was standing between me and the world, between me and *myself*.' And this was, she felt, worth the disruption and pain she'd caused to others. 'I had caused so much upheaval, so much suffering, and for what?' Jones admits. '*So I could put my face in the wind. So I could see the sun's glare.*'

For Jones, her husband's selfhood acted as a filter on hers, and she found the constraint intolerable: 'Everything I experienced – relationships, reality, my understanding of my own identity and

desires – were filtered through him before I could access them.'
Sharing her sense of identity with another in this way was, for
Jones, in zero-sum contest with fashioning herself: 'How much
of my life – I mean the architecture of my life, but also its essence,
my soul, my mind – had I built around my husband? Who could
I be if I wasn't his wife? Maybe I would microdose. Maybe I would
have sex with women. Maybe I would write a book.'[21]

And this relentless focus on self-actualisation at any price
doesn't just affect the divorce rate, but how, why or even if we
form relationships – in ways that turn out to retrieve the normative
patterns of each sex, just in grotesque form. For as we've seen,
the Pill and abortion conveyed the impression that sexual difference could finally be flattened out. Back in 1992, this prompted
Giddens to envisage emancipation from the material constraints
on sexuality as unambiguously positive. For Giddens, this meant
intimacy might finally come to be seen as 'a transactional negotiation of personal ties by equals', which 'implies a wholesale
democratizing of the interpersonal domain'.[22] But for this to add
up to liberation on identical terms for both men and women,
utopians and emancipators such as Greer would have to be right
that the sexes differ in preferences only because of social norms.
In this case, a political and cultural effort to change attitudes to
sex would indeed equalise the 'sexual double standard', and free
women to enjoy erotic freedom on the same terms as men.

What if Greer was wrong, though? As the sociologist Julia
Carter observed two decades after Giddens, the sexual double
standard remains alive and well.[23] For we may have flattened the
sex asymmetry, but this isn't the same as abolishing it.

The feminist theorist Louise Perry argues that the sexual
revolution is predicated on being able to eradicate embodied,
sexed differences between men and women – but has so far failed

to do so. These differences, Perry suggests, are relatively small at the individual level but significant at scale. And they're present both in our physiology and also 'above the neck' in our average interests and preferences.

Notably, despite half a century of arguments that we're all basically the same apart from trivial variations in genital topography, Perry shows that heterosexual men and women persistently exhibit significant average differences in sexual desire and behaviour. Data consistently indicate, for example, that men rate women as most attractive when in their early twenties – regardless of their own age.[24] Men are also considerably higher in 'sociosexuality' – that is, desire for and determination to pursue multiple partners.[25] Women, meanwhile, tend towards 'hypergamy': that is, a preference for partners with social status or resources,[26] a pattern that holds even for high-achieving and high-earning women.[27]

Why? An influential psychology paper published in 1972, between *The Female Eunuch* and *Fear of Flying*, sheds some light on this stubborn dimorphism. According to the 'parental investment theory' advanced by psychologist Robert Trivers, many widely observed differences between men and women can be explained by the sexed asymmetry in how much time and effort is required to pass on our genes.[28]

Higher male levels of 'sociosexuality', for example, can be explained in terms of different 'parental investment'. For, as Perry puts it: '[W]omen can produce offspring at a maximum rate of about one pregnancy per year, whereas promiscuous men can theoretically produce offspring every time they orgasm.'[29] As such, there are two distinct routes men may take while effectively passing on their genetic material: either causing as many pregnancies as possible, or sticking around to raise children with just one partner. Attentive long-term fatherhood increases the likelihood of your progeny surviving. But, as Perry puts it, '[A] man who can game the system by abandoning a woman after impregnating her, and then riding off into the sunset to impregnate many more women, is also successfully spreading his genetic material.'[30]

In contrast, for most of human evolution, passing on your genetic material as a woman necessitated a risky pregnancy and a lengthy period of infant dependency. In that context, it's historically been advantageous to women to choose partners willing to stick around. So women have evolved to show a stronger preference for sex accompanied by emotional closeness, and for long-term partners with resources or social status conducive to raising dependent children in comfort: that is, for 'hypergamy', or what was known in Jane Austen's day as 'marrying up'.

In theory, by de-risking casual encounters for women, the contraceptive revolution levelled the sexual playing field. It opened up the possibility that women, too, could fuck ziplessly, without fear that we'd pay for it with nine months' gestation and the subsequent difficult question of what to do with an unwanted baby. Thus, logically, it also rendered obsolete the 'sexual double standard' that condemns women more strongly than men for irresponsible sexual conduct. But just because we want something in theory, doesn't mean we always end up liking it in practice. As Perry shows, for women in particular casual sex is often just not very enjoyable. Consistently, intimacy is the best predictor of sexual satisfaction: in casual hook-ups, 'only 10 percent of women orgasm, compared to 68 percent of women in long-term relationships'.[31] I'll spare you the grisly details of my own experiments in 'plastic sexuality', except to say that this sounds about right.

And in pretending male and female desire is indistinguishable, when it manifestly isn't, we also obscure equally sexed asymmetries in *who* is most desirable. Numerous studies attest to normative differences that bear out Trivers' theory: for example, women prioritise men with power or resources,[32] while men are, on average, more likely to prioritise female features consistent with fertility.[33] None of this is deterministic, and our desires remain rich and varied; but at scale the differences are significant. A few short decades of sexuality unmoored from reproduction via technology are no match, it seems, for millennia of evolution. On average, what heterosexual men and women desire is still heavily inflected by what we've evolved to desire. And even as these differences have thwarted our efforts to realise the high egalitarian idealism of the sexual revolution, they open new market opportunities for the commercial free-for-all enabled by the pursuit of utopia.

Big Romance mutates

According to the liberatory theory of second-wave feminists such as Greer, freeing marriage from survival and sex from reproduction should have resulted in a liberalisation of the heart, freeing us all to love according to our own desires. But in practice, what followed the arrival of the Pill didn't so much wipe the slate clean for authentic erotic expression, as Greer imagined, as reorder sexed differences in mate choice to the market model. And this doesn't eliminate asymmetries so much as turn them into aspects of market positioning or strategic vulnerabilities. And this in turn meshes with the over-emphasis Big Romance places on finding 'The One', to provide a feast for some, and famine for many.

For a spouse who is less than perfect means, in Big Romance terms, 'settling'. And consumer-magazine feminism declares women should never 'settle' for a partner that's merely good enough.[34] For women, this means ever-escalating expectations for how perfectly their partner should match. This meshes uncomfortably with hypergamy, especially in settings where women match or out-earn men in economic and status terms. For the continued desire to 'marry up' *and* seek emotional fulfilment now means competing with men in the workplace while simultaneously competing with one another for the shrinking pool of men whose economic status still feels like enough of (in Jane Austen terms) a 'catch'. In turn, this means an absolute number of men are simply written off as potential partners.

High expectations are an obstacle even in circles where men and women have explicitly set themselves against this dynamic. In 2020, in response to demand, the cultural critic and entrepreneur Justin Murphy launched a brokerage for arranged marriages among America's young tech avant-garde. Since then it's already arranged pairings. But none have yet tied the knot, and the culprit appears to be Big Romance – or rather, its ultra-demanding cyborg-era 'self-expressive' mutation. Murphy told me that 'from my experience trying to arrange marriages so far, I'm increasingly convinced that it's a problem of unrealistic expectations on the part of both genders'.[35]

In the more everyday world, a study of data from the dating app Hinge revealed that 1 percent of men on the app receive 16 percent of all the 'likes', while 10 percent receive 58 percent of them.[36] But these high-status men now enjoying the attentions of a superabundance of successful-but-still-hypergamous women also have a diminished incentive to 'settle' for just one partner, or indeed to remain monogamous once 'settled'. In the world of online dating, then, sex is hyper-abundant for this 'top 1 percent': anecdotally, one twentysomething friend tells me that some male friends find female approaches so abundant that they are 'quite sick of the attention'.

And if this group gets over half the attention, the discarded remnant is increasingly lonely and resentful. This dynamic has driven a growing all-male 'incel' subculture of unhappy males who see little realistic prospect of forming a family, and blame women for their unhappiness. But even here, the only solution on offer seems to be more of the same. One female journalist who often writes about sex and intimacy recently shared with me an email she received from an 'incel', in which he argues in this vein that more and freer prostitution is the only solution for men's suffering. The asymmetry in sexual access will, he suggests, self-correct if only we can extend freedom and trade further into the sexual domain and 'completely allow sex work', thus 'completing the sexual revolution and letting liberty reign'. The only reason women could possibly object, he argues, is because they want to rig the market so their own promiscuity doesn't diminish their trading value: 'counting on the discouragement of sex work to guarantee enough desperate men to catch them when they're done giving away their best years to other, sexier men'.[37]

Against this hostile backdrop, mirroring male and female ideologies have emerged that seek to weaponise or guard against the other side's normative patterns. The male 'pick-up artist' (or PUA) subculture exchanges techniques oriented at playing on women's desire for affection, vulnerability to negative feedback and appreciation for male self-confidence. Examples include 'negging', apparent compliments with a critical subtext, a tactic that plays on women's greater tendency to be agreeable to put her on the defensive and manipulate her desire for approval.[38] Such patterns in female character and preference are then weaponised to manipulate women into providing sexual access. Conversely, the 'Female Dating Strategy' (FDS) teaches defensive interpersonal tactics that aim to minimise women's vulnerability to such techniques, while maximising a woman's chances of securing the lasting commitment of a 'high-quality man'. For example, FDS adherents are advised to remain aloof, avoid text messaging, and observe the 'three-month rule' — that is, insist a man show three months' worth of consistent interest before having sex with him.[39]

Sexual Reaganism

Across supposedly warring 'sides', then, we find a strong consensus on how we should solve the sex wars. On one side we have 'empowered' women who embrace liberal feminism. On the other we have men who name their critique of gender politics 'the red pill', after the famous moment in *The Matrix* where the hero swallows a red pill which permits him to see the true horror of his predicament. These men and women appear to be antagonists, but in truth both camps embrace a worldview so marinaded in the Hayekian vision of 'spontaneous order' via markets, that (like Reagan-era Republicans) the only solution they can imagine to 'sexual market failure' is further competition, deregulation and self-commodification. This is not the utopia Giddens envisaged — or at least, what he imagined as a liberatory 'transactional negotiation of personal ties by equals' turned out to involve more literal transactions than his utopian vision anticipated.

And the digital revolution offers abundant new technologies that make it ever easier to turn desire into transaction. Much of it hovers in the shadowy terrain between building a fanbase and overtly selling sexual access: a grey zone where often extremely young so-called 'e-girls' build large online followings of besotted male fans, known as 'simps', by posting flirty or outright sexualised self-imagery. In some cases it's just the platform that profits from the clicks, and the 'e-girl' herself simply enjoys the attention. Others, though, are more hard-nosed about paywalling themselves. Belle Delphine, who began her career as an 'e-girl', has millions of followers worldwide at the time of writing. Delphine has been banned from several social media platforms for making sexually explicit content, and has since graduated to hardcore porn. Despite (or perhaps because of) this, many are wildly devoted to her: in 2019, when she marketed her own bathwater to 'simps' for $30,[40] it was a near-instant sellout.

Numerous platforms have sprung up that bring together the tools for building a fanbase and those for selling subscriptions. OnlyFans, launched in 2016, has over 50 million registered users at the time of writing, and over a million content creators serving them.[41] The desire to look at young, hot women is a central driver in fans' willingness to pay up – so, unsurprisingly, the content on sale is almost always pornographic; the most popular creators can rake in hundreds of thousands of dollars a month. Meanwhile, the web-enabled commodification of male desire and resources, and of nubile female flesh, now extends offline too. 'Dating' apps have emerged that explicitly bring hot young women together with older, well-off men in so-called 'sugar daddy' relationships. These are described by one such app, Gentley, as 'a way to have all the benefits of being in a relationship without the actual commitment'.[42]

The collapse of sex into the market is promoted, too, by higher education establishments: universities in Britain and the United States now offer courses on doing online or even in-person sex work. Or perhaps this is pragmatic: one 2021 UK study found 22 percent of students had tried OnlyFans while studying,[43] while an estimated 5 percent of the UK student population, or around 120,000 students, do sex work.[44] And this has accelerated since the pandemic: as Covid shrank the supply of traditional student jobs such as bar work, the English Collective of Prostitutes reported that calls to its helpline from students rose by a third in 2021.[45]

Others, perhaps unwilling to take this approach, less conventionally attractive (for here, too, sexed differences still hold), or simply disgusted by the type of approach they receive from men on dating apps, may reject all sexual attention and style themselves 'femcels'. One describes how 'the only matches I did get were men who wanted to have casual sex. When I didn't respond they'd become rude or abusive.' Another, aged just 19, states that 'It started as a joke' but 'now I think people are saying they're femcel because heterosexuality — as we experience it within this patriarchal system — is broken'.[46]

The standard response to what these young women endure, from within the feminism of freedom, is to agree with this teenage 'femcel' that their suffering is simply further evidence of 'patriarchy'. But what's treated here as a primarily political problem — male supremacy — might equally be understood as an embodied one: the male predisposition to sociosexuality, and desire for physical traits associated with fertility, turned to caricature by the frictionless virtual marketplace and foreclosure of long-term commitment. Viewing it thus of course makes it no less unpleasant, as a single woman, to receive unsolicited sexual propositions from unappealing strangers. But it does imply that trying to solve the problem by 'smashing the patriarchy' is likely to be futile and frustrating for those women who attempt it, and variously baffling or enraging for those men whose desires are thus framed as political oppression.

The 'red pill' view of women is arguably one expression of such bafflement and rage. It's often condemned by feminists for its misogyny, in dismissing all women as sexually degraded, utility-maximising gold-diggers and of relationships as a bitter, zero-sum competition.[47] But as we can see, the market mindset has suffused the domain of sex and relationships far more widely than a few online communities of angry and unhappy men. In that context, the surprise shouldn't be how many men or women view sex in this bleak light, but that there remain any that don't.

From this vantage point, limits and covenants of any kind can only be understood as oppression or bait-and-switch. 'Doing something for nothing' seems mere weakness, and competition the basic mode of human interaction. Thus the 'sexual marketplace' burrows ever deeper into our hearts, minds and bodies, waging war on every form of relationship save the transactional kind, liquefying every such potential and replacing it with freedom, and trade. And half a century of concerted feminist effort to stamp out sexed differences as baseless 'stereotypes', in the name of furthering that freedom, has succeeded only in shaping what's for sale.

Rather than leaving us all as 'humans' free to individuate (and fuck) as we please, this effort destroyed what was left of social norms developed over generations to mitigate normative sexed differences in how men and women approach sexual intimacy. And amid the rubble, those differences persist — just in grotesque form, or re-deployed as weapons in a war that rages both within relationships, and against the possibility of forming relationships.

The adaptive, evolved heterosexual male urge to look at and touch young, fertile female bodies has become the ground for a (literally) nakedly exploitative multi-billion-dollar sex trade, egged on by liberal feminists chanting the market mantra: 'Sex work is work.' For those who reject this in favour of more 'agency', there's the option of monetising their own power to incite desire via digital platforms, a move now straightforwardly presented as feminist empowerment: as the singer Cardi B put it, in the smash hit single 'WAP': 'Pay my tuition just to kiss me on this wet-ass pussy.' Online, in the flesh or by offering a paid-for sexual performance review after a cost-free casual hook-up, women are encouraged by 'sex-positive' feminism to treat as empowering the convergence of sex, freedom and trade.

And men's response to this has been to lean into women's asymmetrical strategic vulnerability: the time-limited nature of youthful hotness as an asset. For while Cardi B may sing gleefully of her ability to 'Ask for a car while you ride that dick', the data from OkCupid attest to how brief the window is in which this is a reliable way to acquire new wheels. The 'manosphere' calls this a woman's 'sexual market value', which is to say her power to attract and secure male resources based on youth, appearance and low 'body count' – that is, few or no previous sexual partners.[48]

And on every side, according to the same market logic of independent, rational actors pursuing self-interest, everyone has consented to each such transaction and no one has the right to complain if they feel hollow, miserable or used afterwards. If women 'undersell' their 'sexual market value' by making themselves available for loveless or degrading encounters, they have no right to complain afterwards if they don't like how they were treated: *caveat emptor*. And if these women are deemed to have consented to being exploited, so too have those 'simps' who lavish emotional energy and sometimes also money on the internet's 'e-girls'.

But here, again, in how they rationalise the resulting dividend of disappointment and loneliness the sexes are not alike. For another well-documented normative difference between the sexes is that men are, on average, physically stronger than women, and statistically far more violent. Around 96 percent of the UK prison population is male; most murderers and violent offenders are male; 93 percent of killers convicted in Britain between 2018 and 2020 were male. Males also account for 98 percent of all reported UK rape and sexual assault, and 82 percent of all Britain's reported violent crime.

No amount of stereotype-smashing will do anything significant to change the brute physical fact that, as Perry puts it, 'almost all men can kill almost all women with their bare hands, but not vice versa'.[49] The reasons for this are (as you might imagine) politically contested, but evolutionary psychologists argue that the higher rates of male aggression observed across many species is linked to males' need to compete for mates,[50] and to protect their offspring.[51] More often than we might like, too, male-typical patterns in sexuality and violence merge.

'Women have no idea how much men hate them,' said Greer in 1970.[52] She imagined that this hatred of and violence towards women was a by-product of sexual shame and repression. But 50 years into our experiment in replacing all forms of shame and repression with a 'sexual marketplace' governed by Hayekian 'spontaneous order', it's far from clear that stripping our culture of sexual shame has done anything to cure us of hostility between the sexes. Far from it. In dissident all-male online spaces, the confused misery of women taught to view self-commodification as empowerment is mirrored by a radioactively resentful male backlash, which grows in strength and bitterness every day – and is spilling over, at an accelerating rate, into real-world violence. Between 1989 and 2010 (the year Instagram launched) there were three mass killings whose motives have been attributed to hatred of women. There have been 12 such attacks since.[53]

War of all against all

Despite half a century of propaganda aimed at convincing us that men and women are identical apart from some trivial physiological differences, sexed differences return as weaknesses to be exploited, as options on dating profiles – or as sexual practices ambivalently endured in the interests of maintaining a connection. For example, as Louise Perry points out, male sexual aggression is now routinely re-coded as consensual 'kink',[54] with sometimes fatal consequences for the (more often female) submissive partner.

And nor, as the philosopher Nina Power argues, does smashing the patriarchy seem to have made women feel less hard done by. For rather than preventing men from behaving badly, the assault on patriarchal constraints and hierarchies has delivered a 'rivalrous' society of 'siblings'[55] in which those men who still want to misbehave are free to do so, without even the constraints afforded by those positive aspects of masculinity that once governed masculine excess: 'the protective father, the responsible man, the paternalistic attitude that exhibits care and compassion rather than simply places constraints on freedom'.[56]

This sibling society in turn enables the least noble aspects of stereotypical masculinity, Power argues: 'The frat boy, the porn-addled young man who acts caddishly and frivolously, isn't a father figure, but literally a "brother".'[57] The return of masculinity under the sign of freedom is thus a cartoonish, infantilised one, hyper-focused on self-gratification and reluctant to assume responsibility or obligations – reluctant, in fact, to find himself in any way embedded in social relations. And under the same order, women are incentivised to monetise their youth and beauty directly, becoming the very figures age-old misogynistic stereotype has long accused women of being – even as they mobilise liberal feminism to shield themselves from the stigma historically attached to that role.

Our nature, then, is not infinitely malleable. For many thousands of years, we've governed our differences via social norms. And despite declaring every such norm obsolete, along with the differences they governed, they've refused to be dismissed. In the words from Horace that serve as the epigraph for this Part of the book: you may drive Nature out with a pitchfork, but she keeps on coming back.

For men and women alike, then, the sexual revolution has not delivered in practice. Rather than grant all a marvellous new world of polymorphous sexual freedom, the surface sheen of Big Romance has served to obscure a collapse of human intimacy into the 'marketplace'. And this hasn't delivered freedom, or happiness, or even equality, but a mutually antagonistic caricature of those features of male and female sexed difference which persist despite our best efforts. For women, this dynamic tends towards variously exploiting youthful beauty and enduring 'zipless fucks' with only a 10 percent chance of orgasm. For men, it offers either a superabundance of 'human spittoons' or embittered celibacy and sometimes misogynistic violence.

And for both, the rivalrous 'sibling society' results not in a level playing field where differences are superseded, but an adversarial relation between the sexes, where they're weaponised. Solidarity and companionship are foreclosed from the outset and that foreclosure is celebrated and amplified alike by liberal feminism, and by the macho culture of 'hoes' and hook-ups. In place of solidarity, we're offered a sexual culture that's supposedly utopian and liberated, with a ring-fenced space for overtly commercial sex, but is in truth industrialised, commodified and monetised by default.

Could the sexed differences in mate choice that produce this grotesque 'marketplace' still be transformed to something utopian, given enough time and political will? Could we still realise Giddens' utopia of 'pure relationship' and 'plastic sexuality'? In order to attempt this, we'd need to reckon with what's left of the link between sexuality and reproduction. For as things stand, the normative long-term aspiration for the average man or woman of childbearing age remains some variant on the theme of a family and kids.[58] And human reproduction is also still (for obvious reasons) an existential necessity for our collective survival.

So if we were serious about severing sexuality entirely from the role it plays in encouraging men and women to make more men and women, we'd need not only somehow to re-programme the core aspirations of a majority of heterosexual adults. And perhaps this is happening, to an extent — though not the polymorphously pleasurable way the utopians envisaged.

A growing subset of young men and women are simply abandoning the field of sex altogether: a recent study shows young men and women in their early twenties today are two and half times more likely than Gen Xers to be abstinent.[59] And perhaps they cannot be blamed. For in the frictionless 'sexual marketplace', neither side can easily afford to treat even raw physical sexual encounters as much more than a low-trust, radically individualist, structurally impermanent experience. In turn, this cloud of suspicion and radical liquidity offers little of the emotional or material stability that might reasonably be hoped for, before embarking on an 18-year commitment to a dependent child (and also to his or her other parent). The full marketisation of sex renders children psychologically (and, increasingly, literally) inconceivable.

But seeing the young vote with their feet and abandon commitment and parenthood in ever greater numbers isn't enough for Progress Theology. After all, reproduction remains an existential necessity for our continuation as a species. As such, it can't simply be abolished. In the next chapter, I'll look at those voices on the progressive vanguard who seek instead to liquefy reproduction, in a war now being conducted on perhaps the most visceral relationship of all: the bond between mother and baby.

5

The Devouring Mother

So hold me, Mom, in your long arms
In your automatic arms
Your electronic arms
In your arms.

Laurie Anderson[1]

Flesh of my flesh

MORE THAN ANYTHING, after my daughter was born, I was trans-
fixed by an overwhelming urge to look after her: a visceral urge so
ancient and pervasive it even shows up in the Old Testament. The
first Book of Kings, written *c.*550 BC during the Babylonian Exile
of the Jews, tells a story of two women who came before King
Solomon for judgement, as they both claimed to be the mother
of the same baby. There were no DNA tests in 550 BC, so the
story goes that Solomon commanded the baby be cut in two, and
half given to each woman. One woman agreed, saying that way
neither would have it. But the second woman cried out, 'O my
lord, give her the living child, and in no wise slay it.'[2] Hearing this,
Solomon gave the baby to the second woman. Her willingness to
protect the baby from harm even at the cost of relinquishing her

own claim to it demonstrated a depth of care for its interests that marked her out as the mother.

It's by no means the case that mothers invariably love and show a willingness to sacrifice for our children, like the nameless mother in 1 Kings. The world is full of difficult relationships between mothers and their children. But a variant of that devotion is so widespread it's ground deep even into figures of speech. 'A face only a mother could love' denotes someone so ugly that only their mother, with her unique capacity for devotion, could still see beauty and feel love.

For me it was a long road to the point where I felt able to embrace such an all-consuming relationship. I came late to motherhood, and was in my late thirties when my daughter was born. In this I'm not unusual: even those women who reach escape velocity from the 'sexual marketplace' now often have fewer children than they'd like. One study showed that the desired average number of children for US families has remained stable since the 1980s at around 2.6.[3] The birth rate, meanwhile, is well below that, at around 1.6,[4] suggesting a widespread gap between ideal and reality.

This is often attributed to uncertainty in housing and employment instability, and these are doubtless factors that contribute (as they did for me in my hyper-liquid twenties) to fearing a baby too great a burden. But it's not just that. Mainstream culture is founded on assumptions that foreclose motherhood, or else see it as, at best, a source of commercial opportunities, or more commonly an obstacle to market participation. But this doesn't mean we've succeeded in liberating ourselves from maternity. Following the pattern I've already set out, in seeking to dissolve motherhood, these ancient instincts are colonised by the market, where they return in the form of an ancient, archetypal nightmare: the devouring mother.

If you'd asked me, mid-twenties, whether I wanted children, I would have said 'I don't know' or 'no', and mumbled something about independence. This wasn't because I was living a particularly high life. 'Independence', for me, was a nice way of dressing up a threadbare and unreliable income, volatile moods, unstable and usually shared accommodation, and (at the rare times I wasn't single) relationships that were also unstable, and sometimes shared as well.

Bluntly, I felt less than competent at taking care of myself, let alone a baby. Not unreasonably, given this, I had recurring nightmares about accidental pregnancy. I was terrified of finding myself facing, via an ineluctable biological process, a set of responsibilities which I felt hopelessly inadequate to meet. In this sense, motherhood structured my twenties – despite being a decade away – through the sheer effort I put into avoiding it.

I tell you all this now, to underline the distance I travelled from that life of financial, interpersonal and psychological fluidity to one where I felt stable enough to become less 'independent'. When she arrived, it wasn't even that I saw her as a separate entity, who needed caring for in some abstract way. It was more basic than that: like having grown an extra limb, and finding that limb suddenly, unnervingly, separated from my own body and needing constant watching and tending to ensure it was still okay. The sense of continuity with my child was all-consuming. I know this only because, after she was born, I stopped feeling it briefly when I grew severely ill with a rare complication following her delivery. When a nurse took her away for care, I remember feeling not a pang of separation but just desperate relief that she was no longer my responsibility. Then, when I began to recover, the sense of connection abruptly came back.

It isn't always the birthing mother who feels this sense of interpersonal merging. But it's also more often the case that the one doing the mothering is the woman who hosted the child in her own body for nine months. 1 Kings says of the baby's mother that 'her bowels yearned upon her son'. Having been literally disembowelled in the process of bringing my own daughter into the world, only to discover that she still felt like part of my body even after exiting it, it feels entirely true to me that my innards might long for closeness to a tiny person who spent nine months among them. And it's clear this is a common experience, and has very little to do with our conscious minds.

Abigail Tucker's 2021 book *Mom Genes*, which looks at 'the science of moms', suggests that what 1 Kings describes has a basis in fact. The 'maternal instinct' is, as Tucker puts it, 'real and powerful, a spontaneously arising set of emotions and actions pertaining to the perception and care of babies'.[5] She's careful to emphasise, though, that this is not exactly intrinsic or universally present in women. Rather, it's set in motion by pregnancy. For it's not just my midsection that will never be the same again, having gestated a baby. I also experienced – as Tucker puts it – 'an unseen and poorly understood cellular-level revolution that rebuilds the female brain'.[6]

Mothers' neurology begins to be transformed during pregnancy, and while acculturation plays a role in this process, it's also a biological change, with similar changes observable across numerous species. Pregnancy permanently heightens mothers' response to images of smiling or distressed infants, for example, a process of 'sensitisation' that makes us acutely aware of babies' needs and cues.[7] And this is especially pronounced for our own babies. Mothers become so swiftly and completely attuned to our particular babies, at a pre-rational level, that – according to some studies – we can recognise our own just by stroking their hand.[8]

And mothers are intricately interconnected with our children, down to a cellular level – a process whose inception Tucker describes with a mixture of wonder and alarm. The placenta which forms to nourish the baby is only partly composed of our genetic material, and its development is invasive: Tucker describes placenta cells 'attacking' a pregnant woman's arteries 'like starved wolves' to access her blood supply.[9] And this invasion never fully ends: our babies' DNA remains in our bodies after birth, sometimes for years, a phenomenon known as 'foetal microchimerism'. During and even long after pregnancy, these cells may identify and repair injuries in the mother's body, appearing in scar tissue and in one case even rebuilding a whole lobe of one woman's liver – a case made even more poignant by the fact that the baby had been aborted.[10]

Foetal microchimerism is both material fact and powerful metaphor for the physiological and emotional interdependence between a mother and baby. Even before they're born, our babies respond to their mothers' physiological arousal – elevated heart rate, changes in the volume of stress hormones and so on. And the reverse is also true: in minute and subtle ways, pregnant mothers also respond involuntarily when their unborn babies are stimulated.[11] This intricate, voiceless dialogue continues after birth as well: mothers and their babies co-create one another, in complex neurobiological feedback loops.

Here, then, is the nuclear core of what transformed my 'independent' twentysomething self into my encumbered, mothering self today: a blurring of the boundaries of 'independent' selfhood difficult to put into words, but rooted in embodied changes triggered by pregnancy. And here too is the problem it poses for bio-libertarian feminism. For this doctrine presupposes a vision of 'progress' understood as every greater freedom, including from all those ways in which 'human' bodies exert any influence on 'human' inner lives.

From this perspective, it's not just legitimate but feminist and progressive to employ technology to make men and women functionally interchangeable. But if we accept these premises, what are we to make of bowels that yearn upon the children they once hosted? Unsurprisingly, bio-libertarian feminists who follow the logic of this all the way down the well of organic embodiment often respond to the problem with something akin to horror.

In her 2019 book *Full Surrogacy Now: Feminism Against Family*, Sophie Lewis describes the transformative impact and invasive power of the placenta, in terms that echo Tucker's mix of admiration and alarm. But Lewis lacks Tucker's wide-eyed wonder. Rather, for Lewis, gestation elicits something closer to pure body horror: as she sees it, 'biophysically speaking, gestating is an unconscionably destructive business'.[12] In her eyes, pregnancy is both relentless army and military weapon: a process that 'never stops, dominates your mood, hijacks your blood vessels and sugar supply, while slowly exploding your anatomy from the inside out'.[13]

In this, Lewis speaks to the shadow side of maternity, where this mixture of the grisly and the miraculous is a kind of secret language shared by mothers of little children. I remember laughing at all manner of bulging, leaking, seeping and otherwise comically gross phenomena with other mothers, when my daughter was *in utero* or newborn. But as things turned out, I *wanted* it all. By the time I became a mother, I'd already grieved one miscarriage, and the arrival of my longed-for baby was deeply welcome despite the discomfort and gore involved in her getting here. Amid the medical emergencies and subsequent mess and pain, I felt for the first time the love idealised in countless artworks by the iconic dyad of Madonna and Child – even if I found myself crying in exhausted pain at endless cluster-feeding, at the same time as gazing in adoration at her tiny, perfect face.

Parasites don't have rights

Equally, though, I was born after the contraceptive revolution. I grew up amid largely unquestioned acceptance that the default 'human' state for both sexes is radical atomisation. And the dissolution of emotional and physical separateness that accompanies pregnancy would surely have felt like a nightmare, had I found myself undergoing it against my will. In those circumstances, I dare say my initial reaction might be closer to Lewis's.

In this light, it's easier to comprehend the sometimes-extreme language employed by contemporary pro-abortion campaigners. One widely shared image from a 2019 abortion rights rally in Alabama, for example, showed young women wearing 'My Body, My Choice' T-shirts, and brandishing a placard that declares: 'PARASITES DON'T HAVE RIGHTS'.[14] It's a common sentiment that was already widely voiced – and contested – before *Roe v Wade* was overturned and with still greater frequency since.[15] My sense is that, even among women who support abortion, very few sincerely view babies as parasites. Language such as this is powered by the (accurate) recognition that women's accession to liberal autonomy on the model set out by Rousseau is only ever provisional. But instead of challenging that vision of liberal autonomy, these feminists depict its loss, via pregnancy, as Gigeresque body horror.

While I didn't experience my unborn child as a parasite, it's clear that, for many, the encroachments a baby makes onto its mother's autonomy would be experienced straightforwardly in these terms. This profound fear of a parasite-baby, which crept through my recurring nightmares, took Hollywood pop-cultural form six years after *Roe v Wade* in the 'xenomorph' created by H. R. Giger for the first *Alien* movie. This acid-dripping mother of nightmares is a nigh-indestructible, insectoid, twin-mouthed horror whose larval form wraps itself around the face of human victims and 'impregnates' them with a hatchling alien which then 'gestates' inside the victim's body and bursts forth from their chest, killing the host in agony.

Such body horror has an echo, too, in the gory and sometimes dangerous nature of pregnancy and childbirth. Among the many changes technology has brought to women's lives are advances that have simply saved many: thanks to developments in obstetric medicine, for example, millions who would otherwise have died during childbirth now survive to raise their children. In the UK alone, perinatal mortality for mothers has fallen from around one in 200 in the 19th century[16] to around one in 10,000 today.[17] I owe my own survival, and that of my daughter, to just such advances: her birth, accomplished surgically, was physiologically not a million miles away from the bloody emergence of a baby Giger xenomorph. So too was the post-partum haemorrhage and subsequent complications that, in an earlier time, would probably have killed me as surely as a chest-bursting xenomorph.

But for the bio-libertarians, tech advances can't stop here. As we've seen, the contraceptive revolution cemented as a core feminist objective a vision of personhood premised on the right to be separate, to not be encumbered, interdependent (or, depending on your perspective, parasitised by an invading alien). As the Catholic feminist Abigail Favale puts it, 'the procreational potential of sex is viewed as a switch that can be flipped, if desired, but whose default setting is "off".[18] For both sexes, but most urgently for women, this is now the foundational condition of 'personhood', and thus a core premise of bio-libertarian feminism.

From this vantage point, pregnancy appears as a monstrous, cancerous, invasive aberration. In the stylised and carefully de-sexed language of an accomplished cyborg theologian, Sophie Lewis captures this revulsion for the visceral, gory, dangerous strangeness of motherhood. 'No wonder philosophers have asked whether gestators are persons,' she says. 'It seems impossible that a society would let such grisly things happen on a regular basis to entities endowed with legal standing.'[19]

In the United States, this framing has taken on new intensity in the light of the furore triggered by the ruling that overturned *Roe v Wade*. One 2022 *Washington Post* op-ed declared that campaigners against abortion aren't 'pro-life' but 'pro forced birth'.[20] That is, what looks to one side like the protection of something sacred – a defenceless life – looks to the other like the monstrous, asymmetric imposition of unchosen obligation, in violation of every ideal of equality, freedom and progress.

From this perspective, Lewis's conclusion is unavoidable: the only progressive response is to denature Nature herself. For as Lewis rightly points out, feminists – the bio-libertarian ones anyway – have campaigned for some time now 'to denaturalize the gender of reproductive work more generally'.[21] That is, women have been campaigning since the second wave began for an order in which caring for babies is everyone's responsibility, not just an obligation placed on mothers. It hardly makes sense to reject the association between women and caregiving, only to re-entrench it at the biological level.

Stubborn bonds

Or does it? For as well as being an obligation – experienced by many feminists as an unfair one – there are also, as it turns out, things mothers *like* about the connection they have with their babies – for all that this is often fraught with ambivalence. This tension comes through clearly in the radical feminist journal *Trouble & Strife*, published between 1983 and 2002. In one 1985 essay, Ruth Wallsgrove describes her experience as a childless feminist woman doing her best to support mothers with childcare, but frustrated that such women 'want support, on their terms' but at no cost to the bond they have with their children: 'they don't want to share'.[22] And children are ambivalent about being 'shared', too. The 'infant attachment' studies conducted by John Bowlby and Mary Ainsworth demonstrated the key role played in child development of the attachment bond small children form with familiar caregivers.[23] And later work by the psychotherapist Sue Gerhardt showed how this attachment bond in turn helps to shape an infant's developing brain.

Caregivers, then, are not easily interchangeable. Another *Trouble & Strife* writer, Diana Leonard, blames this on mothers' own unreasonably high standards of care. 'We shall not get out of this impasse', she argues, 'unless and until feminists/mothers are prepared to problematise the content of childcare: to stop taking what are in fact middle class, western, late twentieth century standards of childcare as a given or as desirable.'[24] Wallsgrove notes that the same goes the other way too: 'non-mothers' find themselves unsatisfied with caring for others' children, and seek that ultimate bond of motherhood. 'Women [...] want to be *mothers*, not non-biologically-determined parents. They want to *have* a baby, not access to someone else's. They want it to know they are its mother, to be identified as mothers socially, even to be the one who *has* to get up in the middle of the night.'[25]

As for feminists demanding childcare, Dena Attar declares that 'We were always a bit embarrassed about that demand' – because, in truth, it sought to address an impossible dilemma: the fact that mothers want time away from children, but also don't want to be separated from their children. 'We had to keep explaining that we didn't mean that babies and children should be left in the twenty-four-hour nurseries all the time. It was just that mothers needed provision to work the hours their jobs required, day or night, and to go to meetings, go out, whatever. Nothing less would really do if we wanted to free mothers to participate as equals in the adult world.'

The solution to this irreducible tension, between the need to liberate mothers from their children in order to 'free [them] to participate as equals in the adult world', and the preference of both mothers and their children to remain closely connected was, she acknowledges, to make the demand purely theoretically: '[W]e kept it as a demand but left it at that, without groups or campaigns or anything much at all.'[26]

Much has changed since Attar wrote those words in 1992. For it's in the interests of both liberal emancipation and economic growth – of both freedom and the market – that this stubborn bond between mothers and children be loosened. Other activities are, after all, more productive than nurturing from an economic point of view – not to mention less constricting. To this end, and aided alike by feminist campaigning and government policy, the decades since *Trouble & Strife* have seen a mushrooming of formal childcare facilities: three out of five UK children under 14 now experience some form of formal childcare.[27]

For Lewis, none of this is enough. The writers in *Trouble & Strife* acknowledged, more or less clearly, that we can't in fact 'have it all', as *Cosmopolitan* editor and prophet of sexual emancipation Helen Gurley Brown claimed in 1982.[28] But since Gurley Brown's book was published, successive generations of mothers have attempted this, only to discover that the so-called 'motherhood penalty' is still stubbornly there. In other words: beyond a certain point, there really is a zero-sum conflict between wanting to be a high-flying professional and a present, attentive primary caregiver.

For the most committed bio-libertarians, though, the solution to this uncomfortable fit between liberal autonomy and maternal attachment isn't to re-examine the cultural privileging of 'autonomy'. Instead, like differences in how men and women choose partners that we saw in the previous chapter, this sexed asymmetry is reframed as evidence of 'patriarchy'. From this perspective, notwithstanding clear evidence for its existence across multiple species, 'maternal instinct' is in fact a self-serving myth concocted by sexist men to keep women subordinate.[29]

Socialise attachment

And if 'maternal instinct' is a patriarchal myth, smashing patriarchy means all-out assault on the oppressive idea that there's anything distinctive or 'natural' about the connection between a mother and her baby. Thus, we find that for Lewis, feminist liberation can only be attained by de-normalising first the 'natural' heterosexual mode of reproduction, second the idea that gestation affords a mother any particular bond with a baby, and finally the idea that gestating, birth and nursing are in any unique sense something done by women. In this, she follows the logic of contraceptive-revolution feminism to its conclusion. Technology may have enabled us to flatten differences between the sexes first in the workplace and then in the bedroom, but this position makes little sense if feminists then set about '(re-)imposing gender on gestation and gestators in particular'.[30] So it follows that the final frontier in the radical equality of all 'humans' is to unmoor such differences from reproduction itself.

When I recovered enough after my daughter's birth to care for her, that fierce desire to be in charge of her care returned in force. But for Lewis, this possessiveness is highly suspect: despite what the radical feminists of *Trouble & Strife* debated in the 1980s and 1990s, and notwithstanding the large body of research showing the importance of infant attachment to a developing child, in her view children 'don't belong to anyone, ever'. But Lewis doesn't travel straight from political critique of natural infant attachment to advocating a free market in babies, any more than proponents of sexual liberation leapt straight to advocating a free market in pornography. She doesn't support commercial surrogacy – the paid 'work' of having a child 'for someone else',[31] not least because in her view this isn't possible as infants 'aren't property'.[32] She is critical of the surrogacy industry, which she calls 'capitalist biotech', noting that this market doesn't seek to solve 'the problem of pregnancy' but rather responds to 'the demand for genetic parenthood, to which it applies the logic of outsourcing'.[33]

Rather, Lewis implies that maternal devotion and infant attachment – a facet of our nature which, an immense body of literature shows, humans share with numerous other species[34] – should be liquefied for utopian reasons. Despite her aversion to the trade that always comes with freedom, Lewis argues that we must demand the biotech, just without the capitalism. Medical advances, in her view, are capable of freeing all humans – and especially women, and (importantly) individuals who identify as women – from those inconvenient constraints of embodiment that hold us back. They just need to be wrestled back from the market. As optimistic about the liberatory potential of new 'reprotech' as she is critical of the way such tech is 'currently monopolized by capitalism's elites',[35] Lewis argues for a utopian world where all may 'reap the benefits of already available techniques'.

And this is essential, from her perspective: for in the Marxist tradition of 'family abolition', the communist struggle begins, quite literally, at home. The very idea of instinctive or given love is not 'natural' but only appears so, to the advantage of capital, and of white bourgeois capitalist women, and to the detriment of everyone else. The claims made upon us by the supposedly pre-political affinities of family are, from this viewpoint, a core part of the systems of oppression that keep us down. In particular, the love parents tend to show particularly for their offspring has its macro-scale analogue in other exclusionary affinities that perpetuate injustice and inequality. For example, Lewis draws an analogy between the exclusionary nature of 'propertarian' family on the small scale, and the exclusionary nature of a nation-state on the larger one, at the expense of immigrants and refugees.[36] It follows, then, that to attain a 'communist amniotechnics' that can 'unbuild the fantasy of aseptic separation between all these spaces and entities',[37] the small-scale, particular loves of family must be dissolved.

In the name of freedom from the 'stratified, commodified, cis-normative, neo-colonial' apparatus of 'bourgeois reproduction',[38] then, Lewis argues for a liquefaction even of those affections and loyalties that are grounded in blood kinship – or, as she puts it, 'capitalism's incentivization of propertarian, dyadic modes of doing family'.[39] This can, in her view, be achieved by swapping the vision

117

of motherhood as something that comes from the guts, as in the Old Testament, with a provisional, de-gendered, denatured, often marginalised or otherwise ambiguous surrogate role of 'gestator'. The endgame is 'gestational communism': a world where babies are not the particular obligation of family units, but 'universally thought of as anybody and everybody's responsibility'.[40]

Disrupt the motherhood market

What Lewis doesn't acknowledge, or perhaps doesn't recognise, is that her utopian vision of all gestation as work – her call for 'full surrogacy now' – is the first move in the now well-established deregulatory two-step. The sexual utopianism of many mid-20th-century feminists gave way less to the sunlit uplands of equal erotic liberation than new kinds of marketisation that now penetrate deep into our hearts, minds and bodies. And the innovations in reproductive technology which Lewis views as rife with thrilling post-natural possibilities for a 'gestational communism' will, in practice, free a few of us to self-actualise as we please. But these are also already reframing embodied human nature as a series of supply and demand problems.

The longing for genetic connection to a baby has already produced well-developed markets for each component part of fertility – male sperm, female egg and a living uterus – in order to service what Lewis calls 'the baby assembly line'.[41] And when progress means the liberation of women from the asymmetric burden of unchosen gestation, logically the same technological levelling must celebrate the liberation of infertile women – or indeed men, a class infertile by definition – from the equally asymmetric burden of unchosen inability to gestate.

This liberation movement, describing itself as pursuing 'fertility equality', echoes Lewis's critique of those feminisms that stop at the embodied process of gestation. One such activist explains in *The New York Times* how their activism simply continues the progressive logic of equality into the wellspring of new life. 'This is about society extending equality to its final and logical conclusion,' says Ron Poole-Dayan, founder of Men Having Babies, a New York-based nonprofit that helps gay men with surrogacy arrangements.[42]

The same article also quotes Catherine Sakimura, deputy director and family law director of the National Center for Lesbian Rights, who calls for a transformation in how 'infertility' is understood – from a biological to a far broader social definition: 'We must shift our thinking', she says, 'so that the need for assisted reproductive technologies is not a condition, but simply a fact.'

The universal solvents of freedom and equality can only do their work by liberating us from 'embedded' life in a web of given social relations. And motherhood is perhaps the ultimate, most literally visceral, given social relation. The only way to make something so particularistic 'open access' is to 'disrupt' it, as the tech bros say: that is, to prise it free from its web of social relations. From this vantage point we might even, as one 2020 *Bioethics* paper speculates, be serving the arc of progress by leaning into 'the liberatory possibilities of (full) ectogenesis' and the ability this would offer to 'separate woman from female reproductive function'.[43]

Could we, as Lewis seems to believe, have the freedom without the market, perhaps by socialising childcare? Public policy on looked-after children would seem to disagree: since Bowlby and Ainsworth's work on 'attachment' showed the importance of stable relational bonds for children's healthy development some decades ago, every UK orphanage has been closed and their role replaced by foster care. The hope was that, in this way, even vulnerable looked-after children might have a chance at developing the kind of stable attachments that will help them to flourish. In other words, even in situations where children *need* non-maternal care, as for example where children have been abandoned or orphaned, accepted best practice has been moving in the opposite direction for decades.

And yet the logic of 'progress' demands the inverse: not fewer, but more interchangeable caregivers. Lewis herself cheerfully acknowledges: 'It's true: I am not thinking of children here.'[44] She is also, perhaps, not thinking of mothers, most of whom do not want their particular loves socialised away. The last serious socialist attempt at institutionalising child-rearing was on the Israeli kibbutz, where babies were housed communally in 'children's houses'. The last children's house closed in 1997, in part because kibbutz mothers who had grown up in that environment baulked at allowing their own babies to be cared for in this way.[45] Meanwhile, more informal efforts at what Lewis calls 'gestational communism' seem mixed at best in their devotion to the welfare of children. Florida-based Ethan Baucom, featured widely in the media in 2019 as one of four male partners in a 'polycule' with Tory Ojeda,[46] was convicted the following year of aggravated child abuse after Ojeda's five-week-old baby, conceived with another of the men in the group, suffered severe injuries.[47]

Still she comes back

Ultimately, the preference, which Lewis condemns as 'proper-tarian', that adults of both sexes display for their own genetic progeny is alive and well in the teeth of every effort either to abolish it, or make it the same across both sexes. Where a transient or short-lived relationship produces a baby, for example, today the parent who accepts primary caregiving responsibility is almost always the mother – a key factor in the 'feminisation of poverty'.[48] And the preference for genetic offspring manifests, too, as Louise Perry notes, in the dark inverted form of the 'Cinderella effect': the danger posed to children by an unrelated male partner of their mother. Such men are 40 to 100 times more likely to kill a child than a genetic father.[49] And this is before we get to the risks posed specifically to girls in this situation. According to one study, one in six girls living with a stepfather experiences sexual abuse, compared with one in 40 living with a biological father.[50]

Nor do children's developmental and attachment needs evaporate, just because utopians advocate introducing more 'liberation' into social structures. It's no disrespect to the lone mothers doing their best in often extremely difficult circumstances to acknowledge that their children face a well-documented uphill struggle to thrive, compared to their peers in two-parent families,[51] and that this is especially pronounced for boys growing up without a father.[52]

Sophie Lewis imagines that a general willingness to be liberated from possessiveness about 'our' babies might produce a utopian 'gestational communism'. She acknowledges that others have pointed out the likelihood that such technologies will be 'co-opted by capitalism' but simply dismisses this as 'pessimistic'.[53] More accurate might be 'realistic', though: to date, the path taken in practice by such 'liberations' indicates strongly that 'accessible to anyone' will continue to come with the unspoken corollary 'at a price'. As the feminist Julie Bindel has documented, commercial surrogacy is far from egalitarian in practice, instead pressing the bodies of impoverished and sometimes illiterate women in developing countries into service as gestational carriers for wealthy Western 'intended parents'.[54]

As well as promising repro-utopia while delivering yet another carcass for the market to pick over, the pursuit of 'equality' into the realm of fertility invites a second comparison with previous disembeddings. Subsistence peasants displaced from common land during the Enclosure Acts flocked to industrialising cities, where they formed the industrial proletariat: a mass of workers forcibly expelled from self-sufficient life into waged subsistence, and compelled to embark on a new power struggle for fair pay and working conditions.

Echoing what happened after the enclosures, the disembedding of gestation implies the proletarianisation of women. But this time we're being displaced not from subsistence life on the land into wage work in industrialising cities. It's physiologically impossible to gestate a baby without involving a woman. So in practice disembedding gestation means de-emphasising the woman in question and describing her instead as a 'carrier', 'surrogate' or 'gestator'. That is, stripping a living, breathing, conscious human woman of human status in favour of her function in the 'baby assembly line'.

To put it another way: the pursuit of progress demands the displacement of women from our own bodies. And these bodies – our bodies – are to be enclosed as the means of production, in what the philosopher Yuval Noah Harari calls the 'second Industrial Revolution', in which the product is 'humans themselves'.[55] We've arrived here via seemingly innocuous technological and cultural shifts that are now fusing into a commercial and political programme with a clear vision for a post-human future in which we are, as Harari says, 'hackable'.[56]

This disembedding of motherhood echoes those that preceded it in a third way, too. As we've seen in previous chapters, when long-held social norms are dissolved in pursuit of 'progress', 'freedom' and 'equality', the result never quite reaches those longed-for goals. We have not yet succeeded in abolishing our profound need to depend on one another for care, or our preference for our own genetic kin. And nor can we abolish motherly nurture. Rather, the attempt to flatten enduring asymmetries in the name of a level playing field for all sees obdurate differences reappear, in grotesque form.

The devouring mother

What happened, then, to motherly nurture, when we disembedded care in the name of freedom? This comes into view when we weigh the effects, at scale, of displacing infant care into institutional settings. This is perhaps the most radioactive third rail of all, and I step on it with trepidation, and a number of caveats. My daughter has spent time in third-party childcare; most childcare workers are boundlessly warm and dedicated; most provide good, loving and beneficial settings. And we all do what we need to do, in order to survive.

But acknowledging all this shouldn't stop us weighing the effects, at scale, of what institutional childcare *does*: namely disembedding the most visceral, intimate and relational of all forms of care, the nurture of little infants. In particular: for children who grow up in that setting, does the experience change what they think care *is*?

One characteristic feature of contemporary politics has been the slow emergence of new, youth-driven preoccupations with 'safety' and 'harm', with both of these understood in emotional and radically subjectivist terms. A great deal has been written about this phenomenon, including by the psychologist Jonathan Haidt, who links it with the rise of overprotective parenting.[57] The psychologist Jordan Peterson personifies this 'safetyism' as a contemporary expression of the devouring mother:[58] a maternal archetype identified in Jungian analysis[59] who destroys her own offspring through nurture, by suffocating their potential.

In contemporary culture, we might see her in the figure of Mother Gothel in Disney's *Tangled* (2010): a witch who keeps Rapunzel captive, so she can preserve her own youth and beauty by drawing on the magic in Rapunzel's hair. Those who dare resist or thwart the devouring mother face her destructive rage. The moment Rapunzel expresses a longing to leave the stifling, false pseudo-maternal imprisonment of the tower for the wide world of self-actualisation, Mother Gothel flips from soft, motherly sweetness to cold-eyed, vengeful fury.

What does it do to the recipient of such suffocating nurture, to be 'cared' for in this controlling way? If Disney is to be believed, nothing at all: Rapunzel seems psychologically unaffected by having spent her entire childhood locked in a tower, while her sole source of human company fills her imagination with horror stories about the dangers of the outside world. But this perhaps reflects a kind of wishful thinking: for a precondition of 'liberation' to work outside the home, if you're a mother, is in many cases handing your own children over to a setting that differs from Mother Gothel's tower mainly in containing more children.

A great deal of research has been done on the long-term effect of childcare on cognitive development and subsequent academic attainment, with most studies concluding that overall effects are either minimal or broadly positive. What if, though, this is measuring the wrong things? Women in the United States have no federal right to paid maternity leave, and one in four mothers are back at work within two weeks.[60] That's a lot of tiny babies in institutional childcare from an incredibly young age. Meanwhile, the American Psychological Association's own literature on building resilience in children emphasises the importance of the primary caring relationship. The APA quotes Philip Fisher, a professor of psychology at the University of Oregon, who says: 'The presence of a supportive, consistent and protective primary caregiver – especially when the underlying stress systems are activated – is the factor that makes the biggest difference in healthy development.'[61]

There's a clear dissonance between this acknowledged infant need for responsive and devoted care, and the now near-universal cultural pressure (and in the case of all but the wealthiest women, usually also *need*) to hand this caring obligation to someone else, so they can get back to work. While studies on the impact of early childcare on attachment produce variable results, one meta-analysis concluded that there's likely to be *some* effect. Importantly, especially where care is poor-quality and infants are very young, long hours in childcare pose a significant risk factor for disorganised attachment.[62] This generalised condition, first described by Bowlby and Ainsworth, results when an infant is dependent for survival on someone who is unpredictable, frightening, abusive or otherwise unable to provide the basic conditions of care and safety.[63] Disorganised attachment strongly associates with significant impairment in adult functioning, increasing the risk of mental health issues, including poor emotional regulation and personality disorders, along with difficulties in managing work, romantic and social life.[64]

There are, to my knowledge, no studies on whether any correlations exist between an institutionalised early infancy and the now widely documented crisis in teen and young adult mental health. But an elevated risk of disorganised attachment, or reduction in the kind of attuned caregiving that promotes resilience, might well be factors in the increasingly emotionally dysregulated quality of youth activism.

And this immense cultural shift might help to explain, too, such activists' common preoccupation with 'safety' and avoiding the risk of 'harm'. For even in the vast majority of cases where day-care staff are attentive and dedicated, the experience is bound to shape those children who grow up in it. And from my own observations, one crucial difference between how my daughter was able to explore the world as a toddler in day care, compared with the home setting, was in the risk-aversion unavoidable in childcare settings.

I would happily allow her to take physical risks, under my watchful eye, that would be unthinkable for a busy day-care worker with multiple charges, insurance liabilities and a business reputation to preserve. Similarly, and doubtless in part responding to demand from loving, absent parents, in a childcare setting the kind of minor accident that would be met with a breezy 'kiss better' from Mummy generates elaborate bureaucracy, complete with forms in duplicate and institutional record-keeping. In turn, I've noticed that for my daughter and her peer group, getting a 'bump note' is a notable event that confers a kind of status – a social norm that's transferred seamlessly from day care to the school setting.

It's difficult to prove a causal link, but it is striking that bureaucratically managed physical and emotional 'safety' has become a key political demand for young adults, around two decades after the rapid spread of nursery-based childcare. To put it another way: in the time it took for a generation to grow up after spending infancy *en masse* in conditions of relatively impersonal, child-centred safety, young adults' model of what life in common looks like has shifted towards expecting an impersonally managed, individual-centred culture with a heavy emphasis on safety.

That is: as women have joined men in embracing the Rousseauian vision of autonomous personhood, and rejecting caring obligations as an obstacle to individual self-realisation, so in turn care has been institutionalised, proceduralised and depersonalised – all the way down to infancy. In the wake of this shift, a generation has grown up that regards the suffocating 'care' of a risk-averse, third-party pseudoparent not as the enemy of their individual flourishing, but as its enabling condition. That, in fact, feels at home in the hygienic arms of an institutional Mother Gothel, and nurtured by her all-encompassing control and preoccupation with risk management. Small wonder such individuals grow up expecting that their universities (and subsequently the companies and organisations that employ them) embrace authoritarian procedures aimed at mitigating 'harm'.

With the Covid-19 pandemic, this impersonal, technocratic model of care reached its apotheosis, as an instrument of government policy across the developed world. It's a vision, again, underwritten by tech: for if all of us are now 'humans' entitled to pass the buck on caring obligations, then the only available caregivers must be machines. In this vision of abundant, automatic, safety-oriented and sexless universal nurture, we're tended to by automated deliveries of food and entertainment. Safety is no longer to be found in the arms of a loving human (m)other but is instead universally available thanks to technology: the 'automatic arms' of Laurie Anderson's prophetic 1982 hit song 'O Superman'.

This antiseptic cyborg devouring mother became abruptly visible in the pandemic-era physical and social infrastructure of masks, screens and social separation. And for some, this is a good thing: the urbanist Benjamin Bratton characterises this vision of care as a template for a new, 'touchless' kind of life in common.

Rather than being a deprivation, Bratton sees 'touchlessness' as central to a recognition that 'societal care' need not be embodied, but can also happen 'at a distance'.[65] This hygienically distant form of nurture replaces the messy, personalised business of embodied love with technology. It's modelled on the industrialised para-mothering of a nursery or hospital: a tenderness of 'impersonal systems upon which each of us relies',[66] one 'built of sensors, chips, simulated genomes, needles, and sterile wipes and realized by the labor of millions of people'.[67]

For Sophie Lewis, meanwhile, 'our inextricably surrogated contamination with and by everybody else'[68] argues not *for* particularistic love in families, but *against* human-imposed political borders. Bratton employs the metaphor of viral contagion to make the same case. For both, universal technological nurture is the ideal: an all-enveloping cyborg mother, in which every human-imposed difference or particular love may be dissolved, in favour of what Bratton calls a 'planetary society' of 'positive biopolitical governance'[69] characterised by 'the ubiquity and universality of its services'.[70]

This emerging order promises to collapse the sexist split between home and work, enabling a retreat back into safely cocooned remote working – albeit at the cost of constant keystroke surveillance by productivity monitoring software.[71] Conflating care with technology, it dismisses embodiment and particularistic affection as unhygienic and reactionary backsliding, inextricable from bigotry and oppression. And perhaps for the growing pop-ulation of now-adult individuals whose early infancy was spent in the relatively impersonal arms of third-party childcare institutions, in a setting carefully scrubbed of danger and contamination and hyper-focused on their entertainment and individuation, it may seem that this is true. If you've grown up in a setting that modelled risk-aversion, proceduralism and institutional love as the default, the sheer *arbitrariness* of in-personal maternal devotion may appear less loving and more cruelly exclusionary.

Devouring the mother

But is this a feminist vision? From a bio-libertarian perspective, undoubtedly. The replacement of caring with technology and process has freed women to soar – at least those with the resources to make use of it. But while women who are either childless or able to mobilise resources and technology to offload nurture are able to 'lean in', as former CEO of Facebook Sheryl Sandberg put it,[72] that subset of women who are mothers, and less full-throatedly committed to the atomised world of emancipation, are doing less well – much like those working-class mothers who, as Marx documented in the 19th century, dosed their babies with opiates to keep them quiet while they worked the long factory shifts needed to put food on the table.

If Covid lockdowns represented a fantasy of amniotic envelopment in hygienic, tech-enabled safety, they delivered a nightmare for actual mothers. A large proportion of working families manage to work and supervise children via a mix of formal and informal care, involving friends and grandparents, as well as formal, paid settings.[73] With all of these abruptly cancelled, millions found themselves stretched to breaking point. In a survey of 1,500 British women conducted by the UK parenting website Mumsnet, 79 percent agreed that 'responsibility for home schooling fell largely to me', while 77 percent agreed that 'it was impossible for me to work uninterrupted' when schools closed.[74]

But it wasn't just those mothers trying to square the absurd circle of working remotely while simultaneously home schooling who felt the removal of in-person social support. Those mothers who'd normally be at home on maternity leave also suffered. Evidence shows a sharp rise in perinatal psychological distress among new mothers during the pandemic, with one international meta-analysis showing perinatal psychological distress in 70 percent of study subjects.[75] On the face of it, you might think those struggling to manage work and school-age children would have fared worse than those on maternity leave, with nothing to focus on but a new baby. Why should new mothers have found lockdown particularly distressing?

Real-life, embodied mothering and the cyborg devouring mother cannot easily coexist. You can't both hold, with Lewis, that infants 'don't belong to anyone, ever' and also support the ordinary state of semi-merged interconnection between a mother and very young child. This isn't just theoretical but highly practical. As Abigail Tucker argues, becoming a mother involves neurological changes – but that doesn't mean mothering is all instinctive. Some of it has to be learned[76] – and a great deal of this is the kind of embodied knowledge that can't easily be absorbed from a book.

After my daughter's birth, I spent around a week in hospital. Though it was due to illness, there was a silver lining: several days spent on a high-dependency ward. There, one care assistant, an older woman of unending kindness and practical wisdom, spent a great deal of time as I recovered trying to talk me through getting my daughter to nurse. Finally, she simply took a handful of my breast, and my baby, and positioned them correctly. After that feeding was easy, because we knew what doing it right felt like. Much of mothering, especially of very small babies, comprises this kind of knowledge – which is difficult in the extreme to transmit via 'touchless' care, however well intentioned that may be.

In contrast, what I've characterised as the cyborg devouring mother offers institutional, all-enveloping safety – but at the price of inhibiting her offspring's potential. We see this writ large in the impact of pandemic restrictions on the very youngest. Infants born during the pandemic scored lower on gross motor, fine motor and communication skills regardless of whether parents had been infected,[77] while another study found that male and poorer children were especially hard-hit.[78] And even with parents at home during lockdown, children under five received less attentive care. According to one UK study, parents spent less time on 'home learning activities' – reading, chatting, playing, singing or painting and drawing – in 2021, compared with 2019. A quarter reported that they didn't chat to their child every day in 2021, compared with 10 percent in 2019. Reading also fell: 53 percent of parents said that they were reading to their child daily in 2021, compared with two-thirds in 2019.[79] Unsurprisingly, 76 percent of UK primary schools reported in 2021 that more children needed support with communication.[80]

And inasmuch as the cyborg mother asks us to relinquish particular relational bonds for impersonal, tech-mediated 'care', she devours mothers' ability to be attuned to and present for their babies. This is literally the case where mothers are compelled by economic necessity or the pressures of career to return to work two weeks post-partum. But it's more subtly visible, too, in those negative impacts on pandemic-era infant development strongly linked to maternal stress.[81] More broadly, this vision of 'care' devours the possibility of mothering as such, crowding out or 'virtualising' myriad mute, pre-rational, instinctive, particularistic or simply impossible-to-monetise ways of relating.

Half a century into the cyborg age, then, whether you view

progress as feminist or not depends a great deal on your situation. If you're female, childless, well educated and ambitious, or wealthy enough to outsource all of 'care' to underlings, then current doctrine may indeed appear 'feminist', in the sense of serving your interests. If you're one of the many women who has, from Wollstonecraft onwards, viewed the women's movement as aimed at seeking a fair settlement between the sexes – including for those women who are mothers – you may by now have some questions.

For the only way literal mothers are able to claw back some social status for themselves within the antiseptic embrace of the cyborg devouring mother is by themselves becoming devourers. No social role embodies this more completely than the 21st century's update of the Madonna and Child: a dyad that recurs with increasing frequency in the media, comprising a 'trans child' whose path is smoothed by an activist mother. I'll revisit this pairing in the next chapter, for it reveals what's at stake in the ongoing drive to subordinate embodied givens – including the maternal instinct – to biomedical mastery. It's the final battlefront in this war on relationships: the drive to liquidate the relationship each of us has with our own bodies.

6

Meat Lego Gnosticism

Trans women as we know them now are the melding of techno-capital with the human race and the expropriation of it towards its own ends [...] Their flesh is how the machinery beneath infiltrates the human race. It breaks these lucky few free from the horrid curse of being human towards the lesbian autoproduction of demons.

n1x, 'Gender acceleration: A blackpaper'[1]

Universal basic dissociation

I DON'T REMEMBER exactly when I stopped just *being* my body, only that the change coincided roughly with puberty. One moment I was a child who ran, climbed, wrestled and played. And the next, I was a squatter in an unfamiliar meat suit: an awkward operator of this unwanted encumbrance, without which I couldn't interact with the world.

That feeling didn't really go away until I was well into my thirties. I don't think I'm alone in this, or very unusual. Many women, feminist or not, have pointed out that the transition to adult female and thus to a body considered 'fair game' for sexual evaluation by men can be deeply uncomfortable.

133

When my household first got online, towards the end of the 1990s, my world changed overnight. Here was a placeless place where I could just *be*, without fretting about whether my tummy made rolls when I sat forward, or if my thighs were rubbing, or whether others were looking at me with desire or disgust. Online, 'me' meant the 'me' I wished I could be: a creature of pure thought.

I often recall that sense of liberation and possibility when I read accounts written by individuals born long after me, of their journey into identification as transgender. One young woman who made that journey, Helena, describes how she found life as a new-minted adult female stressful – much as I had. But where the culture of anything-goes sexuality was only getting started in the 1990s of my adolescence, Helena reached puberty at the height of the 'sex-positive' 2010s, by which time a majority of American adolescents had a smartphone and pornography was endemic.

Helena describes how female adulthood seemed 'hypersexualized and pornified'. But anyone who questioned whether it really was 'empowering' for women 'to do porn, be prostitutes, or have dangerous, kinky, scary sounding sex with many different men' ended up being derided as 'vanilla'. And 'a girl who is vanilla has no chance of really pleasing a man when competing with "empowered" women'. Not unreasonably, she concluded that if the whole world saw this setup as good and feminist, but she didn't experience it as such, the problem must be her: 'I must not have really been meant to be a girl, because if I was, this wouldn't all be so scary and confusing.'[2]

Steven also found puberty distressing, and shared Helena's discomfort with the adversarial behavioural norms now normalised for men and women within the so-called 'sexual marketplace'. For where the prevailing culture offered Helena a supposedly 'empowered' role as the degraded object of male desire, it offered Steven the opposite role, as one of the men who perpetrates this violence. But this came with a sting in the tail: even as these pornified roles constructed men as violent aggressors, and implicitly stigmatised any male who didn't participate, the culture that normalised this violent, transactional dynamic also castigated men for embracing it. The 'social justice' groups where Steven took refuge saw men as ineradicably violent:

> As a white man, I was directly responsible for all of the oppression experienced by women and people of color. I was fourteen years old and had never been in a fight in my life or said a racist or misogynistic word to anyone, but I believed that the circumstances of my birth made me a monster.[3]

For both Helena and Steven, embodied sex loomed large both as a proximate cause of their suffering, and as a potent symbol of the oppressive system that legitimised it. 'I hated my body,' says Helena; 'it must be because I don't like that it's female.' Steven was both terrified of 'what testosterone was doing to me' but also of the in-born stain of 'toxic masculinity'. 'I wanted to transition because my body was my enemy,' he says, 'and my body was the enemy of the world. I hated myself and wanted to punish myself.' Sex, then, had to be forced into medical submission.

Being uncomfortable with physicality isn't new. It's not even uniquely modern: there are many accounts of medieval saints who sought out sometimes extreme physical discomfort, including self-starvation, in order to grow closer to God.[4] But something today is very different: every generation younger than mine has grown up at least partly in a digital social world that is incorporeal by definition.

When I discovered this world in the late 1990s, it proved pivotal to my efforts to prise the 'me' I felt I really was free of the lumbering flesh that carried it so awkwardly through the material world. Online, in search of 'my people', I stumbled into a burgeoning 'genderqueer' subculture that's pervasive now, but was in the 2000s just one tiny corner of an emerging, avant-garde world of online communities. Its London incarnation had two hubs: a weekly bar night, and a small corner of a now-defunct lesbian messageboard. Here, online and off, we imagined alternative selves, played with 'identification' and pronouns, concocted elaborate parallel narratives for ourselves and each other. It felt wonderful and liberating: our inner worlds seemed poised to manifest in the real world through sheer force of imagination. I changed my name to Sebastian for a while. I wondered whether my identity was more male or female. All of us thrilled at the fluidity and playfulness of it all.

The real singularity

This virtual world, then, offered me a space where selves are detachable from embodiment. Around the time I was going by 'Sebastian', Second Life was prompting excitable tech-press headlines about users who spent wild sums on 'land' in its intangible realm.[5] And if that iteration fell by the wayside, the dream hasn't gone away: persistent multiplayer digital universes such as Minecraft and Roblox are among today's most successful games, while in 2021 Facebook founder Mark Zuckerberg bet the house on the 'metaverse'. Zuckerberg's venture has met with mixed success so far, but pundits remain enthusiastic about the prospects for such digitally created alternate worlds.[6]

Over the intervening years, increasingly influential voices in tech, culture and politics have begun to advocate for our complete human mastery of matter via science and technology – and, over time, for the dream that we should merge with our own machines to create new kinds of entity. This was famously articulated by the futurist Ray Kurzweil in *The Singularity Is Near* (2005), which argues that technology is advancing at such speed that by 2029 artificial intelligence would pass the Turing test. By 2045, Kurzweil believes, we'll arrive at a 'singularity' in which this collective intelligence becomes so advanced that it transforms humans in turn.

In truth, though, the singularity isn't near. It's already happened. I was a relatively early adopter of online-first socialising, but not by much. That space is now the primary paradigm by which young men and women make sense of the world. The average amount of time teenagers spend online every week tripled between 2005 and 2009.[7] By 2018, 95 percent of US teenagers had access to a smartphone, and 45 percent reported being online 'almost constantly'.[8]

This rise in smartphone use has been linked by psychologist Jonathan Haidt to rising youth anxiety, loneliness, intrasocial competition and negative body image,[9] and this mental health impact of social media is especially acute for girls.[10] Even workers at Instagram itself recognise this. Summarising its effect on self-perception, a 2019 internal presentation by Facebook, Instagram's parent company, reported: 'We make body image issues worse for one in three teen girls.'[11] The statistics seem to corroborate this: after Instagram launched in 2010, for example, the rate of hospitalisation for self-harm among girls aged 10 to 14 in the United States doubled in five years.[12] A similar pattern is visible in the UK, where over the decade 2007–2017 the rate of hospitalisation for self-harm among girls under 17 rose by 68 percent.[13]

Correlation isn't always causation, but as social media-related body image issues have spiked, so too has adolescent gender dysphoria: the UK's Gender Identity Development Service reported a twenty-fold increase in referrals over a decade, from 138 children in 2011 to 2,383 in 2021.[14] This was primarily driven by adolescents, with 15 being the most common age of referral. Similar patterns are observable in other developed countries including New Zealand[15] and Canada.[16] Reliable statistics are more difficult to obtain for the United States, where healthcare is decentralised, but a 2022 UCLA report shows that estimates for the total number of American transgender youth has risen sharply: 0.5 percent of Americans overall identify as transgender, but this rises to 1.4 percent among youth aged 13–17.[17] According to one recent study, new gender dysphoria diagnoses in American children nearly trebled over five years, from 15,172 referrals in 2017 to 42,167 in 2021.[18]

And the outsize impact social media has on girls' body image may be reflected too in the dramatic reversal in natal sex of children identifying as transgender. Since the mass adoption of smartphones, the sex of minors presenting with gender distress has also reversed, from predominantly boys[19] to overwhelmingly girls. Children referred to the UK's Gender Identity Development Service in 2011 were mostly boys; but by 2021, almost 70 percent were female.[20]

This disembodied form of sociality, then, seems both to be fuelling widespread distress and offering solutions to it – solutions that lean ever further into disembodiment. In this sense, Kurzweil is behind the curve: the generation that's grown up viewing this as normal has already at least figuratively merged with digital technology in transformative ways. As the singer Grimes put it in a 2022 interview:

> We are becoming cyborgs, like, our brains are fundamentally changed – everyone who grew up with electronics, we are

fundamentally different from previous *Homo sapiens*. I call us '*Homo techno*'. I think we have evolved into *Homo techno* which is, like, essentially a new species.

Thanks to this transformation, she thinks, 'We could be, really, whatever we want.' And the already-occurring merger with technology is a potential path to eternal life: 'I think if we choose correctly and we choose wisely, consciousness could exist for a very long time.'[21]

If those reaching adulthood today are already natives of the world bequeathed us by the real singularity, they are greeted with enthusiasm by thinkers who have long sought to merge us with our technologies. For the link between trans and tech is, to some, neither threat nor mental health crisis, but the key to an entire theology. One such visionary is transgender pharmaceutical entrepreneur Martine Rothblatt, who argues that the quest to master one's sexed body is merely the first step in a far greater quest to master embodiment altogether.

Rothblatt recognises that this emancipation is a logical outworking of progress, and by extension of liberal feminism, for 'the course of progress in civilization has been to render as irrelevant as possible the birth status of a particular individual'.[22] Thanks to medical advances that enable humans to remodel their own bodies, Rothblatt argues, biological sex is now merely an accident of 'birth status'. Progress means unchaining individuals from the arbitrary nature of bodily sex, in the name of, as Rothblatt puts it, 'the full cultural liberation of all people'.[23]

In this vision, selfhood and embodiment are wholly separate things: humanness, Rothblatt asserts, 'is in the mind'.[24] Any given 'mind' should be free to edit its own body at will, in pursuit of self-realisation. Growing technological sophistication has, Rothblatt claims, liberated us from adherence to sex role stereotypes. Now, 'thanks to culture and technology, humans are leaving those gender dimorphic behaviors behind as they come to appreciate the limitless uniqueness of their sexual identities'.[25] But it doesn't stop with our 'sexual identities'. Rather, 'freedom of gender is [...] the gateway to a freedom of form'.[26]

And once we realise we're not constrained by our sex, it's only a short step to 'the awakening that we are not limited by our anatomy at all'.[27] Like Grimes, Rothblatt imagines a new species emerging. 'From *Homo sapiens*, literally the "wise man", shall emerge our new species, *Persona creatus*, the "creative person"':[28] a new kind of entity with biological, digital and hybrid members.

Evil nature

Not everyone is thrilled by this prospect. Thinkers particularly in the Roman Catholic tradition condemn the push to master or escape the physical, as a return of the ancient heresy of 'Gnosticism'.[29] This grouping of esoteric Christian sects, active from around the 2nd century AD until their suppression by the Knights Templar in the 13th century, saw life on earth as irredeemably corrupt and dreamed of returning to a higher world of pure thought.[30]

But in truth what we see today is distinct from the ancient Gnosticism. The Gnostics saw material existence as the work of a malevolent deity, the Demiurge, and sought to transcend the material plane through spiritual wisdom ('gnosis'). And they were influenced by the Platonic idea that there exists a higher world of ideal Forms, whose nature is purer and more real than any of their corrupted instances on earth. The Gnostics wanted to escape the corrupt material plane, and live only in this world of pure ideals.

The contemporary phenomenon agrees with the ancient Gnostics on a crucial point: the physical world is evil and arbitrary. Unlike the ancient Gnostics, though, the modern variety seeks to transcend the physical not through spiritual knowledge but through technology. And its moral vanguard is bio-libertarianism, which views any moral or legal effort to restrict the tech-enabled control of our biology with horror and dismay.

This worldview sets women constitutively at odds with our own bodies. To realise ourselves, we must wage war on nature – and even on the idea that we *have* a nature. Indeed, from a bio-libertarian perspective waging war on the idea of 'nature' is precisely what feminism *should* be doing. Firstly, because 'nature' is widely viewed as a mere stalking horse for 'patriarchy'. And secondly because, inasmuch as it exists at all, 'nature' is a set of physiological constraints that we didn't choose and that limit our ability to self-realise. In turn, this invites medical science to expand its sphere of control ever further beyond normal reproduction, and to encompass ever more of our physical nature. The upshot is an order where matters once deemed the proper realm of philosophy or religious faith, such as questions of birth, death or desire, are subcontracted to the machine. That is: if we have technological control, we don't need moral codes any more. Except what this produces is, in practice, a new moral code: a cyborg theology.

This may sound hopelessly abstract. But moral codes – theologies – have real-world consequences, in the human activities they legitimise. And the activities given pride of place by our emerging cyborg theology are those now roaring ahead in AI and biotech. What Christian critics are calling 'neo-Gnosticism' is, from a more secular standpoint, merely the bow wave of this 'progress'.

The end goal of cyborg theology is delegitimising the idea that we *have* a nature: liquefying perhaps the most fundamental social norm of all, and in the process opening profoundly disturbing new market possibilities. In its moralised form, this vision now commands those crucial figures a theology needs, if it's to have real-world political teeth: saints, inquisitors and clergy.

Saints and inquisitors

Rothblatt didn't just theorise the cyborg transformation, but set about helping to deliver it, as an influential early figure in a nexus of campaigning groups now working to entrench the central premise of cyborg theology: that inner identity is unrelated to physiological form. The campaigners have set about reordering legal structures to their metaphysics, by drafting template legislation that replaces legal recognition of sex with legal recognition of self-declared 'gender'. Rothblatt co-authored an early instance of this template, the International Bill of Gender Rights.[31]

Over the decade of the singularity, the 2000s, the worldwide legislative advance of this campaign for 'freedom of form' progressed again. In 2006, a group of lawyers and activists drafted the Yogyakarta Principles, another piece of template legislation proposing 'universal' LGBT rights, including legal primacy of 'gender identity'.[32] As journalist Helen Joyce has documented, this campaign, which presents itself as an outgrowth of feminism and gay rights, now includes bodies such as the American Civil Liberties Union, the Gay & Lesbian Alliance Against Defamation, the UN Human Rights Committee, Stonewall in Britain, and many other campaigns and lobbies.

It's not a campaign conducted via electoral politics. Rather, this would-be cyborg theocracy entrenches its ideology largely through extra-democratic channels – for example, by drafting and campaigning for gender-identity provision in national laws, HR policies or journalistic guidelines, or by shaping social norms via 'education' and the flow of resources to institutions that propagate, communicate or set boundaries on public morals, such as universities, schools, libraries, media organisations and courts.[33] For the most part, too, it seeks to do so without drawing attention to its activities. A 2019 document produced by law colossus Dentons in partnership with the Thomson Reuters Foundation and the International Lesbian, Gay, Bisexual, Transgender, Queer & Intersex Youth and Student Organisation (IGLYO) advises campaigners to 'get ahead of the government and publish progressive legislative proposal before the government ha[s] time to develop their own', and recommends gaining 'a veil of protection' by tying desired changes to 'more popular reform'.[34]

This fusion of coercive power with neo-Gnostic beliefs can now be seen, for example, in US family courts. As the journalist Abigail Shrier has shown, in some places a parent who refuses to allow their child's normal bodily development to be interrupted in the name of identity may be deprived of all parental authority.[35] In other words, some of the US judiciary now see their role as partly inquisitorial: enforcing the fundamentally religious belief that abstract, disembodied selfhood trumps both physiological sex and parental authority.

This theocratic turn today extends beyond family courts, too: in several US states, the cumulative effect of laws governing mental health treatment, insurance and other matters combine to strip parents of all authority where their child's self-declared gender identity is concerned.[36] Nor is the delegitimisation of parents confined to the United States: in Canada, a father has been jailed for insisting that his female child is his daughter, not his son.[37]

And this in turn reveals the cyborg theocracy's most revered and controversial figures: the child saints who now serve as living martyrs to Rothblatt's vision of 'freedom of form'. Every battleground in the utopian assault on human nature converges in this campaign, to extend 'freedom of form' to children. It's a war over what sexuality is, and what it's for. It's a war over whether children should be treated as autonomous – or if not, who has authority to decide what they can and can't do. And it's a war over whether or not we have a 'nature' as such.

Do children have a right to remodel their own bodies in defiance of natural development? This claim pits progress and freedom directly against 'natural' human maturation, now viewed as something unchosen and thus potentially oppressive. And many do indeed now find their own nature oppressive. Steven, for example, experienced puberty as being 'poisoned by a chemical which makes your mind and body monstrous'. Testosterone meant, for him, a toxic slide into corruption: 'Every day, my body was masculinizing. Every day, that slow drip of poison was mutating me into a bestial horror.' He wanted out: 'I wanted to have my testicles removed. They were the source of testosterone, the source of the poison I had to take medication to block. They were symbolic of everything I hated about myself.'

This isn't an isolated account. Male puberty is now viewed as hostile and poisonous by enough individuals to have inspired a T-shirt design, available from multiple sellers, that declares: 'I SURVIVED TESTOSTERONE POISONING'. The 'poisoning' in question is the normal surge in testosterone that occurs as part of normal male puberty. From this perspective, pornographic actor and transgender activist Zinnia Jones argues that normal puberty and medically imposed intervention in puberty should both be treated as requiring informed consent. In a now-hidden tweet, Jones declared that it should be the norm, not the exception, to inhibit the irreversible course of puberty until children opt to undergo it: 'An inability to offer informed consent or understand the long-term consequences is actually an argument for putting every single cis and trans person on puberty blockers until they acquire that ability.'[38]

The transgender surgeon Marci Bowers echoed this in a 2022 Duke University symposium, referring disparagingly to 'people who want to lock others in their gender cages'.[39] Here what Bowers refers to as a 'gender cage' is normal puberty: no longer a normal, naturally occurring process but one now imposed, involuntary and imprisoning. Steven's account powerfully echoes the ancient Gnostics in the disgust he describes feeling, for embodiment itself, viewed only as a source of pollution and misery. 'I saw myself as a being of water and light,' Steven recounts, 'an angel imprisoned in a filthy human body. I resented having to eat, sleep, piss, and shit. I particularly hated having sexual desires and wanted to be rid of them.'

Bowers has expressed reservations about over-diagnosis and hurried medicalisation of transgender youth, but clearly still views medical intervention as appropriate for some children.* And in such cases, implicitly, the 'people' locking such unhappy young 'humans' in 'cages' may include not just legislators, but anyone who opposes trans identities more generally – including a parent less than wholly supportive of their child using medical interventions to obtain the secondary sex characteristics they desire. For needless to say, not every parent is on board with the proposed bio-libertarian solution. The campaign for children's 'freedom of form' thus necessitates a secondary campaign, to undermine the authority parents would otherwise have to prevent their children being remodelled.[40]

---

* Abigail Shrier, 'Top trans doctors blow the whistle on "sloppy" care', Common Sense, 4 October 2021, www.commonsense.news/p/top-trans-doctors-blow-the-whistle.

Gnostic Madonna

In this version of the story, parents who refuse to facilitate their child's bio-libertarian self-actualisation rank among the villains. Virtuous, kind, self-sacrificing mothers and fathers – in other words, the real nurturers – devote their lives to smoothing the path for their child's disembodied 'true self'. And, as is the way with the intricate dialogue of co-creation that is motherhood, the ensuing social production of a 'trans child' is invariably also that of a 'trans parent' – in truth, usually a mother. Susie Green, CEO of youth transgender charity Mermaids, is one such; Marlo Mack, author of a recent book on 'raising my transgender daughter', is another. One such 'trans kid', Jazz Jennings, has been making media appearances since the age of six, alongside one or both parents, to speak about the challenges of growing up transgender – a media career that engulfed Jennings' whole family when extended to a long-running reality TV show, *I Am Jazz*.

I have a measure of sympathy for such mothers. There's no positive social or cultural room for mothers within bio-libertarian 'feminism'. Facilitating a 'trans child' at least affords a partial means of reclaiming the maternal work of care and nurture – not least in the sheer effort required to 'protect' a child from the implications of his or her own biophysical reality. And it affords a means to recoup some parental authority: for the facilitating parents now consent on the child's behalf to interventions with far-reaching consequences.

Rothblatt may claim that gender surgeries are now 'so persuasive that rarely can a "new man" or "new woman" be distinguished from a biological original'.[41] Such magical thinking is commonplace in children, including those who identify as the opposite sex: 'When I was two years old,' said Jazz Jennings, 'I went up to my mom and asked her, "When is the good fairy going to come with her magic wand and change my penis into a vagina?"'[42] In the face of childlike innocence, many parents are uneasy about telling the truth, when the truth means denying something your child wants.

'As a parent, you don't want your child who's only five to have a whole aspect of human experience already shut to them,' says 'trans parent' Marlo Mack.[43] 'I've been kind of cringing when she'll say, "When I'm a mom", or "I'm going to have this many babies", or "When I'm pregnant",' she adds. Mack is right to be uncomfortable: those who can't bear to disappoint their child's innocent cross-sex identification, and opt instead to support the desire even in the face of natural puberty, are setting their children on a path to adulthood deprived of the capacity to have children of their own. Young men and women who transition in adolescence may freeze eggs or sperm,[44] gambling on the 18 percent success rate of fertility treatment from frozen eggs.[45] But the chances of success remain low. Implicitly, then, 'trans parents' hope that Meat Lego technology will enable their child to flourish while keeping as many doors as possible open. But in practice, taking this path means taking the decision to close other doors for your child.

Mounting evidence suggests that when such children reach adulthood, sexual desire and pleasure may be severely inhibited or wholly unavailable. Seventeen-year-old Jazz Jennings was documented in 2018 in *I Am Jazz* discussing having never experienced an orgasm, or any sexual desire to speak of at all.[46] Even gender surgeons such as Marci Bowers (who treated Jennings) have expressed concerns that children whose normal puberty is interrupted early enough by cross-sex hormone treatment may remain, like Jennings, seemingly incapable of orgasm as adults.[47] The same course of treatment also forecloses normal adult fertility, as adult gametes never develop. And, in many cases, hormone treatment followed by surgery leads to a cascade of further medical interventions: for example, Jazz Jennings underwent 'gender confirmation surgery' with genitals so underdeveloped thanks to artificially arrested puberty that they could furnish no material to construct a 'neovagina'. Instead, multiple painful surgeries were required to form one from colon tissue.[48]

For those who transition later, too, side effects are legion. Evangelists for the war on nature ground their case for surgical gender medicine in a horror-response to unchosen physical changes. But the bio-libertarian claim of medical mastery over nature brings its own dividend of body horror. Around a quarter of female-to-male transgender individuals undergo 'top surgery', which is to say double mastectomy;[49] in the three years ending 2021, at least 776 of these were performed on minors aged 13 to 17.[50] In addition to this significant and irreversible intervention, a regime of cross-sex hormones can cause blood clots, male-pattern baldness, Type 2 diabetes, pelvic pain and vaginal atrophy to the point where hysterectomy is usually necessary after a few years.[51]

One paper in the *Indian Journal of Plastic Surgery* notes that phalloplasty usually involves creating a 'penis' from a flap of the patient's forearm skin, which leaves behind an area of scarring and sometimes nerve damage. The 'neophallus' can be made erect only via an artificial stiffening device 'associated with high infection and failure rates'. The whole procedure is at considerable risk, the authors report, of 'flap failure, urethral fistula, urethral stricture and stiffener related problems'.[52] If the neo-Gnostic worldview imagines us all as pure, disembodied selves, our bodies are mere parts to be disassembled and reassembled at will, like Lego bricks made of meat. The gap between Rothblatt's vision and its messy, fleshy execution is the stuff of nightmares.

Meat Lego priestesses

You'd expect the Meat Lego vision to meet more concerted institutional resistance. But the burden of proof seems to be eternally
on those who oppose this radical project of tech-enabled emancipation. In Britain a number of individuals have experienced social
sanctions, from loss of employment to visits from the police, as a
consequence of having expressed scepticism about trans activism.
How has this worldview so swiftly acquired, if not mass acceptance, at least such substantial institutional backing?

What I've called the real singularity, which is to say the now-
normal experience of disembodied online sociality, is doubtless
a factor in widespread youth support for Meat Lego Gnosticism.
And yet terminally online teenagers hardly wield the political
clout needed to rewrite international legal systems. What else is
in the mix? Gender-critical feminists sometimes point the finger
at 'patriarchy', while from a different vantage point, others note
the relatively small number of ultra-rich individuals and foundations[53] that supply much of the funding, not to mention the NGOs
working – as noted above – pre-politically to entrench it. Baffled
conservatives, meanwhile, may be tempted to blame it all on Marxism
in universities, or progressive activists with asymmetrical haircuts.

While each of these explanations appeals to different sets of
political prejudices, none accounts for the seemingly unstoppable
top-down push to deregulate our bodies, in the name of a 'civil
rights' of pure consciousness. They fall short because the truth
implicates all of feminism – as well as its technological foundation.

A 2016 survey conducted across 23 countries revealed that
support for transgender rights is stronger among those with
higher earnings and education levels, just as it's strikingly higher
among women.[54] We can reasonably infer from these findings that

high-earning graduate women, which in the contemporary world means knowledge workers, are the group most likely to support the idea that individuals should be free to live as their preferred gender regardless of physiology.

This makes sense, when you consider that female knowledge workers are unlikely to be confronted, in the course of working life, with any stark contrasts between their ability to perform professionally and that of their male peers. There is, after all, no obvious reason why a clever and ambitious woman should not be as effective a barrister as her male colleague. Many feminists have pointed out that this doesn't work in anything like the same way for enslaved, agrarian, developing-world or otherwise less privileged women.[55] Nor does it even necessarily apply in manual work, which is usually to say more working-class occupations.

But it doesn't matter how often the class politics of sex dimorphism and work is pointed out. The critique never sticks, because for a minority of women the idea that we really can detach self-realisation from biology remains both plausible and compelling. This class of female knowledge professionals is also, as we saw in the last chapter, the subset of women liberated to fly high by the tech-enabled detachment of sex from reproduction, and motherhood from care, that now comprises the bulk of mainstream 'feminism'. And from the perspective of a woman who understands feminism in this way, there are few upsides to disturbing the idealist vision of men and women as interchangeable.

For the moment we acknowledge that sexed differences 'below the neck' have political or economic salience, this increases the risk that someone might resurrect the discussion of such differences 'above the neck' too. And in turn, this poses a clear threat to my right to be treated in the workplace as indistinguishable from male colleagues. The fact that this is true only for knowledge workers, and stops being true even in this case when women have babies, will likely concern such women less than pursuing professional parity for themselves and other women of the same social class.

The group of international lobbyists whose main focus is institutionalising cyborg theology in the guise of 'trans rights' is not, in truth, very large. But this lobby has had such a widespread impact, in such a short period of time, because its priest class is drawn from that far larger group of women who benefit from its doctrines – and who predominate within the wider ecosystem of institutions that shapes the modern moral universe.

The elite of the United States today is increasingly female dominated:[56] women outnumber men at undergraduate level in most universities, 60 percent to 40 percent in some elite colleges.[57] Even in the once heavily male-dominated military–industrial complex, as of 2019 four of the five biggest defence contractors – Northrop Grumman, Lockheed Martin, General Dynamics and the defence arm of Boeing – had female CEOs.[58] And the institutions that set and manage social and cultural norms – such as education, media, law and HR – are all increasingly female dominated. Female law students outnumber male ones two to one.[59] Women outnumber men in journalism.[60] Seventy-five percent of nonprofit workers in the United States are female,[61] and the UK proportion is nearly as high, at 68 percent.[62]

Such workers are chiefly graduates, notably from the arts and social sciences[63] – subjects where women outnumber men two to one in the UK[64] and which lean strongly towards a progressive worldview.[65] And if the disproportionately female graduates of disproportionately progressive elite liberal arts courses, who then disproportionately make up the nonprofit sector, have seized enthusiastically on a set of moral principles and institutional changes that downplay the role of biological sex in a way that benefits elite women overall, so a second key terrain for the contest over the political salience of sex dimorphism is corporate HR. This is the division of the business world tasked with managing the acceptable social (and, by extension, moral) parameters of everyday working life. Sixty-three percent of UK HR workers[66] and over 70 percent of those in the United States[67] are women.

And if elite progressive graduate women are in charge of shaping public morals via nonprofits and HR departments, they're also busy doing so for the next generation in schools: here, too, 85 percent of UK primary school teachers are women, and around 65 percent of secondary school teachers.[68] In the United States, 76 percent of teachers are women.[69] And as all US states require teachers to hold at least a bachelor's degree,[70] these are also uniformly drawn from the female demographic most likely to be enthusiastic about trans rights. And as is increasingly evident, the moral and institutional power this class is able to mobilise to shore up its interests is considerable.

These are the priestesses of cyborg theocracy. And they have the pulpit. But if they reap the benefits of their vision, its costs are borne elsewhere.

Collateral damage

The principal beneficiaries of this emerging order are elite professional women. Meanwhile, the costs get higher the further you go down the socio-economic hierarchy – for it gets ever more difficult to ignore the persistent salience of biological sex the further away from knowledge-class work you get and into groups that still mainly work in, or are forced to spend most of their life in, the physical world.

Naturally this includes female athletes; much gender-critical feminist activism has focused on defending their interests against the plainly unjust impact on women of making competitive sport effectively unisex. But nowhere is this more evident than right at the bottom of the social hierarchy, in prisons. Despite overwhelming evidence that male-pattern criminality is both more prevalent and more severe than that committed by women,[71] and despite studies that suggest transgender women retain male offending patterns,[72] a growing number of jurisdictions segregate prisons on the basis of self-identified gender rather than sex. In practice, this means that women incarcerated mainly for non-violent petty crimes may find themselves housed alongside – or even in the same cell as – sometimes violent and significantly physically stronger male-bodied individuals.

Some of these may also be sexually predatory. In the UK, the notorious 2018 case of Karen White caused shockwaves. This intact male-bodied sex offender, previously known as David Thompson, assaulted two female inmates after being incarcerated in a women's prison, following a self-declared identification as a woman[73] – a case that forced a re-evaluation of 'gender self-identification' in the UK Prison Service.[74] In Illinois, meanwhile, where self-identification is now standard in prisons, one woman sued the prison service in 2020 after being raped by a male-bodied fellow-prisoner.[75] And in 2022, as I write, reports are emerging that since a successful bid by the American Civil Liberties Union (ACLU) to force the Edna Mahan Correctional Facility in New Jersey to house transgender women, two female prisoners are now pregnant as a consequence of sex with another male-bodied prisoner, who identifies as a woman.[76] (The ACLU is 60 percent female-staffed.)[77]

But if athletes and incarcerated women are acceptable collateral damage to the cyborg theocrats, so too are the distress, scars and regret now increasingly common among unhappy young people who embrace cyborg sainthood. A growing proportion of this group, which experiences elevated rates of autism and often other mental health comorbidities,[78] then finds the gap between Meat Lego promise and Meat Lego reality to be filled with horrors. Helena imagined, she says, that transition would transform her into 'this outgoing male jock archetype' who would 'be handsome, have lots of friends, and love life'. In reality, though, she was 'lonely, enmeshed in toxic and stressful relationships, on academic probation, in legal trouble due to substance use, and feeling possessed by some sort of demon I now recognize was at least partially the testosterone's worsening grip on my mind'. Eventually she dropped out of college, found a dead-end job and, in the grip of escalating psychiatric difficulties, resorted to hitting herself and self-harming with blades to cope.

Many now live with the too-late realisation that what they thought of as their meat avatar can't be edited and re-edited at will, like the digital kind. One young woman, who transitioned at 18, declares online 'I miss my breasts so much'. She now lives, permanently, with choices she believed she'd never regret: 'I was always 10000000% sure I made the right decision. But the past couple years I've finally realised and it's so fucking hard to comprehend this and accept it.' Nearly ten years on, she's left only with a sense of irretrievable loss.[†]

Steven, meanwhile, has recurring nightmares about the irreversible moment of genital surgery. 'They called the surgery an "orchiectomy",' he says, 'but these days I think of it as a castration.

[†] 'I miss my breasts so much', Reddit post by u/grublove, 31 May 2022, www.reddit.com/r/detrans/comments/v1u391/i_miss_my_breasts_so_much/ [retrieved 11 November 2022].

I sometimes have nightmares about waking up afterwards. In my dreams I scream and scream, I run through the hallways howling and begging for them to undo it, to fix me, to make me right again.'

Are these stories just unfortunate outliers, unrepresentative of an otherwise successful approach? Well, the authors of a 2019 study that claimed to show significant improvements in mental health for individuals undergoing gender surgery were eventually forced to issue a correction, acknowledging that the statistics did not in fact show any evidence of such improvement.[79] Even Jazz Jennings, who remains a prominent figure for youth transition, doesn't seem to have developed into a happy adult, deferring a place at Harvard in 2019 due to ongoing struggles with anxiety, depression and binge eating.

One source said: 'Jazz has told friends that she has things anyone in her position would want: money, the perfect female body. But she's just not happy. Somewhere down the line, she's lost herself.'[‡] Others are more literally and completely taken from their mothers, into the 'care' of the devouring cyborg one. California teenager Yaeli Martinez was taken into state custody around the age of 16 after her mother, who had raised her, insisted her gender dysphoria was not an effect of her 'true self' but mental illness. After becoming a ward of state Yaeli began medical transition. But the treatment did not provide relief; instead, her mental health deteriorated, and she committed suicide in 2019, by lying down in front of a train. She was just 19. 'They killed my daughter,' Martinez says. 'They had to pick pieces of her off of the track.'[§]

---

‡ Jane Flowers, '"I Am Jazz" returns to TLC in January – What's jazz been up to in the meantime?', TV Shows Ace, 8 November 2019, tvshowsace.com/2019/11/08/i-am-jazz-returns-to-tlc-in-january-whats-jazz-been-up-to-in-the-meantime/.
§ Tori Richards, 'Mother of trans teenager: Los Angeles County killed my daughter', *Washington Examiner*, 22 March 2022, www.washingtonexaminer.com/news/mother-of-transgender-teenager-los-angeles-county-killed-my-daughter.

The great terraforming

But it's not just the cyborg priestesses who benefit from ignoring this collateral damage. It's also, as radical feminists have argued since the 1970s, everyone now making money from the rocketing demand for meat avatar customisation.[80] *Forbes* estimates a US market in gender medicine worth over $200bn a year: 'larger than the entire film industry'[81] – and argues from this that more investment should be made in 'trans tech'.

And this barely scratches the surface of the true economic upside of abolishing the idea that humans have a 'nature'. For as we've seen, liquefying social and biophysical norms doesn't make them go away. Re-imagining our bodies as Meat Lego won't free us from our bodies. Instead, we'll simply demolish what's left of the cultural and legal norms that evolved over time to manage aspects of human nature that remain beyond our power to change or eradicate. And it will free the market to move into that space.

This marketisation of human bodies is well under way. Female students in the United States already sell their eggs to infertile couples undergoing IVF to cover college tuition, the $40,000 average[82] table stakes for joining the knowledge-worker class.[83] Enclosed and commodified via a range of for-profit medical practices, from assisted fertility to commercially available breastmilk for babies born by surrogacy,[84] the often-exploitative conditions experienced by commercial surrogates are well documented.

And the further you go down the hierarchies of power and money, the greater the potential this introduces for (as Nikola Tesla put it) man-made horrors beyond our comprehension. In 2022, a doctor at an Indian transgender clinic announced the first experimental transplant of a female uterus into a male-to-female transgender patient.[85] Dr Narendra Kaushik stated that he planned to take the uterus from either a dead donor, or a female-to-male patient undergoing a hysterectomy.

Should demand outstrip the supply of unwanted body parts taken from cadavers or female-to-male transgender individuals, there are plenty more to be had: in Maharashtra, where the daily wage is less than $3 and farm workers are hired on a contract basis, women often undergo hysterectomy to make themselves more productive and employable.[86] When there already exist semi-legal ways in India for the impoverished to sell organs on the transplant market, it's not hard to envisage how such a woman might see little downside to making a profit from necessity by selling hers.

This might seem far-fetched, but is only a logical consequence of existing practices: women seeking to freeze their eggs are already offered discounts or free service in exchange for 'donating' eggs, which are then sold to other clinic clients.[87] The step from 'donating spare eggs' to 'donating spare body parts' is one of degree, not kind.

And if this deregulatory drive follows the usual pattern, transgender medicine is less an end goal than an emotive wedge issue for the wider commercial potential of biotech. It's a growth area, despite the global economic shock of coronavirus: according to a 2021 McKinsey report, in 2020 the average share price for European and US biotech firms increased at more than double the rate of the S&P 500.[88] And much as the financial boom of the 1980s and 1990s required the deregulation of finance, unlocking the potential for biotech requires the further deregulation of nature. A 2016 op-ed published by CNN, criticising the use of the term 'natural' in campaigns to promote breastfeeding, inadvertently makes the whole argument. It cites experts who worry that celebrating what's natural runs the risk of fuelling suspicion against anything which isn't – a category that includes 'vaccines, genetically modified foods and assisted reproductive technologies'.[89]

If we can denature biological sex in the name of identity, if we can denature maternal love, if we can problematise embodiment itself, we can hardly uphold a distinction between humans and other life forms in pursuit of the same utopia. This reality is in fact already here, borne on the wings of experimental identity medicine, where surgeons in Brazil are experimenting with vaginoplasty procedures using skin from a tilapia fish.[90]

But if this feels like crossing a boundary, immense potential is unlocked by simply declaring that there is no such boundary: that 'nothing is natural'. In 2021, a US–Chinese scientific team published a report detailing the successful creation of embryonic human/monkey chimeras in a laboratory.[91] The news triggered outrage, as an unnatural attempt at 'playing God'.[92] But the goal of the research into human/monkey chimeras was, as the researchers explained, the advancement of regenerative medicine including 'the generation of organs and tissues for transplantation'. When the demand for donated organs so far outstrips the supply of willing donors, it's not difficult to see the incentives to pursue such research. And if we see all of biology as plastic, with no meaningful constraints of norm or nature, human/animal chimeras are not monstrous but exciting and rich with potential. (One might even see it in social justice terms, as a means of relieving pressure on those impoverished farm-working uterus donors in Maharashtra.) Popular revulsion at meddling with what's 'natural' is a key constraint on this emerging field.

And if Yuval Noah Harari imagines that the product of the latest industrial revolution is 'humans themselves', then this can hardly proceed very profitably unless the wider culture has accepted the moral case for treating us as hackable. Nor is Harari the only blue-sky thinker brainstorming the political implications of this vision. S. Matthew Liao, NYU Ethics Chair and editor-in-chief of the *Journal of Moral Philosophy*, suggested at the 2016 World Science Festival that we might address the carbon emissions resulting from livestock farming for meat by manipulating the human genome to make humans allergic to meat.[93]

No one has yet succeeded in uploading a human consciousness into a computer, and there's good reason to think we won't ever achieve this.[94] But while this dream shapes the imaginary for influential figures in culture and politics, it will conjure the fantasy of *Homo techno* or *Persona creatus* among the rich and powerful, even as it displaces the peasantry from the 'commons' of our own bodies, so these can be commodified.

The principal advocates for this movement, wittingly or not, are those progressive knowledge-class women who are still net beneficiaries of the war on embodiment. But while feminism has provided much of the moral cover for this dystopian possible future, I am not saying this is all women's fault. The technological and cultural shifts that got us here happened slowly, and every step made sense on its own terms. But taken together, it's now fusing into a commercial and political programme that threatens to launch us into a world of hackable, fungible, wholly commodified and de-sexed 'humans'. This would-be cyborg theocracy promises all of us liberation from every last constraint – from 'the horrid curse of being human' itself, as the anonymous 'n1x' put it at the beginning of this chapter, offering in its place something superficially like the spiritual escape offered by the Gnostic sects.

It's an enticing prospect of radical self-fashioning, as imagined by Rothblatt, or eternal digitised life as envisaged by Grimes. This fantasy has lurked in the scientific imaginary since the beginning of modernity – but it's never seemed more appealing, or plausible, than today. And for those with the resources to bend nature to their will, the war on nature is mostly upside. Grimes is a case in point: she has two children with entrepreneur Elon Musk, the world's richest man, and had the second by surrogacy because she found the first birth traumatic. Who wouldn't celebrate such freedom? What should concern us, though, is less the fantasy of breaking free from the prison of materiality but the impact of this war on nature for those who lack such economic or cultural power (including many of those commercial surrogates to whom wealthy women may opt to subcontract gestation).

As ever-growing numbers of us stare, entranced, at the iridescent promise of a wholly disembodied and self-fashioning personhood, far fewer look past that fantasy to wonder what will happen to the meat suits we're promised we can leave behind. And here, what we'll get is unlikely to be emancipation – at least not one without terrible collateral damage. The pharma millionaires and transhumanist visionaries ushering us towards this world are indifferent to the needs of ordinary women. We see glimpses of the disparities this will create, in the asymmetrical distribution of freedom and trade in the gulf between Grimes and the womb-less farm-workers of Maharashtra. We see it, too, in emerging evidence of political prisoners killed to order and their organs harvested to service the Chinese transplant industry.[95]

For if everything that makes us human resides in our consciousness, and there's nothing natural or integral about our bodies, then we really are just meat. And inert, soul-less meat – living or dead – can legitimately be hacked, spliced with fish-skin or pig or monkey DNA, chopped and remodelled at will, or dismembered for commercial or political ends. At scale, meat can be managed via bio-engineering: modified like battery-farmed poultry to better tolerate poor living conditions, perhaps, or to crave new forms of synthetic protein proposed by futurists as the best means of ensuring adequate food supplies as the human population grows.

I don't want to live in this world. It's one in which a few will flourish and many suffer. It's also one that holds many sex-specific nightmares for women, whom the new era is already working to dismember, both culturally and legally. The endgame is the horrors that will follow on our total re-conceptualisation as de-sexed 'people', as 'sex workers', as 'lactators', 'menstruators' and 'gestators', or simply as 'donor tissue'.

It's war

If what's left of the women's movement is not to be wholly consumed by Meat Lego Gnosticism, feminists must follow in the footsteps of detransitioners and seek a measure of peace with our own bodies. This is easier said than done. For me, as I've recounted, it has been a long journey and one that's far from complete. Nor is it straightforward politically, for it's likely to come at some cost to those women who benefit from 'personhood' on the bio-libertarian template. This class may need to lose a measure of the benefits that such 'equality' and 'progress' has afforded them. Suggesting they do so is likely to provoke, to put it mildly, a defensive reaction. And this class of women currently has the mic. I suspect many will fight tooth and nail to keep it, using every form of overt and covert political street-fighting at their disposal. In pursuit of their class interests, they'll use weight of numbers across education, NGOs and corporate HR departments to tip the scales in favour of the legal fiction that sex doesn't need to exist.

But all is not entirely hopeless. For pointing out, as I have, that a subset of women has an interest in supporting the post-human order isn't to say that all women do, or even that bourgeois knowledge-class women necessarily will. So I'll dedicate the final section of this book to a programme for taking feminism back for and with those many women (and men) revolted by the prospect of living under Meat Lego Gnosticism.

It's time to wrest the movement from the sterilised steel claws of the Fourth Industrial Revolution, and from those women still cheering that revolution on for short-term political gain. We need a feminism that's fighting today's battles, not those of the industrial era. No more freedom, no more technology, no more atomisation. We need a movement that honours the interests of women, and of men, as irreducibly sexed fusions of self and body, against an emerging order that seeks to de-sex and disembody us all. One that understands 'progress' is now our enemy. A reactionary feminism.

INTERLUDE

Detransition

The true reactionary is not a seeker after abolished pasts, but a hunter of sacred shades on the eternal hills.

Nicolás Gómez Dávila

WE ACCEPTED TECHNOLOGY'S PROMISE to make us all pure, free, unencumbered selves. We've pursued that promise, and allowed the wider political, economic and cultural order to name the pursuit 'feminism'. And we're now well beyond the point where this is delivering more freedom, or even more happiness. The further we've slid, collectively, into the pursuit of absolute freedom underwritten by tech, the less we've come to need one another, and the more transactional, hostile and nihilistic our relationships have become: with each other, with our kids, and with our own bodies.

It should be clear by now that trying to squeeze a few more drops of freedom from the rotting carcass of the industrial era is not going to help us abolish human nature. Nor will it do anything about 'patriarchy'. It's some time now in the West since we abandoned actual 'patriarchy', in the sense of abolishing social and legal forms such as primogeniture, coverture, or even the family wage or differential treatment for women in social interactions. And despite this, efforts to 'smash' this nebulous thing appear only to have moved the goalposts in terms of where and how it manifests. And this is because most of what flies under the 'patriarchy' banner in the 21st century is simply those ineradicable sex differences that return, like zombie caricatures of themselves, in

165

a hyper-liquid market society.

More efforts to smash our nature will not make this kind of 'patriarchy' go away. The feminist movement in all its fractious multiplicity is an umbrella term for women's specific responses to the technologies and ideologies of the industrial era – responses that were often justified. But the industrial era's core understanding of personhood is accordingly baked into those responses: the autonomous self. The notion of women's rights implies this atomistic understanding of personhood, but most of the developed world no longer lives in the industrial era. If we go on clinging to that era's memes of freedom and progress, we'll get more atomisation.

Wherever cyborg culture is ascendant, the universalising, atomising, abstract 'rights' model that underwrites 'freedom' and 'progress' no longer benefits women, or any of us. Instead, it drives an ever more frenzied push to liquefy human nature, that in the end serves only the hydra of freedom and trade.

But if we accept where we are, and pursue instead a story of interdependence, and reconciliation, perhaps we might find another way. That also means learning to live with ourselves, including those ways in which our sex shapes who we are, how we live and what we desire. It also means balancing the atomistic framework of 'women's rights' against the more contextual, relational and grounded one of 'women's interests'. This is by definition not a universalist project. To be clear, I see this as a 'yes, and' rather than a 'no, but': I am emphatically not advocating abandoning 'rights', where these are still an appropriate frame, but rather staying aware that they're a tool that works in some contexts, not a universal, metaphysical reality that can be realised everywhere. Though human nature is not infinitely malleable, human culture varies immensely, and the same policy can serve women's interests in one material context and undermine them elsewhere. We only need to consider, for example, the ways in which 'women's rights' have been used as a vector for neoliberal US foreign policy goals to see that a more grounded and culturally sensitive assessment of women's interests may sometimes deliver more genuine benefits to women than a blind and absolutist fixation on 'rights'.

Feminism against progress, then, is anti-universalist, contextual and relational. This recovery of context and relationships begins with restoring our relationship with ourselves: that is, resisting the culture of chronic dissociation. In this light, we have much to learn from those men and women who found themselves elevated to sainthood by the cyborg cult, only to turn back again.

No one embodies more completely than these 'detransitioners' the difficult experience of taking at face value the great lie of Meat Lego Gnosticism: that we could be freed from dependence on our bodies (and, implicitly, one another). Many detransitioners now live with irreversible medical decisions made on that journey. I don't want to add insult to injury by objectifying them again, in service of a different political argument. But in describing their descent, all the way into Meat Lego body dissociation and back again, those courageous individuals willing to tell their story concretise a relationship to technology that in truth implicates all of us.

In less material ways, many of us have done something analogous, as we invited 'progress' into the deepest parts of our relational lives. Many mourn traumatic experiences or irreversible decisions we made along the way, too, based on promises of mastery that turned out to be insubstantial. My own 'liberated' youth left me with a wagonload of sexual trauma, for example, and I know I'm far from alone in this. I believed the stories about extended fertility, empowerment and freedom, too. Except as it turned out I didn't in fact have all the time in the world. I think often about my decision to defer having children as long as I did, and wonder whether I'd be a mother to more than one if I hadn't. I'm grateful for my one child, but others aren't as lucky. Some in my position may never have even one child, and mourn that absence every bit as keenly as the nameless young detransitioner quoted in the last chapter mourns her amputated breasts.

In the bitterly adversarial battlefield of online sex wars, there's no shortage of men keen to laugh at those of us who took at face value the claim that we could liberate ourselves from our sexed reality, only to regret what we lost in the attempt. It's not enough, though, just to laugh and point and say it serves women right for believing we could be free. That promise, and those technologies, profoundly structure all our understandings of what's possible.

Detransitioners often face social ostracism at the hands of their formerly supportive trans 'community'.[1] Studies suggest detransitioners also often struggle to access medical support for detransition.[2] Small wonder: they serve as living reproof to the claim that abstract, disembodied 'selfhood' is an infallible judge of its own identity. And under Meat Lego Gnosticism, this is outright blasphemy.

So, too, is another common feature of detransitioners' stories: the reconciliation with embodiment. Ash, one young male detransitioner, describes how what helped him let go of cross-sex identity was reconciliation with the pleasure a body can bring, including sexual pleasure. 'Then I realized, why would I want to get rid of *this*?' he says. 'This [body] is so cool and does interesting things.'[¶] Similarly, Abigail Shrier recounts the story of Chiara, a young woman who desisted after her family sent her to live on a horse farm for a year, where 'the physical labour helped her reconnect to her body'.[**]

¶ Lisa Selin Davis, 'A desister's tale', Quillette, 11 February 2022, quillette.com/2022/02/11/a-desisters-tale/.

** Shrier, *Irreversible Damage*, location 3481.

I never went as far as these young men and women into body dissociation, but their stories echo my own slow, ambivalent recovery of a sense that selfhood and physicality can't be separated. I've recounted how becoming a mother played a part in that journey. There was much more besides, and motherhood is by no means the only way back into a relationship with ourselves. This makes arguing for such a journey difficult to do in the abstract. But realising my body isn't something I'm *in* but something I *am* is near the heart of the case for reactionary feminism. It's also the core of any meaningful resistance to Meat Lego Gnosticism. We're less likely to submit to a regime that treats men and women as defective 'humans' in need of tech fixes, if we know 'bodies' can't be treated as separate from 'selves' without doing deep violence to both. And if I was just lucky enough to reach escape velocity before it was too late, it's my hope that some of those who read this will be young enough to step back from the dissociative self and its commodification of body parts, before sustaining as many scars as I did.

I may disappoint more conservative readers, though, in my suggested approach. For while abortion serves as a metaphysical keystone for cyborg theocracy, I don't wish to make the argument that the only proper starting point for a fightback against this theocracy would be seeking abrupt and radical abortion restrictions.

Here, first of all, it's important to disaggregate US and European abortion politics. The issue plays out very differently across different cultures: the United States is both more polarised and also (in places) considerably more liberal than much of Europe, with abortion permitted all the way to term in some states.[3] By contrast, in European Union countries the median gestational limit is 12 weeks.[4] In the UK it's a relatively settled issue, with broad consensus supporting some abortion access[5] but consistently more women than men supporting a reduction in the current 24-week gestational limit.[6] And maximalist support for abortion to term is supported only by a minority, especially among women.[7]

Even so, legislation itself is never fixed. In the United States, activists continue to push for an end to all restrictions on abortion. And American culture wars, complete with American-style polarisation, have a habit of spreading beyond the United States. In this context, it's probably too optimistic to hope that if we just sit quietly the issue will go away. But while we should anticipate and resist any political activism in favour of further liberalisation on abortion, resisting calls for legislative liberalisation in Britain is quite a different matter from pushing for total de-liberalisation.

The downstream effect of making birth control widely available has been de-stigmatising extra-marital sex; abortion serves as the material backstop for that change in social norms. Banning the backstop would not put the broader changes back in the box. As things stand, so much of the world is ordered along the sexually libertine and implicitly anti-natalist lines enabled by these technologies that abrupt prohibition of that backstop would be most likely to immiserate women still further.

But while I don't advocate beginning with the law, nor do I think we can rely on it. And crucially, we must do what we can to swim against the wider atomising tide. This technology was sold as freedom for women, and on that basis the activist wing of cyborg theocracy continues to push for maximalist reproductive control, even at the expense of unborn lives. We must hold onto the recognition that the 'freedom' it enables has become the key-stone of a new kind of prison: a Meat Lego order that downplays the political, social or cultural importance of sex dimorphism, even as it sets about shattering the reproductive functions at the core of those differences into component pieces, and reordering them to the market.

On its own, banning abortion wouldn't heal the dissociative relation we have to ourselves, a split now well established downstream of this legal and cultural reality. But at its most utopian, reactionary feminism dreams of a world where every baby is welcome, and this welcome is not in zero-sum competition with an understanding of personhood so atomised that mothers are by definition un-personed in the course of embodying that welcome.

Even those who aren't in favour of banning abortion can surely support the dream of transforming how we live together, so abortion may come to feel ever less indispensable as an emergency backstop. More and less ambivalently pro-life feminists against progress can, perhaps, converge on a vision of the future where the proper support and regard is there to enable all mothers to flourish *as* mothers, without being diminished as adult human women. So a good acid test for a prudential, embodied, relational feminism against progress is as follows: does a given action or policy bring us closer to this world? If the answer is no, it isn't reactionary feminism.

I don't think what follows is definitive. All of it should be applied prudentially. It doesn't replace 'women's rights', at least as long as we continue to live under a regime that's ordered in those terms. Nor is it an argument for excising modern science and technology from our lives. The cyborg era affords new possibilities, even as it brings new dangers. What we need is a more critical relation to the technologies we use, lest we find instead that they're using *us*.

Tech determinism is itself a moral choice, that – once taken – frames every other moral choice we're in a position to make. If we assume that we have no agency in the face of 'progress', we've already handed ourselves to cyborg theocracy. I think, though, that we can shift our focus from a controlling approach underwritten by tech, in the name of freedom, to a practice-based approach underwritten by a willingness to accept that we can't, in fact, abolish human nature. Instead, if we want to retain any ability to live together, we need to be proactive about embracing – even exaggerating – that nature, an inescapably dimorphic whole. This is a fundamental act of resistance to the cyborg theocracy that would reduce us all to polymorphously gendered, interchangeable assemblages of fungible body parts.

So this isn't a playbook for some long march back through the institutions. That's a topic for more directly political thinkers. Rather, it's an argument for *less* determinism in our relation to technology. The evangelists of progress enjoin us relentlessly to 'liberate' ourselves ever further, through the market. But if you're reading this with a formless sense that there's something off about that path, and a despairing hope that another life ought to be possible, take it from someone who has liberalled about as hard as it's possible to liberal: you've been lied to. And another life *is* possible.

To live it, you'll need to be the change you want to see in the world. You'll be swimming against the tide. But there's still time for men and women to step aside from the enticing highway to post-humanism, and look anew at how we might live together in the ruins of progress. There are several facets to this: interpersonal, social, institutional and arguably spiritual. All of them converge in the question of how – or if – men and women can form families, against an economic, political and ecological backdrop that grows ever more uncertain.

This means rebuilding solidarity from the ground up. What follows is a more speculative sketch of how a feminism against progress might support that rebuilding. This part of the book will apply most directly to those still young enough to be weighing how, or if, to make marriage and family part of their own life plans. I've included stories from women and men who are already rebuilding: some still very young adults, some without immediate family role models to draw on, and all struggling to build lives, relationships, families and wider social networks on the other side of total atomisation.

All have grown up in the cyborg era, but rejected its promise of frictionless, tech-enabled atomisation, and the attendant fantasy of Meat Lego transhumanism. Many were themselves raised by hyper-individualistic parents, and have little in the way of familial role models for their efforts. They're trying anyway. So am I: I'm a survivor of the End of History, and I still struggle with its legacy, in body dissociation and a reflexive aversion to constraints of any kind. I doubt I'm the only one trying to reverse-engineer a workable mode of life in common, from what feels like a heap of rubble. So I offer the rest of this book tentatively, in the hopes that my reflections on that effort to date make the road a little smoother for anyone else out there who is trying to build.

PART THREE

Reactionary Feminism

7

Abolish Big Romance

Warriors and workers of all countries, unite, while there is still time, to prevent the coming of 'the realm of freedom'. Defend with might and main, if it needs to be defended, 'the realm of necessity'.

Leo Strauss[1]

WE'RE NOW WELL BEYOND Peak Progress. The decades since the turn of the millennium have seen two international banking crises, terrorist attacks, a return of great-power politics, a global pandemic, war in Europe, rocketing inflation and (at the time of writing) an energy crunch. And whatever your views on how to address it, man-made climate change is growing difficult to deny, even for those ideologically committed to pretending it isn't happening. The permacrisis shows no sign of abating: our current trajectory promises to make life poorer, tougher and more uncertain for all but the richest.

If the world is growing less stable, we're going to need to rely on one another: where resources falter, strong relationships can make up some of the shortfall. But we face this unsettled future less well supported on this front than ever, thanks to a culture that sweeps us ever further into atomisation. And this is especially a problem for mothers: as Abigail Tucker shows, the happiest mothers are those with good social support networks.[2] If this is true in prosperous times, it's orders of magnitude more so in tough ones. Swimming against the atomising current, then, is an urgent priority for reactionary feminists. This applies even (or perhaps especially) to those of us raised as good little hyper-individualists, in a culture hell-bent on liquefying and commodifying every form of relationship.

Resistance means opting for beneficial constraints, which enable us to live well. Happily, on this front there already exists a vintage social technology we can deploy, as a first step in resisting the atomising pressures of cyborg theocracy, if we can only upcycle it for the 21st century: marriage. It's not a magic bullet to solve every challenge we face; nothing will ever do this. Nor, as even happily married people will tell you, is every marriage a utopia. But women who are mothers flourish in a less liquid social fabric – and married family units, the smallest possible commons outside the market, are essential to creating that stability.

In parts of the world where cyborg theocracy is now dominant, this is a virulently countercultural view. For where markets rule, they come with songs of praise to being alone. Think of Honor Jones, writing about how she loved her husband – but still divorced him, because their marriage wasn't self-expressive enough, and he was an obstacle to her personal fulfilment. The siren call of atomisation comes from everywhere, and legitimises itself in many ways: girl-power self-actualisation and embittered men's rights activism, for example, are mirroring ideologies driving the same decline into loneliness and mutual hostility.

For both of these perspectives, marriage is tantamount to prostitution: a fake contract that enables exploitation of one sex by the other. Far better to deregulate relations between the sexes altogether, and let everyone embrace market forces as they see fit. And whether it serves to legitimise abandoning relationships that don't measure up to the 'self-expressive' gold standard, or as a cynical foil for calls to marketise still further, Big Romance is centrally implicated in this dynamic.

How do we detransition from here? Some conservatives dream of abolishing second-wave feminism, which is to say returning to a pre-1960s understanding of marriage, and with it the 'traditional' relation between men and women. This is usually understood to mean the sex roles typical of the industrial model, in which women serve as principal domestic consumers, while relying on their husband's goodwill and good character to offset the loss of agency this implies under the order of 'economic sex'. In other words: we should keep everything the same, except what women do.

Such proposals seem blind (or indifferent) to the fact that this would be subject to all the structural downsides that drove women to abandon this model in the first place. And in any case, those material conditions are long gone. In most social strata both sexes work, and in many US cities women under 30 out-earn their male peers, at least until they become mothers,[3] a fact that makes interdependence optional rather than necessary for most couples. In this context, dual-earner households are now the norm in both the UK and the US, and the 'two-income trap' means supporting a stay-at-home parent is economically unfeasible below a certain earning threshold.

But the weakness of these proposals isn't that they're unworkable, or even that they're 'traditional', but that they're not traditional enough. For most of history, men and women worked together, in a productive household, and this is the model reactionary feminism should aim to retrieve. In any case, half a century into the cyborg era, there's little prospect of reviving the industrial-era housewife as the principal template for sex roles — and there's no need, because for knowledge workers at least the sharp split between 'home' and 'work' that drove the emergence of such roles is blurring again. And the blurring of that divide in turn opens up new possibilities, hinting at a way of viewing lifelong solidarity between the sexes that owes more to the 1450s than the 1950s. It does so by bringing at least some work back into the home, and in the process ramping up the kind of interdependence that can underpin long-term pragmatic solidarity.

Remote work, e-commerce and the 'portfolio career' are not without risks. They can bring increased employer surveillance or economic precarity, for example. But cyborg developments also offer scope for families to carve out lives where both partners blend family obligations, public-facing economic activity and rewarding local community activities in productive mixed-economy households, where both partners are partly or wholly home-based and work collaboratively on the common tasks of the household, whether money-earning, food production, childcare or housekeeping.

Some are already pioneering this model. One young woman I interviewed is Willow, 25, a writer based in rural Canada, who married at 23 and is co-creating a domestic economy with her husband Phil that's clearly an update on the pre-modern arrangements we saw in Part 1. Along with her writing projects, she and Phil work together on carpentry projects, where they divide the work roughly into 'first fix' (which requires more strength, and which Phil does) and finishing work (which requires more patience and manual dexterity, where Willow excels). Their baby is too small for Willow to do much in the workshop at present, but she's active in finding him clients and sometimes also apprentices, as well as tending a smallholding, and will return to carpentry in due course.

From an industrial-feminist perspective, Willow's approach is unconscionably in hock to patriarchy: she married young, views childcare as largely her domain and is not the main money-earner. But from the perspective of a feminism against progress, Willow is pursuing her interests as an embodied woman, in her relational context, rather than as an atomised, abstract 'human' in an inconveniently female body. Having decided relatively young that she wanted children as well as economic and political agency, and that she didn't want a conventional career that compelled her to spend long periods away from her children, she set about creating a household where she can have these things – and can have them at the point of maximum energy and fertility, in her early twenties. As such, Willow had little time for the now-pervasive advice given to young women, to defer marriage and kids 'until you're ready'. She heard them out, she says, but 'in my heart I didn't have any concerns'. Rather, as she puts it: 'Getting married was the foundation of the life I wanted to build.'

Willow is right at the start of creating her household – but others are well established on the same track. Ashley, 36, is a decade into building hers: she and her husband live in Uruguay, where both do part-time remote language teaching while managing a homestead where they teach courses on low-carbon living, and caring for three young children. This lifestyle enabled Ashley to realise the goal she and her husband set for their life together: 'centring family as the core of our meaning-making'.

In retrieving something like the pre-modern model for family life, where the household is the centre of both family and economic activity, Willow and Ashley are paradoxically ahead of the curve. They're weaving work and children back together, in a way that hasn't been possible for mothers since the Industrial Revolution. With it, too, they're pioneering the reactionary feminist alternative to mainstream conservatives' futile call for return to 'traditional' (which is to say industrial) sex roles. Willow and Ashley are absolutely not abolishing feminism; both view their approach as making space for themselves to be women as well as 'humans'. What they are abolishing is Big Romance.

In a material context where women are structurally at an economic and political disadvantage, as we have seen historically, it makes sense to promote and pursue emotional closeness as the key benchmark of a beneficial long-term relationship. Very starkly: if your husband loves and respects you, the fact that in absolute terms he has economic power over you is less likely to threaten your well-being. Over time, though, the liberal feminist demand to enter market society on the same terms as men has been broadly achieved.

But as we've seen, memes often take a while to catch up with material conditions. And part of what makes contemporary sex relations so muddled and unhappy is the persistence of Big Romance, in its 'self-expressive' form, long after its material basis has all but disappeared. For with this change, Big Romance stopped mediating relations between men and women and began actively militating against them. If we're to rebuild solidarity, a very first step is in backing out of the blind alley, currently followed by feminists and anti-feminists alike, in which heterosexual marriage is decried as a malign bait-and-switch indistinguishable from prostitution.

In other words, not ditching marriage but revisiting the premodern approach to what marriage is *for*: less personal fulfilment, or even romantic love, than an enabling condition for building a meaningful life. For Ashley, marriage isn't primarily about warm and fuzzies. It's about building. 'I see our marriage as an act of production,' she says. 'We're co-producing a family culture, and are intimately involved in the raising and education of our children.' And it's not that their relationship isn't intimate and affectionate, she says – but this is a by-product of the work they do together: managing the homestead, renovating buildings, producing food at home and involving their children in the work.

Taking this approach profoundly strengthens their partnership, while the concreteness of their shared end goal makes even the drudgery feel worth it: 'The act of co-production in a marriage seems really unromantic, on a day-to-day basis: you're working and doing all this drudgery,' she explains. 'But if you weren't doing it in the home, you'd be doing it for a boss, and how is that supposed to be more liberating?' As she sees it, it's precisely in the dull everyday work that you create meaning together: 'If the drudgery of daily life is in the service of building a resilient relationship, home and relationship with your children, this is the work of life. It's much more meaningful overall than just being a slave to a corporation.'

And far from familiarity breeding contempt, Ashley argues that working closely together every day creates a strong base for navigating difficulties. If you see one another all the time, and the goal is building together, minor interpersonal quarrels are more easily set aside. As Ashley puts it: 'When you're there day in and day out with a person, working on the project of life, those superficial realities tend to fall away in importance, and working together and making life work together becomes much more important.'

In her view, the romance comes not through the ego-fulfilment of a perfectly congenial partner, but working *with* someone to build something that will outlast them: 'It's much more romantic in the end when you realise this home, this life, these children, if they're thriving it's a result of our shared ability to create something greater together through our interdependence and cooperation than we would be able to separately, as part of our marriage.

We're working towards something bigger than ourselves. We're building a legacy.'

Isn't this a rather bleak and utilitarian view of a long-term relationship, though? To this I can only say that in my own experience, in practice the Big Romance focus on maximum emotional intensity and minimum commitment is bleaker. Honor Jones described life refracted through her husband as stifling, but I spent the best part of 15 adult years living as a single atom before I married. I've done all the things Jones lists as upsides of the atomised life. From where I'm sitting, what she characterises as stifling isn't a bug, it's a feature. I've found the closing-down of limitless optionality more liberating than not, in the sense that what I do every day has become meaningful to the extent that I've been willing to accept constraints on what I *could* do.

That's all I'll say about the profound personal value I place on being, and staying, married. To describe something, as a professional writer, is in a sense to make it *yours*, and my marriage doesn't belong to me. It belongs to an *us* that's unavailable for public consumption – not by virtue of being private property, but by virtue of being a miniature commons. And a commons is, by definition, not available for consumption by anyone with the freedom to contract, or the money to buy, but only to those who share and sustain it.

And when we think of a marriage as a commons it becomes clearer what's needed to sustain it. Treating a marriage as something that can be leveraged for individual benefit will destroy it. So, too, will treating personal fulfilment as the yardstick for success: not least because the standards set by Big Romance are now impossible to meet. If a relationship needs to bear the full weight of mutual self-actualisation, as well as life in common, then every crumb underfoot, and every flaw you see in your partner, will feel like a boulder on the road to a better 'me'.

In contrast, if it's a foundation for cooperation on the domestic economy, and the intimate work of creating a safe and stable space for children, it has room to be a little imperfect. And you stand a far greater chance of building something lifelong, whose benefits will multiply down the generations. But this points to the other corollary of abolishing Big Romance: the feminist case against easy divorce. Lest anyone mistake me, this isn't a conservative argument. With only two marriages for every divorce, there is very little left to conserve. And I'm not claiming either that everyone *must* get married. There have always been women who don't want to be mothers, who don't want relationships with men, or who don't want relationships full stop. Nor am I arguing that anyone should remain in a violent or otherwise abusive relationship 'for the sake of the children'. The case against easy separation isn't a case against every separation.

Mine is, rather, a reconstructionist argument: not retrieving past forms but (as Gómez Dávila says) hunting for sacred shades on the eternal hills. Marriage is a remarkably flexible template: the decision by 'family abolitionist' Sophie Lewis to marry an individual of the opposite sex (albeit one who identifies as a woman)[4] is as much a testament to the enduring social value and adaptability of heterosexual marriage as the most ardent 'tradwife'. What matters isn't who does what, or what anyone is wearing, but absolute loyalty. If you want to pass through the looking glass into a world beyond the marketisation of everything, you have to treat your miniature commons as indissoluble: not a contract but a covenant.

And if you're among the great majority who wants kids, you're best off getting married – that is, by definition, 'settling'. That means, for both sexes, being realistic about who might choose you: it's a tragedy, as the cultural critic Justin Murphy puts it, for 'imperfect people' to eschew marriage to one another 'because they want people lacking their own degree of imperfection'. His advice to all those men who 'really want love and a wife' but 'can't find a "good-enough" girl to date, let alone marry' is to 'lower your fucking standards'.[5]

Choosing one person also means continuing to choose them: that is, opting to ignore all the ways the grass might be greener somewhere else – and continuing to do so, even when things are a bit 'meh'. Every marriage has ups and downs, and some of them can last for years. According to Dr Paul Amato, a sociologist at Penn State University, 'high-conflict' marriages are characterised by heated argument or even violence, and in these cases divorce may be beneficial for children. But around half of divorces are also in what Amato calls 'low-conflict' marriages: that is, the relationship was not perfect but they muddled along well enough. 'For 55 percent to 60 percent of couples,' he says, 'these are not bad marriages. They are just not ecstatic marriages.'[6]

And where things are not ecstatic, which is to say for most marriages at least occasionally, the reactionary feminist emphasis is not on warm and fuzzies, or aesthetics, or trying to litigate how any given family negotiates household roles. It's absolute, unshakeable loyalty. You can get a long way on stoicism and common purpose – but to do so, you have to foreclose separation as a possibility. As Justin Murphy puts it: 'Marriage is often crazy ups & downs but if you really, in your heart of hearts, tied yourself to the ship – there's not much you can control. Just never, ever stray – let alone cheat – and just steer the fucking ship.'[7]

This has all been said before. But against the endless lionisation of the world's Honor Joneses, it needs saying again. If you want kids, and you want stability, and you want family life, and you want a lifelong partner, that means sometimes taking the rough with the smooth. If you're still labouring under the misapprehension that there's a perfect partner out there waiting for you, in whose company this needn't be true, and with whom everything will be hearts and flowers forever, I have a bridge in Brooklyn to sell you.

Of course this isn't to say detransition from Big Romance will be easy. Anecdotally, every millennial couple I know with young children struggles with the gap between ideal and reality, especially where parenting has disrupted the relationship: new resentments, new asymmetries, sometimes simmering tensions. But it's exactly in functional but less-than-perfect families, as Amato argues, that statistics show children are most deeply hurt by divorce – because, actually, it was good enough for them. In many cases, little more than a change in attitude can make it good enough for us as well.

Lest anyone accuse me of arguing against women's emancipation and well-being, in the name of family stability, studies show a third of men and women who get divorced subsequently regret it.[8] More freedom doesn't always equal more happiness. And sticking with an imperfect-but-functional partnership doesn't self-evidently mean never-ending misery. Life is long, and I've seen even extended rough patches in relationships smooth back out into affection, respect and intimacy.

We need to tilt the scales back towards erring on the side of stability rather than that of freedom. For it is increasingly clear that Big Romance is not just harmful at the societal level but miserable at the personal one. What was once companionate marriage, a call for *some* interpersonal respect in the interests of offsetting a real imbalance of power, has become, as Ashley puts it, a vision of marriage as 'two individuals who have consumed one another, and have status as a result of what they're able to consume'. From this perspective, the pursuit of flawless future bliss in the 'self-expressive marriage' is presented as a guarantee of 'standards'. But it serves largely as defence against imperfect present happiness – and solidarity. And unless we re-learn how to rely on one another, we're not going to make it.

In response, many who grew up in the post-1960s world of autonomy and self-actualisation are now rebelling against the culture of absolute self-centredness. For such reactionary feminists, abolishing Big Romance means seeking and sustaining marriage as a kind of radical solidarity – even when this is challenging. By shifting our focus from emotional fulfilment to long-term thinking and the practical work of building together, we can reclaim marriage as a post-romantic covenant between two willing partners: the key and foundation for a productive household, like Ashley's or Willow's.

There are many obstacles. Those from liberal families who embrace early marriage often face social disapproval. Most of us have been wounded by contact with the sexual 'marketplace', and bring that baggage with us into our marriages. And many have grown up with few or no childhood templates on which to base a thriving post-romantic partnership. For all these, reverse-engineering something that works more or less from scratch is a daunting prospect. There will be false starts and stumbles. But we have to try. This is in women's interests, inasmuch as motherhood is infinitely less gruelling in a less liquid society. It's in men's interests, too, inasmuch as men also want and need companionship, belonging, solidarity and children. And for all of us, even when they're not perfect, such households offer infinitely more opportunity to thrive than the exploitative, medicated, disembodied, disembedded excesses of bio-libertarian hyper-modernity.

But what use is it telling women to abolish Big Romance and

get married, if there's no one to marry? In response to this we must run the gauntlet of every feminist who has ever conceived of women's interests as necessitating the exclusion or defeat of men. What comes next happens alongside men. And that means, paradoxically, allowing the sexes to spend a little *less* time together.

8

Let Men Be

It's impossible for the erased males to command any respect from the people … and still less from their women.

Bronze Age Pervert[1]

WHERE HAVE ALL the good men gone? Well, part of the answer is that, outside the elite and labouring classes, they're increasingly out-competed by women. The cyborg era has shifted power between the sexes – but that shift is unevenly distributed. Men predominate today at the very top and very bottom of the socioeconomic layer cake, in super-elite and dangerous or physically strenuous work. But many sectors are now majority-female – and this is concentrated in the middle.

This majority-female mid-tier knowledge class produces the priestesses of cyborg theocracy. Their bio-libertarian worldview seeks to replace embodied men and women with the tech-enabled, self-fashioning, post-human 'person'. This is the worldview that saw Bristol University student Raquel Rosario Sánchez disciplined by university officials in 2021 for organising a feminist consciousness-raising session that explicitly excluded males, despite the fact that the right to do so is protected under the 2010 Equality Act.[2] And the same worldview reaches impressive heights of absurdity, and cruelty, where it colonises settings in which embodied sex clearly remains a factor. Recall, for example, the ACLU campaign to force New Jersey's prisons to accommodate males who identify as women, and the two women subsequently impregnated by a male fellow-inmate at New Jersey's Edna Mahan Correctional Facility.

Gender-critical feminists have worked fiercely to defend *some* exceptions to this abolition of sex, in contexts such as women's prisons and sports teams where physical embodiment still matters. They're right to do so. But there's also a cognitive dissonance at work here, which parallels the common gender-critical feminist enthusiasm for biomedical mastery of sex difference in some contexts but not others. It's a dissonance usually pointed out only by embittered anons in the manosphere: that is, there exists a precedent for current assaults on all-female spaces, and it was driven by the women's movement.

The 20th century saw a multitude of 'boys' clubs' go co-ed, in the interests of women's equal participation in public life. As we've seen, since Harriet Taylor Mill many liberal feminists took the (male-standard) public-facing liberal subject, and with him the public culture created by men, as the default aspirational templates for *all* liberal subjects. If you accept this premise, of course excluding women from social networks crucial to public-facing liberal subjects looks like men reserving goods for themselves that rightfully ought to be available to 'people'. And from this it follows that for women to have a fair crack at personhood, men must move up and make room for women in their social spaces.

Reactionary feminism goes further than the gender-critical kind. 'Gender neutrality' is inimical to all our interests, for it aims to replace men and women with fungible, interchangeable 'people' composed of fungible, interchangeable body parts. This means defending sex segregation alongside gender-critical feminists, especially at the margins where it's self-evidently cruel, destructive or absurd. But if we're to avert the Meat Lego horrors that follow in the wake of 'gender neutrality', and also re-establish solidarity between the sexes, we need to extend sex realism to every domain where it's salient.

In those social strata where work is knowledge-based, there's little material reason for the sexes to be segregated. In such contexts, ambitious women have long sought to challenge sex segregation. For even today, such spaces matter in public life: a University of Bristol study showed that informal networks such as private members' clubs or golf clubs were more influential in securing directorships than formal qualification for a position.[3] The Garrick, for example, one of the last all-male London members' clubs, is currently subject to a legal challenge by women demanding admission. Cherie Blair recounts her outrage when, as a young barrister in 1976, she was left standing outside the club while her supervisor took Tony Blair, her fellow-pupil, inside the Garrick, saying: 'It's outrageous that so little progress has been made since then.'[4]

But until trans activism began inserting males into all-female spaces, the dissolution of sex segregation remained asymmetric. All-male groups have largely turned co-ed, while at least some equivalent institutions for girls remained single-sex. One paradigmatic instance of this dynamic is the Boy Scouts. Founded in 1908 by Robert Baden-Powell, with the aim of teaching boys the skills and mindsets needed for good citizenship, it was rapidly followed in 1910 by the Girl Guides, a separate organisation that, like the Scouts, rapidly expanded beyond Britain. Scouts and Guides existed in tandem as single-sex organisations until 1976 when, impelled by the demand from girls for access to the adventurous experiences and outdoor fun offered by scouting, the first Scout troops began to admit girls. By 2007, all scout troops were compelled by the umbrella organisation to make provision for girls to join, and by 2011 girls were joining at a higher rate than boys.

Girl Guide groups, meanwhile, still exclude boys (or at least boys who identify as such). This asymmetry provokes little comment, at least overtly: for example, one 2019 *Guardian* article celebrated the rapid rise in girls' participation in scouting, especially across diverse communities and ethnicities. The father of a new scouting recruit, Florence, says, 'We don't like the idea of gender segregation [which] doesn't happen in the real world.' The same article, meanwhile, quotes Guiding deputy chief executive Ruth Marvel, who states that while Girl Guiding has considered going mixed, internal polling reveals the overwhelming consensus of their membership is that they'd prefer to remain girls-only.

The main justification for this asymmetry is that there exists an imbalance of power, status and resources between men and women, and as such women need single-sex support to flourish while the same isn't true for men. As Marvel argues: 'What we offer is more relevant than ever in terms of giving girls opportunities to genuinely explore who they are and what they want to be, and without having anyone telling them that that's not OK.'[5]

At a material level, too, women's lesser physical strength and vulnerability to male violence and sexual aggression is cited to justify the preservation of female single-sex spaces. This is the rationale that drove radical feminists to found domestic violence shelters, rape support groups and other all-female support bodies in the mid-20th century: the very single-sex spaces now threatened by the cyborg call to give 'gender' precedence over embodiment.

Those women who protest, like Cherie Blair, at the negative professional consequences of exclusion from elite male social groups, are very much creatures of the upper crust. And provided they never look outside elite social strata, those knowledge-class women glaring enviously at the men who still bestride the professional heights might be forgiven for thinking male supremacy is as robust as ever. Men still dominate the highest-status professions, and women remain under-represented in those board-level positions attainable by the right golf club membership.[6] In the elite professional circles frequented by a Cherie Blair or a Hillary Clinton, men are still obviously dominant. From this perspective, the ongoing battle to dissolve sex segregation still has a long way to go – and as such, single-sex spaces even in less privileged social strata than that frequented by Garrick members must be subject to the same desegregation. A bit of collateral damage is well worth the greater goal of 'ending patriarchy' – which is to say, the impossible task of eradicating all differences between the sexes.

Further down the food chain, though, departure from the industrial era into the cyborg one wasn't a moral shift so much as a brute economic one. Offshoring replaced manufacturing work with less secure or well-paid positions in warehouses or the gig economy. And this has resulted in a devastating loss of agency, purpose and dignity that's disproportionately affected working- and lower-middle-class men, even as female employment in the same social strata has risen.

But anyone who wonders even in passing whether desegregating the sexes might also have some downsides for men – particularly further down the class hierarchy – will be dismissed as the worst kind of reactionary. Take, for example, the horrified progressive response to a 2021 call by Missouri senator Josh Hawley, for a politics that seeks to restore the well-being of lower-class men.[7] The *Washington Post* declared that this was 'more about prejudice than masculinity',[8] while for *Rolling Stone* it was 'a call to return to the days when men could indulge their masculine urges without consequence', by 'demeaning women, groping them, or worse'.[9]

Boys' clubs are *prima facie* evidence of patriarchy, however rich or poor you are. As such, they have to go: in 2014, one of the last all-male working men's clubs, the Anstice Memorial Institute in Shropshire, closed down rather than succumb to institutional pressure to admit women. When in 2010 the club's Grade II-listed building was revealed to have structural problems, the club sought funding to pay the £50,000 cost of repairs – but was turned down by National Lottery funding on the grounds of its sex-discriminatory membership policy. After 246 of the 300 members voted not to change the rules, the club opted instead to shut down.[10]

Can we make the case that anything is changed for non-elite men as a result of losing access to opportunities for all-male socialisation? Perhaps. The evolutionary biologist Joyce Benenson argues that women and men socialise in distinct ways, a disparity that's a mix of innate bias and peer socialisation but is fundamentally structured around evolved strategies for survival. This in turn, she argues, creates a set of behavioural biases reproduced both by social norms, but also by our evolved sexed preferences.[11] The upshot of these distinct strategies, Benenson claims, is that human males tend towards social patterns in which they cooperate with peers and compete with out-groups.[12] In contrast, human female survival strategies turn on excluding other females in the search for mates, then enlisting peers and elders to help with the care of dependents.

If Benenson is right, a single-sex group going co-ed will have to adjust its patterns of socialisation. Does this matter? Well, in 2022, Merseyside farmer Lisa Edwards received fierce backlash when she accused the 94-year-old Liverpool Agricultural

Discussion Society of sexism for restricting membership to men. After 90 percent of group members voted to remain single-sex, group member Olly Harrison argued: 'There are conversations that are different between men and women.' Given the high incidence of mental distress and suicide in farming, Harrison claimed, and the fact that some conversations among men can only happen away from the presence of women, 'To take away a space to chat is wrong.'[13]

Over recent decades, across many sectors beyond farming, there's been a steady rise in 'deaths of despair' – the bleak term for deaths from suicide, drug and alcohol abuse and other self-inflicted conditions associated with loneliness and lack of hope.[14] Such deaths are most prevalent among working-class men, and social scientists attribute the grim phenomenon to the loss of dignity and economic opportunity. But can we entirely rule out the possibility that this could also be linked to the concurrent decline in male friendship?

According to one 2021 study, in 1990 55 percent of American men said they had at least six close friends. By 2021 only 27 percent reported six or more close friends: half that number. Loneliness has rocketed: 15 percent of American men have no close friendships at all, a fivefold increase since 1990.[15] This leaves many men dependent on a partner for social connection and wider friendship, which in turn leaves them desperately vulnerable if the relationship ends. Suicide is the biggest killer of UK men under 45, and 75 percent of all suicides are men.[16] The highest risk group for suicide in the UK is male divorcees, followed by widowers.[17] In contrast, there's no correlation between suicide risk and marital status for women.[18]

The push to make everything unisex is now rebounding into women's single-sex spaces, to women's detriment. As far as Girl

Guiding's leadership team is concerned, theirs remains an all-girls movement. In 2017, though, Girl Guiding changed its policies to accommodate male-bodied trans 'girls' and Guiding leaders within what was previously a single-sex environment, prompting resignations and fierce pushback among Guiding leaders concerned about potential safeguarding risks.[19]

But long before cyborg theocracy set its sights on all-female prisons or the Girl Guides, the price of elite women's demand for equal opportunities was delegitimising single-sex sociality – with unacknowledged impacts especially on working-class men. And yet, should any straight white man show signs of distress, liberal feminism will dismiss this as further evidence of patriarchy: 'a social pathology of aggrieved entitlement and misogyny', as *Ms.* magazine put it in 2019.[20]

In this context, perhaps we shouldn't be surprised to find straight, white, working-class men less than fully committed to advancing knowledge-class women's political interests. In 2016, 71 percent of white working-class men voted for Trump over Hillary Clinton. This has been linked by some researchers to entrenched working-class male sexism.[21] But such responses could also be read as reasonable pushback by this demographic against putative rule by perhaps *the* quintessential knowledge-class female liberal, a group viewed not entirely without justification as class enemies.

In turn, such women grow ever more anxious to suppress a now palpable undertow of male hostility, which reads through the lens of progress as mere poisonous, reactionary backsliding. But from another angle, the Hawleyesque plea for the well-being of working-class men is straightforwardly in women's interests – specifically, of those women who might otherwise form families with such men. It's right in absolute terms, of course, to care about the well-being of a large part of the world's population.

Every woman has male friends, partners, children and loved ones. But a brute calculation of ordinary women's interests should also support a call for more and better jobs for men; more dignity; less porn and video games; more responsible men forming families.

Two things follow from this. Firstly, that in some contexts there's nothing anti-feminist (at least not for a reactionary feminist) about defending men's interests as distinct from those of women, and in conjunction with them. And secondly, that this extends to supporting a measured rollback of radical 'gender neutrality' across the board, in favour of sex segregation where appropriate – for both sexes. For in some contexts, the gender-critical arguments for segregation by sex are every bit as applicable when the sexes are reversed. The most obvious of these is an historically all-male setting, where men's greater physical strength and propensity for violence are not a bug but a feature: the military.

In search of a male perspective on whether (or how) all-male social dynamics are affected by a shift to co-ed environments, I interviewed Matt, 34, a former soldier from Missouri. His description of an all-male US Special Forces unit maps onto Benenson's description of male social groups, as structured by a dominance hierarchy ordered towards cooperation in defeating an out-group. As he tells it, the team was characterised by 'a natural hierarchy' that formed 'often outside of the rank structure'. Proper behaviour in that hierarchy was policed indirectly, by 'teasing and ribbing' which served to 'spotlight weakness, selfishness, dishonesty and disloyalty' and demand better behaviour. This social dynamic forged a powerful in-group: over time, he says, 'we became a well-oiled machine'.

Matt told me that in most contexts he welcomes the sexes mingling. But integrating women in such groups, he recalls, would 'immediately disrupt the balance within the group and introduce a level of dysfunction'. 'I've seen great female soldiers,' he says, but mixing the sexes changed the social dynamic in ways that radically impaired their effectiveness, resulting in a 'breakdown in trust and cohesion' that was 'just devastating'. That is, the extreme situation of military combat called for a measure of realism about limits to radical gender-neutrality, whether in material terms or in terms of the social dynamic. And Matt's description of how shifting from all-male to co-ed fighting units affected cohesion shows striking parallels to the gender-critical feminist case against trans women in female prisons.

In both settings, members of the minority sex were perceived to be receiving special treatment. One inmate at Edna Mahan complained that trans women received priority for hormone treatment, and were given make-up and other personal items for free where female inmates had to pay for them.[22] Correspondingly, as Matt tells it, in his military unit male leaders treated the women differently: 'Sometimes it was paternalistic, other times it was that they just weren't taken seriously, and sometimes it was exploitative.'

In both settings, too, sexual desire swiftly and disastrously complicated an already high-pressure social setting. For while same-sex desire will inevitably find some expression in a single-sex prison or fighting unit, self-declared same-sex-attracted individuals are only an estimated 3.1 percent of the population.[23] By contrast, the vast majority of members of both sexes are heterosexual, meaning the probability of sexual interactions – consensual or otherwise – will escalate considerably in a co-ed setting. And in a high-pressure environment such as a prison or battlefield, the complexities this introduces can be explosive.

As Matt describes it, 'Almost always the female would have a sexual relationship with someone in the group, and then move onto another, and another.' In one unit, Matt says, '[O]ne of the girls had had a sexual relationship with the commander, the first sergeant, and several of the soldiers, all in a six-month period – and she was married.' Morale was, he said, further undermined by the jealousy and suspicion felt by soldiers' wives at the presence of female soldiers. Again, Matt's account parallels the gender-critical case for sex realism in some settings: accounts are already emerging of the explosive consequences of introducing heterosexual desire into women's prisons: harassment, reported rapes, pregnancies and even heterosexual marriages between inmates.[24]

By the same token, normative differences between male and female physical strength, and propensity for violence, mean introducing members of the opposite sex into either female prisons or all-male fighting units predictably increases the risk to the wider community – in mirroring ways. In the context of female prisons, Helen Joyce notes the striking difference in male and female offending patterns: bluntly, men are vastly stronger and more physically violent than women.[25] Very simply, then, introducing males into an all-female prison increases the danger to the women there.

Conversely, in a fighting unit on the military frontline – a setting that's historically almost always been all-male – physical strength and a capacity for violence are (as Matt notes) positive traits. Women are statistically less likely to be very strong or very violent; adding them to such a unit may thus increase the danger to the surrounding males by physically weakening the team overall. In the interests of making the social status accorded to soldiers an equal-opportunity thing, the physical standards required of new recruits have been diluted;[26] but on the battlefield, Matt says, this can be lethal. 'They were smart enough, no doubt, but they just didn't have the physical capacity and they couldn't be trusted to carry a 90-lb ruck with ammo and, if the situation merited it, the machine gun.' And this can be a matter of life or death: as Matt puts it, the cost of substandard performance on a battlefield 'is ultimately people getting killed'.

Both settings, then, ignored clear normative differences between the sexes in terms of behaviour and physical attributes, while disregarding – again for egalitarian reasons – the interpersonal complexities introduced by sexual desire. The results were painfully predictable, and just as vehemently disavowed by utopians in the name of progress. Instead, bio-libertarian true believers continue reordering public life to their own interests, via the bulldozer of 'gender neutrality', and dismissing male objections as reducible to mere misogyny.

If you think 'progress' means making men and women completely interchangeable, perhaps you'll shrug off elevated risks to a formerly single-sex community as a reasonable price to pay for broad positive changes. Against this, we might say with one gender-critical feminist on Twitter: 'How many rapes of women in prison by "trans women" is ok for you?'[27] It's beyond the scope of this chapter to assess whether an egalitarian military is a positive end goal – but if you believe it is, we might ask with Matt: how many additional maimed or dead soldiers can you justify on the road to that end goal?

We could read gender-critical feminists, or soldiers who prefer all-male fighting units, simply as bigots and reactionaries. But in truth they're realists. Reactionary feminism diverges from the gender-critical kind only in extending the logic of measured sex realism to all-male spaces as well as all-female ones. This is particularly important where it comes to advocating for the interests of less wealthy men, whose suffering should concern us all.

But even acknowledging this is now difficult, not least because male resentment of 'gender neutrality', and the asymmetric power dynamic it encodes, is now so virulent it often manifests precisely as hair-curling misogyny. The anonymous Bronze Age Pervert, for example, whose words form the epigraph to this chapter, attributes 'the hypocrisy of all political life in our time' to 'the liberation of women', which he calls 'an act of complete insanity'.[28] Inspired by this and similar sentiments, then, it's not difficult to find extreme masculinists online arguing that women should be compelled to withdraw entirely from public life, and reduced to a subordination far more total than any which has ever historically obtained in the West.[29]

But even in the unlikely event that such proposals were to win out, this would do nothing to resolve our woes. For while, in Bronze Age Pervert's view, feminism is 'the revolt of women against the outrage of democracy', it's more accurate to say both feminism and democracy are facets of a wider social response to industrial technology. Given this, as with the more main-stream Right, any proposed resolution that amounts to 'keeping everything in the social order the same, except what women do' would produce much the same social order, just swapping the current subculture of mutinously resentful men for one of women.

A more constructive way forward begins with reactionary feminists leading the way in celebrating those social structures in which younger men learn from older ones how to be in the world – without demanding to be included in them. It's not really for me to say what forms male mentorship might take, though I suspect few of them would look like something women would easily recognise as a support group. There are some 'men's groups', in the sense of having as their primary focus just being men in the absence of women, but these are often in practice money-making schemes powered by charismatic individuals, and of questionable benefit to their adherents.

The groups that excite suspicion are those that focus on excelling at a specific activity, and view a single-sex social dynamic as an important factor in pursuing that goal. One such is F3 Nation, a group that organises peer-led free outdoor workouts for men, in the name of building character and fostering male leadership. Founded in 2011, the organisation now has some 40,000 active members and over 3,000 groups meeting across the United States, with branches spreading internationally. The focus on *doing* rather than *talking* again underlines how all-male sociality is unlikely to look like the 'men's groups' that emerged in the 1960s to mirror female 'consciousness-raising'. And it's telling that such groups are routinely greeted with the same hostility that met Josh Hawley's defence of men. One Twitter user who saw an F3 Nation group passing on a night event instantly assumed the group was 'paramilitary-themed'[30] and made the leap straight to 'fascist/white supremacist dogwhistling'.[31] Comments on the group's Facebook page regularly accuse them of 'toxic masculinity' or being a 'cult'.

No wonder: for under Meat Lego Gnosticism all 'humans' must be interchangeable. The aim is to replace every single-sex group with a unisex jumble of meat-parts, segregated by unfalsifiable 'identity'. And traducing male sociality is as much part of this as invading university feminist consciousness-raising groups. The idea that we might opt to structure social groupings by something (from this perspective) as arbitrary as embodied sex is a heresy as extreme as detransitioning, or treating self and body as a single whole. And heresy must be stamped out. The brute institutional force arrayed against Rosario Sánchez, simply for proposing a single-sex women's group, suggests the cyborg theocrats understand what's at stake.

As long as feminism refuses to look at both sides of this coin, embittered denizens of the manosphere will go on claiming that the incursion of male-bodied 'women' into all-female spaces is simply legitimate payback. Such men observe the assault on women's spaces with a grim satisfaction. But should Meat Lego Gnosticism prevail, the ramifications will affect all of us. It may be tempting to tell those women fighting the assault on women's spaces that they made their bed and should lie in it. But such cynics should recall that a world where human nature has been abolished puts everyone's children at risk of being 'upgraded' by the limitless ambitions of Big Biotech. On the other side, gender-critical feminists need to consider the possibility that the price for full-throated male support in defending single-sex spaces is returning to at least partial sex segregation even in some contexts where we'd prefer inclusion, such as parts of the military.

It might seem perverse, in a book about feminism, to make the case for men being freer to exclude women. But elite women have always been the guardians of moral and cultural norms. It's a safe bet that most of the women reading this book will belong broadly to this subset of our sex: the one that, today, reaps the greatest benefits of the immense shift we've made to social lives that are mixed-sex by default, and is also the most insulated from its negative side effects. I'm not arguing for such women to leave public life. We simply need to recognise that the effort to eradicate all-male social spaces, norms and aesthetics, or to treat such phenomena as malign by definition, is antithetical to women's broader interests.

And working to restore appropriate sex segregation doesn't even imply a world very different from the one we have now. It's simply one that extends sex-realist arguments for segregation beyond women's prisons to every context – of which the military is only the most obvious – where those arguments apply.

Reactionary feminism can lead by example in *just not caring quite so much* if men sometimes leave us out, and do their thing without us. This might seem trivial in material contexts where work means a laptop job, and it doesn't make much difference either way. But the direction set by elite women reverberates down the social hierarchy, and has far more profound impacts further down the socioeconomic hierarchy, where sex matters most.

Fundamentally this means recognising that good men are forged not just by women but also by beneficial competition with other men. We cannot, after all, wring our hands about men's ailing mental health while reacting with fear and hostility to every fraternal organisation that focuses on practical activities and produces, apparently as a side effect, more confident and well-adjusted men. And if helping men to flourish (and keeping intact male-bodied individuals out of female prisons) means more single-sex societies across the board, and that in turn means a handful of Cherie Blairs are shut out of elite social clubs, that's a trade all of us should be willing to make.

If I'm right about the end of progress, we will need one another if we want to thrive. That obviously includes men. A world of growing instability, fragmenting peace and order, resource competition and faltering subsistence is not one in which the welfare (or even physical safety) of women and children can be taken for granted. Against that backdrop, a world where every baby can be welcomed without a loss to women's personhood is self-evidently impossible unless it's also filled with good husbands and fathers. Not sperm donors, porn-addled pick-up artists, passive-aggressive 'male feminists' or bitter, proletarianised male labourers doing grunt work by day and seething online at night. Capable, confident men. If we want to see more of these in the world, we need to step back a little, and let them create one another.

A final, less tangible benefit of stepping back is the aid this affords both sexes in reclaiming desire from the machine. For the true root cause of the so-called 'sex recession' is the conquest of sexuality by the all-exposing 'marketplace', and reactionary feminism takes direct aim at this commodification of desire. Reclaiming our right to segregate in everyday life by sex – whether pragmatically, as in prisons or the military, or simply because we *prefer* it – affords a chance to withdraw from the tyrannical glare of compulsory gender-neutrality. In other words: it returns a measure of mystery to the opposite sex.

And this in turn creates more space for desire to flourish. But attending to the paradox of desire between the sexes also means turning our fire directly on the technology that has enabled radical hyper-sexualisation, and with it an exhaustion of desire in the 'sexual marketplace'. A feminism against progress, in other words, is feminism against the Pill.

9

Rewilding Sex

You get on TikTok. Booty. Booty. Ass. Shake ass. Instagram.
Ass. Titties. Ass. Titties. Ass. Titties. I'm not excited no more.
I'm booty'd out. Y'all have shown me so much ass I'm numb to
it. It's like seeing so many deaths you just become numb to it.
I'm not even excited to see booty no more. It's like aw, bro, you
see her ass? I've just seen 37 other ones this morning. OK, it's
big. It's a ass.

Y'all have taken the joy of ass-gazing outta my life.
And that's something I prided myself on growing up. I
used to love to just ass-gaze. Now, I'm just numb to ass.
Just keep it in your pants, man.

@gotsnacks_ on TikTok[1]

THE NOTORIOUS *INFOWARS* HOST Alex Jones once opined that
he didn't like the government 'putting chemicals in the water
that turn the friggin' frogs gay'. CNBC called this a 'disturbing
and ridiculous conspiracy theory',[2] and Jones is noted for wild
and sometimes actionable claims. But if we read 'gay' in the
colloquial sense, as offensive shorthand for 'feminised male',
Jones's assertion contains a glimmer of truth. Chemicals really
are going into the water that so disrupt the endocrine systems
of small aquatic creatures, including frogs, that males sometimes

undergo sex reversal[3] or adopt homosexual behaviour.[4] It's just that the synthetic estradiol that damages fish and amphibians isn't being added to the water as a sinister government conspiracy. The truth is more banal: traces of estradiol are peed into the sewage system by every woman who uses hormonal birth control, and this compound is difficult to remove in sewage treatment. So if you're on the Pill, it's not the government messing with frogs' sexual behaviour. It's you.

The catastrophic ecological impact of hormonal birth control is one of the many cognitive dissonances in liberal feminism, a movement that generally prides itself – at least superficially – on alignment with progressive causes including concern for the environment. But the lure of consequence-free sex is so powerful that no matter how often the ecological destructiveness of the Pill is reported, this fact somehow never seems to register in the popular consciousness. It's the only way we can go on viewing as 'consequence-free' something that in fact has serious consequences – just largely borne not by humans, but by frogs and fish.

That doesn't mean there are no consequences for us, though. The Pill is an ecological catastrophe on an immense scale, thanks to the literal poisons it leaks into the water table. And after 50 years of its reign, the figures are in: its effect on the delicate social ecology of sexual relations has been every bit as bad. The Pill plays a central role in opening the door for a host of figurative poisons, which have percolated into every facet of our intimate relations. And on both ecological and social fronts, bio-libertarian feminism simply chooses to look past these side effects, because progress means individual autonomy at any price.

In the view of internet historian Katherine Dee, changing attitudes to the Pill stand in for wider concerns about the sexual revolution. Many young women from across the political spectrum, she argues, internalised the contemporary 'liberated' approach to sex – but have, as Dee puts it, come to feel they were 'duped'.[5]

Increasingly, such women are blaming hormonal birth control for a slew of side effects that make them miserable. One young woman tweets: 'Sometimes I wonder if I'm actually mentally ill or if it's just that I've been on birth control my entire adult life.'[6] Another agrees: '[I] thought I was so mentally ill until I went off birth control.'[7] Nor is it just women noticing the psychological effects: one popular online (male) voice argues that 'hormonal birth control is plausibly the greatest driver of unhappiness among modern American youth and certainly far more psychoactive than ppl realize', based on the fact that every woman he's dated who has 'switched or stopped birth control' has 'undergone noticeable personality changes'.[8] They're looking for alternatives, too: videos with the #naturalbirthcontrol hashtag on TikTok have been viewed more than 30 million times.[9]

On the face of it, the complaints are about biological side effects. But we can also read, beneath this, a broader statement: the Pill is making me miserable. And this is a far broader critique. For in de-risking sex, this technology has made it ubiquitous, and in the process stripped desire of anticipation, excitement and mystery: in a word, emptied it of eroticism. In its place we're offered an increasingly coarse, commodified and grotesque landscape of all-you-can-eat lust.

This marketisation of sexual desire has been under way now since the 1960s. And digital culture has accelerated those ways we're able to buy sexual stimulation, or sell ourselves as commodities. The resulting hellscape of sexual anomie is the true face of what calls itself 'sex-positive' feminism, a movement that doesn't seem to have prevented Gen Z from slumping into a 'sex recession'.[10] Indeed, as Louise Perry argues, it may even be driving it. Pornography degrades the capacity for mutual pleasure: doctor Harry Fisch calls porn 'the single, largest non-health issue that makes relationships crumble', linking porn over-use with erectile issues and inability to orgasm.[11]

This phenomenon is known as 'death grip syndrome'.[12] In Perry's view, pervasive digital access to porn is generalising this, in what she calls a 'cultural death grip': a widespread societal indifference to sexual stimuli.[13] As @gotsnacks_ puts it on TikTok, in the epigraph to this chapter: 'I'm booty'd out.' Or, in the case of those women of my generation who were the first to walk into full-spectrum cyborg-era sexual 'liberation', we might say brutalised to the point of no longer wanting to remain silent.

Former *Playboy* columnist Bridget Phetasy describes this experience in an essay titled 'I Regret Being a Slut'. Here, she recounts how when she was younger, 'I would have said one-night stands made me feel "emboldened".' The truth, though, was that 'I was using sex like a drug'. Phetasy reports that she now regrets all but a handful of her youthful sexual encounters, nearly all of which were 'either meaningless or mediocre (or both)' and most of which 'left me feeling empty and demoralized. And worthless.'

In her view, the greatest damage she did to herself lay in the indifference she cultivated, as a cover for how unhappy it made her feel to be treated as worthless: 'I told myself I didn't care,' she writes. 'I didn't care when a man ghosted me. I didn't care when he left in the middle of the night or hinted that he wanted me to leave. The walks of shame. The blackouts. The anxiety.' Eventually, she recounts, she hit rock bottom when she received a text message that read 'Goodnight baby I love you' — swiftly followed by another that read, devastatingly: 'Wrong person.'[14]

By today's standards, Phetasy and I merely dipped our toes in the shallows of what Giddens optimistically called 'plastic sexuality' and 'pure relationship'. Since then, the collateral damage has grown steadily worse. The expectations set by free-access porn now routinely result in teenage girls enduring acts they don't enjoy, in exchange for the barest signs of affection.[15] One teenage girl was reported in 2019 to have been left with anal injuries so severe, after trying to imitate pornography, that she will need a colostomy bag for life.[16]

And among adults, a BBC Scotland survey suggested that over two-thirds of men under 40 have spat on, slapped or choked their partner during consensual sex – with many indicating that this was inspired by porn consumption.[17] And fetish practices far more extreme than slapping or choking are now so mainstream that magazines for school-age girls write about 'kink' for their youthful readers.[18] In turn, this percolates out into real life, with young women on social media recounting experiences of abuse perpetrated in the name of 'kink'. In one particularly shocking (since deleted) example, a young Twitter user described how, when she was a teenager, the 38-year-old man with whom she had a 'consensual' BDSM relationship introduced 'breath play': 'he was piss drunk & put me in a rear naked choke & I passed out'. On another occasion, she recounts, 'I'd woken up to him shoving crushed up Adderall in my vagina.'

None of this would be possible unless, in the name of freedom and progress, we'd accepted a view of women as sterile by default, with fertility as an optional extra. Even for those women who somehow avoid such violent or degrading sexual demands, default sterility means continual pressure to accede to loveless sex. The problem Virginia Ironside discovered in the 1960s – that being on the Pill made it hard to refuse sex – has only grown worse since, with many women now 'consenting' to unwanted sex largely out of politeness.[19]

None of this is in women's interests. 'Liberation' shouldn't mean violence, anal injuries, and casual hook-ups with a 10 percent chance of orgasm. Phetasy now denounces the culture she imbibed, which reduced 'sex-positivity' to a promiscuity that left her empty and demoralised. Crucially, she argues, 'sex-positive' doesn't automatically mean love doesn't matter: 'You can still be sex-positive and accept that for you, sex can't be liberated from intimacy and a meaningful relationship.'[20]

I'm less courageous than Phetasy in describing my own adventures in 'liberation'. All I'll say is that she speaks for me as well. I don't think we're outliers, either: as Louise Perry puts it in her 2022 *The Case Against the Sexual Revolution*: 'Loveless Sex Is Not Empowering'. The torrent of acclaim the book received across the political spectrum suggests that there are many other women out there who feel the same.

Realistically, we can't simply stuff the technology back into its box. But reactionary feminists can – once again – lead by example by rejecting it. Don't take the Pill. Don't encourage your friends to take the Pill. Quite aside from harming aquatic life, and facilitating the pervasive pornification of mainstream culture, the Pill causes mood issues, weight gain and libido loss. It's also a crucial precondition for bad sex, because it de-risks casual hook-ups. Why would you take a pill that makes you fat, miserable and sexless, merely to increase your chance of a loveless fuck where 90 percent of the time you won't even come?

Objectors may point out that this raises a coordination problem. If mainstream sexual culture now assumes that women will by default be sterile and sexually available, then how is any heterosexual woman who refuses this dynamic ever to find a partner? Won't men simply pass them over for someone who plays by the usual rules? One of my interviewees doesn't think so. Katie,

25, a researcher from Washington, DC, says that in her experience, dating while refusing birth control was 'not at all awkward or weird'. Rather, in her view, it serves to filter out frivolous would-be partners: 'If you're serious about it, and they're serious and thoughtful too, then it's not an issue.' That is, the men for whom it's a dealbreaker are those who anyway only wanted sex: 'If they were focused on things that were solely about a physical relationship – sure that'd make it hard.' Katie's principles have evidently not proved an obstacle to finding a partner: she recently married.

Other objectors might accuse me of trying to legitimise a conservative 'purity culture', under the guise of feminism. And it's true that religious conservatives have long been critical of the Pill. But while reactionary feminist prescriptions – rejecting the Pill and casual sex – are similar, I'm not arguing for female 'purity' in the sense of imagining that women could or should somehow remain free of sexual desire. Indeed, the 'purity' approach seems mainly to incentivise rebellion: Phetasy's story began with an upbringing in which she was taught to prize this 'purity', to fear sex and to be ashamed of her own desires: 'My burgeoning sexuality would unfold as a reaction to these repressive religious orthodoxies, old-school notions of sexual status, and trauma.' I don't want to re-tread timeworn arguments about some imaginary state of feminine purity. Women get horny. Get over it. We aren't going to heal the dissociative harms of the sexual revolution by embracing a different kind of body dissociation and pretending to a 'purity' few of us feel.

Instead, we must heal our polluted erotic ecologies by rewilding sex. In the field of conservation, 'rewilding' refers to practices such as reintroducing apex predators or reducing intervention in a landscape, such that complex ecologies are able to re-emerge and find equilibrium again. In one famous example, reintroducing wolves to Yellowstone National Park in the United States resulted, via a complex chain of inter-species interactions, in a river changing course.[21] Applying a similar mindset to our sexual ecologies means a similar willingness to make space for dangerous elements of the natural order. Specifically, we need to recognise that 'risk-free' heterosexual sex can only be had at the cost of reproduction. And eliminating that biological purpose takes much of the dark, dangerous and profoundly intimate joy out of sex.

Pornography itself is a reliable guide to what's truly forbidden. And the volume of content that now focuses on either the idea of procreation, reframed as 'breeding fetish', or on physical evidence of pregnancy, such as lactation, reveals perhaps that even the most fundamental organismic urge – the drive to reproduce – has not been abolished by opt-in fertility, but merely commodified. If we can reclaim this profound facet of our nature from its capture by Big Porn, we stand a chance of reclaiming the charge, and the intimacy, of sex from a 'booty'd-out' culture grown numb to even grotesque stimuli. But just as in the wolves of Yellowstone, this also means reclaiming the danger.

To restore that danger, we must acknowledge that for all but the small minority of same-sex-attracted people, desire and reproduction can't be disaggregated, any more than 'self' and 'body'. Shorn of its connection to the source of life itself, that darkness and danger will find twisted expression in depraved fetishes and sexual violence. By contrast, consensual, genuinely consequential sex is profoundly intimate: not least because a woman who refuses birth control will be highly motivated to be choosy about her partners. Pregnancy risk is, after all, a cast-iron reason to reject having sex with anyone out of politeness.

The most direct way for women to reclaim this beneficial sexual self-discipline now is by saying 'thanks but no thanks' to the technology. While this means, for those who take this path, an explicit insistence on sex only in the context of trust and intimacy, it doesn't necessarily follow that women should refuse sex before marriage. But *caveat emptor*: if you're playing with this kind of fire, outside the context of a committed relationship, you'd better be absolutely certain you can trust your male partner.

If you are sure of that trust, there's a strong likelihood you'll enjoy sex more when you do have it – and not just because women are so much more likely to orgasm in a committed relationship. In a lifelong partnership, the possibility of conception can itself be deeply erotic. And one of the open secrets of 'natural family planning' methods is that sex really is better when you don't disrupt it with artificial hormones. Studies have shown that women's sexual libido peaks just before ovulation, a cycle that makes perfect sense from the perspective of what sex is ultimately *for*[22] – but if the menstrual cycle is disrupted by hormonal birth control, this effect disappears. And if you don't want to conceive a baby, having sex anyway assumes a level of faith in your male partner's self-control that on its own implies real intimacy.

And along with the pro-pleasure, pro-love case for rewilding sex is the pro-embodiment one. Rejecting birth control is the first and most radical step women can take, in healing the disconnect introduced by technology between us and our own bodies, in the name of freeing us from sex difference. As Abigail Favale notes, relying on cycle tracking to manage fertility increases women's awareness of our fertility cycles, and with it attunement to our own bodies. In this sense of increasing our agency in terms of fertility awareness, and bringing women into harmony with our own embodied existence, rejecting the Pill is not less but *more* empowering.

215

The true, deep wildness of sex can only be reproduced, in the sterile order of de-risked consumer sex, by the stylised violence of 'BDSM'. Add the real, material 'power exchange' of fertility back into sexual intimacy, and I'm willing to bet the popularity of 'kink' would evaporate overnight. Or, rather, return to its proper place. In turn, then, we might see fewer incidences of girls passing out in a rear naked choke-hold or having crushed Adderall stuffed into them; fewer incidences of death from 'rough sex'; fewer prolapses; perhaps also fewer men driven to ever more extreme stimuli in search of the one thing that's truly forbidden: sex with the real danger left in.

We can have this again. To get there, we must reject the totalitarian sexual–industrial complex. We can reclaim our sexual cycles, our capacity for eroticism, our attunement to our own bodies, and our right to refuse exploitative, loveless and degrading approaches. And in refusing this degraded parody of our most intimate embodied experiences, we can open ourselves to better ones – not with The One, but with *a* one: someone who is willing to step up. Not to Big Romance, or the fantasy of perfect communion, but as far as solidarity, intimacy, family and building a life together.

Afterword

Ghost Books

The fact that the masses are spontaneously being drawn into the movement does not make the organisation of this struggle less necessary. *On the contrary, it makes it* more necessary.

Lenin, *What Is to Be Done?*

IN THE COURSE OF DRAFTING *Feminism Against Progress*, I learned that one of the most difficult things about writing a book is choosing what to leave out. Trying to say everything risks leaving the reader less enlightened than muddled and irritated. But seeking to avoid this means crafting an argument haunted by the ghostly outlines of several other books that didn't get written.

One of those ghost books explores the chronic and increasingly obvious tension between the high-tech, consumerist underpinnings of feminism on the bio-libertarian model, and the new age of rising energy costs, dwindling resources and looming scarcity. If, as Phyllis Schlafly observed, it was as much the washing machine as feminism that liberated women,[1] it stands to reason that, should resource constraints ever make washing machines prohibitively difficult to manufacture or expensive to run, we will need to re-evaluate what women's liberation looks like. This goes for innumerable other technologies, too, from disposable nappies and formula milk to birth control itself.

Another ghost book looks at the impact of our shift from the print to the digital age, not through the lens of everyday life and relationships, as I have at a few points in this book, but in the context of our broader politics. For if the printing press radically transformed politics, faith and culture, it seems more than probable that an information revolution every bit as radical as the printing press will have effects on an equivalent scale. To my eye, we're beginning to see the enormity of those effects, some of which are already shaking the very foundations of our cultural and political settlement.

Centrally, the digital revolution is undermining settled foundations of liberal democracy, including freedom of speech, public debate within a rational frame, and a shared belief in objective reality. All of these changes, in turn, have already decisively altered our political process. It's far from original to observe that electorates are growing increasingly disillusioned with the democratic process, as it becomes ever clearer that political forces wholly unaccountable to electorates shape and constrain the space within which elected politicians are able to operate. It's my view that this is a structural feature of the cyborg age, and likely irreversible.

A third ghost book addresses the question of what *politically* should be done about everything I've discussed in *Feminism Against Progress*, and especially as concerns the tightening political and ideological mesh of Meat Lego Gnosticism. In Part 3 of this book, I've focused on the small scale: family life, loved ones and sex. It's a central premise of both my work and my life that the intimate scale is of no less importance than the grand sweep of history, so I feel no need to defend or apologise for this. Even so, it invites the question of what, if anything, reactionary feminism has to say about women's interests at scale.

To answer this would be to rewrite Part 3 of this book from the other end of the telescope. The question might be as follows: what would it take at scale, across relationships, family life and sexual intimacy, to create a world in which every baby is welcome *in conjunction with* and not *at the expense of* his or her mother? I've not sought to make definitive claims partly because, for reasons already explained, reactionary feminism is best understood not as a universal set of principles but as an heuristic for situations that are always contextual and relational. But the answers I would give are also structured by these other two phantom books.

For one thing, reactionary feminism at scale needs half an eye on the long-term likelihood that the enabling technologies which underpin bio-libertarianism will become scarcer and more expensive in the medium term, stratifying what 'feminism' means ever more sharply by social caste. If this is so, then reactionary feminists who are genuinely concerned for the interests of women beyond the elite will need to think as concretely as possible about what it means to support family formation, relationships and mutually respectful sexual intimacy, in the absence of all those reinforcing technologies that currently underwrite our condition of relative freedom. What this means in practice will vary by local context, but may well produce some counter-intuitive policies from an industrial or cyborg feminist perspective. To take just one example, in the absence of reliable and universally available birth control, 'no sex before marriage' is a far more feminist proposition than its inverse.

And getting from 'propositions' to social change at scale means leading by example, but also an awareness of the teaching role played by laws and other regulatory frameworks, and a willingness to use those frameworks towards reactionary feminist ends. And this, of course, touches on the question of political power.

Here the question of what is to be done is once again shaped by the phantom books I've sketched above. For if, as I suspect, the cyborg age is a post-democratic age, it follows that feminist politics capable of acting effectively in this age must adjust accordingly.

This is less alarming than it sounds, and is in fact already happening. In Chapter 6, I outlined a cyborg metaphysics I've characterised as Meat Lego Gnosticism, and described the ongoing process of institutional capture that has been steadily working to entrench its principles within that pre-political matrix of power which increasingly serves, in the cyborg era, to discipline the dwindling power of electoral politics. I've called this convergence of cyborg metaphysics and institutional power 'cyborg theocracy'.

Though the situation we face on this front is perilous, it's far from hopeless – provided reactionary feminists don't make the mistake of seeking to effect change purely via public debate (too muddled and cacophonous in the digital age, not to mention increasingly subject to censorship) or via electoral politics (already substantially defanged). Such pushback as has already been effective seeks rather to do battle with cyborg theocracy on its own territory, which is pre-political.

In the UK, for example, where relatively effective resistance has been mounted to the encroachment of gender ideology, this has generally not been directly via electoral politics, but some way upstream: grassroots mobilisation with the aim of effecting change *before* issues percolate up to electoral level. The campaign against 'gender self-identification' saw years of activism oriented towards ensuring the mass of ordinary women's voices were heard on proposed changes to the Gender Recognition Act. In the end, the consultation was flooded with responses, and in the ensuing highly politicised environment the proposed change to 'self-ID' has been (at the time of writing) shelved. In the course of that campaign, new institutions, protocols, resources and campaigning networks have formed to campaign politically in defence of sex realism – all of which have in turn served to extend the pushback beyond the 2004 Gender Recognition Act.

A key battlefield has been seeking to roll back the onward march of institutional capture, effected via schemes such as Stonewall's Diversity Champions. As Helen Joyce has outlined, this innocuous-sounding structure in practice serves to entrench cyborg theocracy across bodies such as universities, corporations and the public sector.[2] It's a paid-for accreditation scheme whose official purpose is signalling a body's support of LGBTQ+ rights via compliance with Stonewall's suggested institutional changes, most of which are propagated via HR departments and include changes that are in practice highly political, such as removing sex-segregated toilets or erasing female-specific language from maternity policies.

The scheme is graded via competitive rankings, and its demands have grown more extreme over time. Shifting the standing of such schemes from 'self-evidently good' to 'uncomfortably politicised' has been a key focus for fighting back, and has met with some success as public bodies such as the Equality and Human Rights Commission and the BBC have withdrawn from participation in the scheme.

Needless to say, though, this is a many-headed hydra. The approach taken by gender-critical feminists should serve as a template for reactionary feminist politics across the board. But it's also not enough just to resist: alongside trench warfare aimed at slowing the spread of cyborg theocracy in institutions, reactionary feminists need to take positive steps to institutionalise a worldview capable of supporting men and women as we are, not as radically malleable Meat Lego post-humans. That means building rival institutions capable of exercising influence within the pre-political (or, if you prefer, post-democratic) space of NGOs, educational institutions and regulatory frameworks – and having the courage to use the resulting power to reactionary feminist ends. It's not enough simply to defend the liberal status quo of negative freedoms to do or say what we please. If this is not to be turned against us, in the liquefying interests of tech-enabled freedom and trade, the cyborg era necessitates a positive restatement of human nature, and a defence of that nature in all our interests – even where doing so invites accusations of being 'illiberal'.

To give just one example, this means we can't just declare, as the UK's Attorney General did in 2022, that schools are under no obligation to accommodate requests from pupils to use pronouns that are at odds with the pupil's biological sex.[3] Such statements are a start, but in practice will serve only to slow the spread of cyborg theocracy. Turning the tide means obliging those in educational authority to teach children the truth, namely that there are two sexes and it's physically impossible to oscillate between them. Reactionary feminists and our fellow-travellers need a concrete change plan for seizing and wielding the power necessary to institutionalise this and related changes.

The details of such a plan are for more strategic political minds than mine to devise, but in its absence a reactionary feminist politics will amount to little more than a despairing and ultimately doomed rearguard action. For the reality is that all politics is now illiberal – or, more accurately, post-liberal. Those who insist on sticking to liberal tactics in spite of this shift have already conceded the fight.

If this seems a gloomy note to end the book on, this is only because the situation is truly desperate. But I'm not without hope. Many today see the urgency of the situation, sense that the wider political context is changing beyond all recognition, and find themselves willing to consider measures that (from the standpoint of late-industrial liberalism) appear extraordinary.

This is as it should be. There is very little left to conserve, but that in turn means there's everything to build. It doesn't matter if your orientation is the personal one of your immediate home and community, or the political one of the social fabric more broadly. The personal and the political are, as ever, the warp and weft of that social fabric. And for as long as there's been a history of women, that history records us weaving.

Notes

1. AGAINST PROGRESS

1   'Labour's 1997 Party Political Broadcast – Things Can Only Get Better' [video], YouTube, uploaded by Great British Politics, 5 June 2015, www.youtube.com/watch?v=gi5j7jjhm4M&ab_channel=GreatBritishPolitics [retrieved 5 January 2022].
2   Judith Butler, *Gender Trouble: Feminism and the Subversion of Identity* (New York and London: Routledge, 1990).
3   Deborah Summers, 'No return to boom and bust: what Brown said when he was chancellor', *Guardian*, 11 September 2008, www.theguardian.com/politics/2008/sep/11/gordonbrown.economy.
4   Steven Pinker, *Enlightenment Now: The Case for Reason, Science, Humanism, and Progress* (London: Penguin, 2018).
5   Christopher Lasch, *The True and Only Heaven: Progress and Its Critics* (New York: Norton, 1991).
6   Adrian Vermeule, 'All human conflict is ultimately theological', *Church Life Journal*, 26 July 2019, churchlifejournal.nd.edu/articles/all-human-conflict-is-ultimately-theological.
7   Norma Swenson to Ivan Illich. Quoted in Fabio Milana, '*Gender*: Notes to the text', *International Journal of Illich Studies* 5:1 (2016), journals.psu.edu/illichstudies/article/view/60133/60063.

2. FEMINISM, ABORTED

1   Barra Roantree and Kartik Vira, 'The rise and rise of women's employment in the UK', Institute for Fiscal Studies, 27 April 2018, ifs.org.uk/publications/12951/.
2   Kristin A. Goss, 'Volunteering and the long civic generation', *Nonprofit and Voluntary Sector Quarterly* 28:4 (December 1999): 378–415, journals.sagepub.com/doi/pdf/10.1177/0899764099284002.

3   Christopher Lasch, *Women and the Common Life: Love, Marriage, and Feminism*, ed. Elisabeth Lasch-Quinn (New York: Norton, 1997), pp. 95–6.

4   Jean-Jacques Rousseau, *Emile, or On Education*, tr. William Harold Payne (1762; New York: Appleton, 1895), p. 263.

5   Gaëlle Ferrant, Luca Maria Pesando and Keiko Nowacka, 'Unpaid care work: The missing link in the analysis of gender gaps in labour outcomes', OECD Development Centre, December 2014, www.oecd.org/dev/development-gender/Unpaid_care_work.pdf.

6   See, for example, *The Motherhood Pay Penalty*, Trades Union Congress, March 2016, www.tuc.org.uk/sites/default/files/MotherhoodPayPenalty.pdf.

7   Jemima Olchawski, *Parents, Work and Care: Striking the Balance*, The Fawcett Society, 2016, www.fawcettsociety.org.uk/Handlers/Download.ashx?IDMF=ee914eef-9b45-4f6e-84c5-57c0547727b4.

8   See, for example, Tejvan Pettinger, 'Economic inactivity – definition and causes', Economics Help, www.economicshelp.org/blog/160372/economics/economic-inactivity.

9   'Women shoulder the responsibility of "unpaid work"', Office for National Statistics (ONS), 10 November 2016, www.ons.gov.uk/employmentandlabourmarket/peopleinwork/earningsandworkinghours/articles/womenshouldertheresponsibilityofunpaidwork/2016-11-10.

10 @JoeBiden on Twitter, 23 November 2021, twitter.com/JoeBiden/status/1462961600999133185?s=20 [retrieved 6 January 2022].

11 See, for example, Eva Feder Kittay, *Love's Labor: Essays on Women, Equality, and Dependency* (New York: Routledge, 1999).

12 The Associated Press, 'Robertson letter attacks feminists', *The New York Times*, 26 August 1992, www.nytimes.com/1992/08/26/us/robertson-letter-attacks-feminists.html.

13 Scott Yenor, *The Recovery of Family Life: Exposing the Limits of Modern Ideologies* (Waco: Baylor University Press, 2020).

14 Germaine Greer, *The Female Eunuch* (1970; London: HarperCollins, 1990), p. 80.

15 Ibid., p. 110.

16 Jill Filipovic, 'Women are having fewer babies because they have more choices', *The New York Times*, 27 June 2021, www.nytimes.com/2021/06/27/opinion/falling-birthrate-women-babies.html.

17 Neil Smelser (ed.), *Karl Marx on Society and Social Change* (Chicago: University of Chicago Press, 1973), p. 5.

18 Karl Polanyi, *The Great Transformation: The Political and Economic Origins of Our Time* (1944; Boston: Beacon Press, 2001), p. 44.

19 Ibid., p. 48.

20 Elizabeth Wayland Barber, *Women's Work: The First 20,000 Years – Women, Cloth, and Society in Early Times* (New York: Norton, 1996).

21 Toni Mount, *The Medieval Housewife and Other Women of the Middle Ages* (Stroud: Amberley, 2014).

22 Ivan Illich, *Gender* (1983; London: Marion Boyars, 1990), p. 75.

23 Geoffrey Chaucer, 'The Parson's Tale', lines 927–9, in Larry D. Benson (ed.), *The Riverside Chaucer* (Oxford: Oxford University Press, 1987), p. 321.

24 See, for example, Giles of Rome, *De regimine principum*, book II (c.1277).

25 See, for example, Matthew 20: 25–28: 'You know that the rulers of the Gentiles lord it over them, and their great ones exercise authority over them. It shall not be so among you. But whoever would be great among you must be your servant, and whoever would be first among you must be your slave, even as the Son of Man came not to be served but to serve, and to give his life as a ransom for many.'

26 Susan Carol Rogers, 'Female forms of power and the myth of male dominance: A model of female/male interaction in peasant society', *American Ethnologist* 2:4 (November 1975): 727–56.

27 Illich, p. 20.

28 Friedrich Engels, *The Condition of the Working Class in England* (1845). Cited in Valerie Bryson, *Feminist Political Theory* (London: Palgrave, 2016), p. 60.

29 Karl Marx, *Capital*, vol. 1, tr. Ben Fowkes (1867; Harmondsworth: Penguin, 1976), pp. 521–2.

30 Louise A. Tilly, 'Women, women's history, and the Industrial Revolution', *Social Research* 61:1 (Spring 1994): 115–37.

31 Illich, p. 50.

32 Ibid., p. 48.

33 Barbara Welter, 'The cult of true womanhood: 1820–1860', *American Quarterly* 18:2 (1966): 151–74.

34 Emma C. Embury, 'Female education', *Ladies' Companion* 8 (January 1838): 18.

35 Friedrich Engels, *The Origin of the Family, Private Property and the State* (1884; Chippendale: Resistance Books, 2004), p. 67.

36 See, for example, Mechthild Nagel, 'Patriarchal ideologies and women's domestication', in Mechthild Nagel and Anthony J. Nocella (eds), *The End of Prisons: Reflections from the Decarceration Movement* (Leiden: Brill, 2013), pp. 147–67.

37 Lasch, *Women and the Common Life*, chapter 5.

38 Nancy F. Cott, *The Bonds of Womanhood: 'Woman's Sphere' in New England, 1780–1835* (New Haven and London: Yale University Press, 1977), pp. 68–70.

39 See, for example, Sue Gerhardt, *Why Love Matters: How Affection Shapes a Baby's Brain* (London: Routledge, 2004).

40 See, for example, Abigail Tucker, *Mom Genes: Inside the New Science of Our Ancient Maternal Instinct* (New York: Gallery Books, 2021).

41 'Manuscripts and special collections: Property ownership', University of Nottingham, www.nottingham.ac.uk/manuscriptsandspecialcollections/learning/medievalwomen/theme3/propertyownership.aspx.

42 Linda K. Kerber, 'Separate spheres, female worlds, woman's place: The rhetoric of women's history', *Journal of American History* 75:1 (1988): 9–39.

43 Mary S. Gove Nichols and Thomas L. Nichols, *Marriage: Its History, Character, and Results; Its Sanctities, and Its Profanities; Its Science and Its Facts, Demonstrating Its Influence, as a Civilized Institution, on the Happiness of the Individual and the Progress of the Race* (Cincinnati: Valentine Nicholson & Co., 1854).

44 Reva B. Siegel, 'Home as work: The first woman's rights claims concerning wives' household labor, 1850–1880', *Yale Law Journal* 103:5 (1994): 1073–217, openyls. law.yale.edu/bitstream/handle/20.500.13051/8808/42_103YaleLJ1073_ March1994_.pdf?sequence=2&isAllowed=y.

45 Harriet Taylor Mill, 'The Enfranchisement of Women' (1851). Reprinted in Ann P. Robson and John M. Robson (eds), *Sexual Equality: Writings by John Stuart Mill, Harriet Taylor Mill, and Helen Taylor* (Toronto, University of Toronto Press, 1994), pp. 178–203.

46 Ibid., p. 190.

47 Ibid., p. 179.

48 Ibid., p. 192.

49 Ibid., p. 186.

50 Ibid.

51 Charlotte Perkins Gilman, *Women and Economics* (1898; Mineola, NY: Dover, 2012), p. 120.

52 Quoted in Siegel, p. 1166.

53 Erika Bachiochi, *The Rights of Women: Reclaiming a Lost Vision* (Notre Dame, IN: University of Notre Dame Press, 2021), p. 111.

54 Ibid., pp. 106–16.

55 Ibid., p. 207.

56 Ibid.

57 Betty Friedan, *Life So Far: A Memoir* (New York: Simon and Schuster, 2006). Quoted in Bachiochi, p. 210.

58 Bachiochi, p. 270.

59 Ruth Bader Ginsburg, 'Some thoughts on benign classification in the context of sex', *Connecticut Law Review* 10 (1978): 813–27.

60 Greer, p. 252.

61 Ibid., p. 11.

62 Dorothy Sayers, 'Are women human?: Address given to a woman's society, 1938', *Logos: A Journal of Catholic Thought and Culture* 8:4 (Fall 2005): 165–78.

63 Daphne Clair de Jong, 'The feminist sell-out', *New Zealand Listener*, 14 January 1978. Republished in Mary Krane Derr, Rachel MacNair and Linda Naranjo-Huebl, *Prolife Feminism: Yesterday and Today* (Bloomington, IN: Xlibris Corporation, 2005), p. 234.

64 Nick Lavigueur and Alice Cachia, 'This is how many children were cared for by substandard childminders', YorkshireLive, 18 December 2018, www.examinerlive. co.uk/news/west-yorkshire-news/how-many-children-were-cared-15562634.

65 Martin Kitara, 'Almost half of single parents living in poverty', Turn2us, 1 June 2016, www.turn2us.org.uk/About-Us/News/Almost-half-of-single-parents-living-in-poverty.

66 See, for example, the UK's Millennium Cohort Study, which shows that the children of single parents fare worse over the long term on a number of metrics. Centre for Longitudinal Studies, University of London, cls.ucl.ac.uk/cls-studies/millennium-cohort-study.

67 See, for example, Harry Benson and Stephen McKay, 'Family breakdown and teenage mental health', Marriage Foundation, November 2017, marriagefoundation.org.uk/wp-content/uploads/2017/11/MF-paper-Family-breakdown-and-teenage-mental-health-FINAL.pdf.

68 Mary Eberstadt, *Primal Screams: How the Sexual Revolution Created Identity Politics* (West Conshohocken, PA: Templeton Press, 2019).

3. SEX AND THE MARKET

1 Lasch, *Women and the Common Life*, pp. 31–67.

2 Venetia Murray, *An Elegant Madness: High Society in Regency England* (New York: Viking, 1999), p. 51.

3 Daniel Defoe, 'The Complete English Tradesman' (1726), in *The Novels and Miscellaneous Works of Daniel Defoe*, vol. 17 (London: D. A. Talboys, 1841), p. 213.

4 Quoted in Lasch, *Women and the Common Life*, p. 49.

5 Hannah More, 'Strictures on the Modern System of Female Education' (1799), in *The Works of Hannah More*, vol. 3 (London: Bohn, 1853), p. 277.

6 Mary Wollstonecraft, *A Vindication of the Rights of Women* (1792; e-book edition, e-artnow, 2013), pp. 56–7.

7 Andrea Hunt, 'Companionate Marriage', in Constance L. Shehan (ed.), *The Wiley Blackwell Encyclopedia of Family Studies* (New York: Wiley Blackwell, 2016).

8 Jane Austen, *Pride and Prejudice* (1813; London: Macmillan Collector's Library, 2003), p. 387.

9 Ibid.

10 Ana Vogrinčič, 'The novel-reading panic in 18th-century England: An outline of an early moral media panic', *Medijska istraživanja* 14:2 (2008): 103–24, hrcak.srce.hr/file/49661.

11 Letter, 1797, in *The Monthly Mirror: Reflecting Men and Manners*, vol. 4 (London: T. Wright), p. 277.

12 One 1795 writer in the magazine *Sylph* declared: 'I have actually seen mothers, in miserable garrets, crying for the imaginary distress of an heroine, while their children were crying for bread: and the mistress of a family losing hours over a novel in the parlour, while her maids, in emulation of the example, were similarly employed in the kitchen. I have seen a scullion-wench with a dishclout in one hand, and a novel in the other, sobbing o'er the sorrows of Julia, or a Jemima.' (Quoted in Julia Epstein, *The Iron Pen: Frances Burney and the Politics of Women's Writing* (Madison: University of Wisconsin Press, 1989), pp. 219–20.)

13 Engels, *The Origin of the Family, Private Property and the State*.

14 Alexandra Kollontai, 'The social basis of the woman question' (1909), in *Selected Writings of Alexandra Kollontai*, tr. Alix Holt (London: Allison & Busby, 1977). Transcription by Andy Blunden available at www.marxists.org/archive/kollonta/1909/social-basis.htm.

15 Ibid.

16 Ibid.

17 Simone de Beauvoir, *The Second Sex* (1949; New York: Vintage, 2011), p. 761.

18 Helen Gurley Brown, *Sex and the Single Girl* (New York: Bernard Geis Associates, 1962).

19 Jennifer Scanlon, 'Sensationalist literature or expert advice?', *Feminist Media Studies* 9:1 (2009): 1–15, p. 12.

20 Shulamith Firestone, *The Dialectic of Sex: The Case for Feminist Revolution* (1970; London: Verso, 2015), p. 187.

21 Virginia Ironside, '"We paid the price for free love": The flip side of the sexual revolution', *Daily Mail*, 18 January 2011, www.dailymail.co.uk/home/you/article-1346813/The-flip-1960s-sexual-revolution-We-paid-price-free-love.html.

22 Gloria Steinem, 'A bunny's tale', *Show Magazine* (May 1963).

23 Elizabeth Gail Currans, 'Performing gender, enacting community: Women, whiteness, and belief in contemporary public demonstrations', University of California, Santa Barbara dissertation, September 2007, p. 50.

24 Friedrich Hayek, *New Studies in Philosophy, Politics, Economics and the History of Ideas* (Chicago: University of Chicago Press, 1978), pp. 63–4.

25 Roy F. Baumeister and Kathleen D. Vohs, 'Sexual economics: sex as female resource for social exchange in heterosexual interactions', *Personality and Social Psychology Review* 8:4 (2004): 339–63.

26 Marshall McLuhan, *Understanding Media: The Extensions of Man*, critical edition, edited by W. Terrence Gordon (1964; Berkeley: Gingko Press, 2003), p. 19.

27 Michael J. Rosenfeld, Reuben J. Thomas and Sonia Hausen, 'Disintermediating your friends: How online dating in the United States displaces other ways of meeting', *Proceedings of the National Academy of Sciences* 116:36 (2019): 17753–8, doi.org/10.1073/pnas.1908630116.

28 David Courtwright, *The Age of Addiction: How Bad Habits Became Big Business* (Cambridge, MA: Harvard University Press, 2019).

CYBORG THEOCRACY

1 Patrick Deneen, *Why Liberalism Failed* (New Haven and London: Yale University Press, 2018).

2 Margery Wolf, 'Marriage, family, and the state in contemporary China', *Pacific Affairs* 57:2 (1984): 213–36.

3 'Urban population (% of total population) – China', World Bank Data, data.worldbank.org/indicator/SP.URB.TOTL.IN.ZS?locations=CN.

4 Zhan Hu and Xizhe Peng, 'Household changes in contemporary China: An analysis based on the four recent censuses', *Journal of Chinese Sociology* 2:9 (2015), doi.org/10.1186/s40711-015-0011-0.

5 Ma Jian, 'China's barbaric one-child policy', *Guardian*, 6 May 2013, www.theguardian.com/books/2013/may/06/chinas-barbaric-one-child-policy.

6 Ye Liu, 'China's one-child policy helped women make a great leap forward – so what now?', *The Conversation*, 4 November 2015, theconversation.com/chinas-one-child-policy-helped-women-make-a-great-leap-forward-so-what-now-50143.

4. WAR ON RELATIONSHIPS

1 Cardi B, 'WAP', feat. Megan Thee Stallion. James Foye / Belcalis Almanzar / Austin J. Owens / Jorden Thorpe / Megan Pete / Frank Brent Rodriguez. WAP © Sony/atv Songs Llc, Sony/atv Ballad, Sony/atv Allegro, Songs of Universal Inc., Washpoppin Inc., Future Sights And Sounds Music, Hot Girl Music, Songs of Holup Publishing, Avex USA Hits, Songs of Keyzbaby (2020).

2 Anthony Giddens, *The Transformation of Intimacy: Sexuality, Love, and Eroticism in Modern Societies* (Stanford: Stanford University Press, 1992), pp. 11, 3.

3 Greer, p. 18.

4 Ibid., p. 25.

5 Ibid., p. 23.

6 Ibid., p. 22.

7 Ibid., p. 11.

8 Ibid., p. 285.

9 Erica Jong, *Fear of Flying* (New York: Signet, 1973), p. 22.

10 Esther Lee, 'This was the average age of marriage in 2021', The Knot, 15 February 2022, www.theknot.com/content/average-age-of-marriage.

11 'Marriages in England and Wales: 2019', ONS, 19 May 2022, www.ons.gov.uk/peoplepopulationandcommunity/birthsdeathsandmarriages/marriagecohabitationandcivilpartnerships/bulletins/marriagesinenglandandwalesprovisional/2019.

12 Amy Polacko, NBC News THINK, 31 December 2021, www.nbcnews.com/think/opinion/new-year-s-eve-celebrate-women-who-choose-stay-single-ncna1286803.

13 Bella DePaulo, Psychology Today, 3 December 2019, www.psychologytoday.com/gb/blog/living-single/201912/5-reasons-why-so-many-women-love-living-alone.

14 Molly Smith, 'Women who stay single and don't have kids are getting richer', 31 August 2022, www.bloomberg.com/news/articles/2022-08-31/women-not-having-kids-get-richer-than-men.

15 Sheila Jeffreys, *The Industrial Vagina: The Political Economy of the Global Sex Trade* (London: Routledge, 2008).

16 Jerry Barnett, 'The price of sex', Sex and Censorship, 13 January 2019, sexandcensorship.org/tag/sex-work.

17 incels.wiki/w/Marriage.

18 Lyman Stone, 'Male sexlessness is rising but not for the reasons incels claim', Institute for Family Studies (IFS), 14 May 2018, ifstudies.org/blog/male-sexlessness-is-rising-but-not-for-the-reasons-incels-claim.

19 Rachel M. Schmitz and Emily Kazyak, 'Masculinities in cyberspace: An analysis of portrayals of manhood in men's rights activist websites', *Social Sciences* 5:18 (2016), doi.org/10.3390/socsci5020018.

20 Eli J. Finkel, 'The all-or-nothing marriage', *The New York Times*, 14 February 2014, www.nytimes.com/2014/02/15/opinion/sunday/the-all-or-nothing-marriage.html?_r=0.

21 Honor Jones, 'How I demolished my life', *Atlantic*, 28 December 2021, www.theatlantic.com/family/archive/2021/12/divorce-parenting/621054/.

22 Giddens, p. 3.

23 Julia Carter, 'The sexual double standard: Languages of inequality', Working Paper Series 2, University of Bradford, 2012. Available at repository.canterbury.ac.uk/download/60cdf6e2604b68e4625e26660fc8a9c44dcab94a6b7ad180f2a6b9ccdc74a2e0/168858/The-sexual-double-standard---Languages-of-inequality.pdf.

24 Pamela Engel, 'CHARTS: Guys like women in their early 20s regardless of how old they get', Business Insider, 20 October 2014, www.businessinsider.com/dataclysm-shows-men-are-attracted-to-women-in-their-20s-2014-10?.

25 Louise Perry, *The Case Against the Sexual Revolution: A New Guide to Sex in the 21st Century* (Cambridge: Polity, 2022), p. 48.

26 David M. Buss, 'Do women have evolved mate preferences for men with resources?', *Ethology and Sociobiology* 12 (1991): 401–8, deepblue.lib.umich.edu/bitstream/handle/2027.42/29156/0000200.pdf.

27 See, for example, 'Better-educated women still prefer higher-earning husbands', IFS, 7 November 2016, ifstudies.org/blog/better-educated-women-still-prefer-higher-earning-husbands.

28 Robert L. Trivers, 'Parental investment and sexual selection', in Bernard Campbell (ed.), *Sexual Selection and the Descent of Man, 1871–1971* (Chicago: Aldine-Atherton, 1972). Available at roberttrivers.com/Publications_files/Trivers%201972.pdf.

29 Perry, p. 49.

30 Ibid., p. 38.

31 Ibid., p. 82.

32 Daniel Conroy-Beam et al., 'How sexually dimorphic are human mate preferences?', *Personality and Social Psychology Bulletin* 41:8 (2015): 1082–93.

33 Dario Maestripieri et al., 'A greater decline in female facial attractiveness during middle age reflects women's loss of reproductive value', *Frontiers in Psychology* 5:179 (2014), doi.org/10.3389/fpsyg.2014.00179.

34 'Baird: Why women should not settle', Newsweek, 21 January 2010, www. newsweek.com/baird-why-women-should-not-settle-71043.

35 Personal communication, 19 June 2022.

36 Dan Kopf, 'These statistics show why it's so hard to be an average man on dating apps', Quartz, 15 August 2017, qz.com/1051462/these-statistics-show-why-its-so-hard-to-be-an-average-man-on-dating-apps.

37 Sender and addressee withheld. Personal communication, 7 March 2022.

38 Ali Pantony, '"Negging" is the toxic dating trend no one asked for, but Danny on Love Island is proof that, sadly, this sort of emotional manipulation is very real', Glamour, 20 July 2021, www.glamourmagazine.co.uk/article/negging-dating-term.

39 Erin Taylor, 'Reddit's Female Dating Strategy offers women advice – and a strict rulebook for how to act', The Verge, 14 February 2020, www.theverge. com/2020/2/14/21137852/reddit-female-dating-advice-strategy-women-rulebook-memes.

40 Katie Bishop, 'Who is paying $30 for "gamer girl" Belle Delphine's bath water?', Guardian, 12 July 2019, www.theguardian.com/technology/2019/jul/12/belle-delphine-gamer-girl-instagram-selling-bath-wate.

41 'Ultimate guide to OnlyFans', Influencer Marketing Hub, influencermarketinghub.com/glossary/onlyfans.

42 @GentleyDating on Twitter, 15 April 2022, twitter.com/gentleydating/status/1515010282418061317?s=21&t=UL_b3NRBX8tlYL19wFUi3Q [retrieved 10 November 2022].

43 Imogen Braddick, 'Rise of students posting explicit pictures and videos on OnlyFans platform to fund university costs', Evening Standard, 9 September 2020, www.standard.co.uk/news/uk/onlyfans-students-university-fees-a4543246.html.

44 Jessica Simpson, 'Whorephobia in higher education: a reflexive account of researching cis women's experiences of stripping while at university', Higher Education 84 (2022): 17–31, doi.org/10.1007/s10734-021-00751-2.

45 Niamh Cavanagh, '"Have to survive": Desperate students selling sex and signing up to OnlyFans as traditional bar jobs dry up and Covid forced shops to close', Sun, 11 April 2021, www.thesun.co.uk/news/14612715/desperate-students-selling-sex-onlyfans-covid.

46 Alexandra Jones, 'The rise of femcels – meet the women who refuse to have sex', Evening Standard, 10 March 2022, www.standard.co.uk/insider/what-are-femcels-female-involuntary-celibates-b987250.html.

47 See, for example, Susanne Kaiser, Political Masculinity: How Incels, Fundamentalists and Authoritarians Mobilise for Patriarchy (Cambridge: Polity, 2022), pp. 19–24.

48 rationalwiki.org/wiki/Manosphere_glossary.

49 Perry, p. 29.

50 Patrik Lindenfors and Birgitta S. Tullberg, 'Evolutionary aspects of aggression: The importance of sexual selection', Advances in Genetics 75 (2011): 7–22, doi. org/10.1016/B978-0-12-380858-5.00009-5.

51 Mark van Vugt, David De Cremer and Dirk P. Janssen, 'Gender differences in cooperation and competition: The male-warrior hypothesis', *Psychological Science* 18:1 (2006): 19–23.

52 Greer, p. 280.

53 en.wikipedia.org/wiki/Misogynist_terrorism.

54 Perry, p. 126.

55 Nina Power, *What Do Men Want?: Masculinity and Its Discontents* (London: Allen Lane, 2022), p. 42.

56 Ibid., p. 41.

57 Nina Power, 'Why we need the patriarchy', *Compact*, 22 March 2022.

58 The proportion of childless US adults aged 18 to 49 who think it 'not too likely' or 'not at all likely' that they'll have children rose from 37 percent to 44 percent between 2018 and 2021 according to Pew Research. But this still leaves a majority who think themselves likely to have a family. See Anna Brown, 'Growing share of childless adults in U.S. don't expect to ever have children', Pew Research Center, 19 November 2021, www.pewresearch.org/fact-tank/2021/11/19/growing-share-of-childless-adults-in-u-s-dont-expect-to-ever-have-children/.

59 Kate Julian, 'Why are young people having so little sex?', *Atlantic*, December 2018, www.theatlantic.com/magazine/archive/2018/12/the-sex-recession/573949/.

5. THE DEVOURING MOTHER

1 Laurie Anderson, 'O Superman' (1982).

2 1 Kings 3:26.

3 Lyman Stone, 'How many kids do women want?', IFS, 1 June 2018, ifstudies.org/blog/how-many-kids-do-women-want.

4 'US birth rate falls 4% to its lowest point ever', BBC News, 6 May 2021, www.bbc.co.uk/news/world-us-canada-57003722.

5 Tucker, p. 10.

6 Ibid., p. 6.

7 Ibid., p. 37.

8 Ibid., p. 39.

9 Ibid., p. 64.

10 Ibid., p. 5.

11 Ibid., pp. 157–8.

12 Sophie Lewis, *Full Surrogacy Now: Feminism Against Family* (London: Verso, 2020), p. 11.

13 Ibid., p. 43.

14 Dan MacGuill, 'Did pro-choice protesters carry a sign that likened fetuses to "parasites"?', Snopes, 12 June 2019, www.snopes.com/fact-check/parasites-rights-abortion-sign/.

15 See, for example, @arsenic_delight on Twitter, 16 May 2022, twitter.com/arsenic_delight/status/1526031950061965312?s=21&t=fsD_j30y0LUqA48SaPU3qQ [retrieved 10 November 2022].

16 Geoffrey Chamberlain, 'British maternal mortality in the 19th and early 20th centuries', *Journal of the Royal Society of Medicine* 99:11 (2006): 559–63, www.ncbi.nlm.nih.gov/pmc/articles/PMC1633559/.

17 'Maternal mortality rate per 100,000 maternities, and maternal mortality ratio', sdgdata.gov.uk/3-1-1/.

18 Abigail Favale, *The Genesis of Gender: A Christian Theory* (San Francisco: Ignatius Press, 2022), p. 101.

19 Lewis, pp. 2–3.

20 Catherine Rampell, 'These GOP politicians aren't pro-life. They're pro forced birth', *Washington Post*, 10 May 2022.

21 Lewis, p. 24.

22 Ruth Wallsgrove, 'Thicker than water? Mothering and childcare (1985)', in Deborah Cameron and Joan Scanlon (eds), *The Trouble & Strife Reader* (London and New York: Bloomsbury Academic, 2010), p. 28.

23 John Bowlby, *A Secure Base* (1988; Abingdon: Routledge, 2005), pp. 12–14.

24 Diana Leonard, 'Baby talk (1992)', in Cameron and Scanlon (eds), p. 38.

25 Wallsgrove, p. 29.

26 Dena Attar, 'The demand that time forgot (1992)', in Cameron and Scanlon (eds), p. 31.

27 'Childcare and early years survey of parents in England, 2018', Department for Education, assets.publishing.service.gov.uk/government/uploads/system/uploads/attachment_data/file/766498/Childcare_and_Early_Years_Survey_of_Parents_in_England_2018.pdf.

28 Helen Gurley Brown, *Having It All: Love, Success, Sex, Money, Even If You're Starting With Nothing* (New York: Sidgwick & Jackson, 1982).

29 Chelsea Conaboy, 'Maternal instinct is a myth that men created', *The New York Times*, 26 August 2022, www.nytimes.com/2022/08/26/opinion/sunday/maternal-instinct-myth.html?smtyp=cur&smid=tw-nytimes.

30 Lewis, p. 42.

31 Ibid., p. 11.

32 Ibid.

33 Ibid., chapter 1.

34 See, for example, Gianluco Esposito et al., 'The calming effect of maternal carrying in different mammalian species', *Frontiers in Psychology* 6:445 (2015), doi.org/10.3389/fpsyg.2015.00445.

35 Lewis, p. 20.

36 Ibid., p. 165.

37 Ibid., p. 167.

38 Ibid., p. 21.

39 Ibid., p. 22.

40 Ibid., p. 168.

41 Ibid.

42 David Kaufman, 'The fight for fertility equality', *The New York Times*, 22 July 2020, www.nytimes.com/2020/07/22/style/lgbtq-fertility-surrogacy-coverage. html.

43 Kathryn MacKay, 'The "tyranny of reproduction": Could ectogenesis further women's liberation?', *Bioethics* 34:4 (2020): 346–53, doi.org/10.1111/bioe.12706.

44 Lewis, p. 55.

45 Noam Shpancer, 'Child of the collective', *Guardian*, 19 February 2011, www. theguardian.com/lifeandstyle/2011/feb/19/kibbutz-child-noam-shpancer.

46 Sarah Finley, 'Polyamorous woman, 20, reveals she fell pregnant by one of her FOUR partners after they all went on vacation together – but she says they will ALL raise the baby as a "family"', *Daily Mail*, 5 December 2019, www.dailymail. co.uk/femail/article-7759411/Polyamorous-woman-20-fallen-pregnant-one-FOUR-partners-went-away-together.html.

47 Dan Scanlan, 'Jacksonville man jailed in abuse of 5-week-old baby', *Florida Times-Union*, 25 March 2020, eu.jacksonville.com/story/news/local/2020/03/25/jacksonville-man-jailed-in-abuse-of-5-week-old-baby/112253316/.

48 MacKenzie A. Christensen, 'Feminization of poverty: Causes and implications', in Walter Leal Filho et al. (eds), *Encyclopedia of the UN Sustainable Development Goals: Gender Equality* (Cham, Switzerland: Springer Nature, 2019).

49 Perry, p. 168.

50 Diana E. H. Russell, 'The prevalence and seriousness of incestuous abuse: Stepfathers vs. biological fathers', *Child Abuse & Neglect* 8:1 (1984): 15–22.

51 Kathleen Kiernan, Sam Crossman and Angus Phimister, *Families and Inequalities*, The Institute for Fiscal Studies Deaton Review of Inequalities, June 2022, ifs. org.uk/inequality/families-and-inequalities.

52 Sara McLanahan, Laura Tach and Daniel Schneider, 'The causal effects of father absence', *Annual Review of Sociology* 39:1 (2013): 399–427, doi.org/10.1146/annurev-soc-071312-145704.

53 Lewis, p. 167.

54 Julie Bindel, 'Outsourcing pregnancy: A visit to India's surrogacy clinics', *Guardian*, 1 April 2016, www.theguardian.com/global-development/2016/apr/01/outsourcing-pregnancy-india-surrogacy-clinics-julie-bindel.

55 'Death is optional: A conversation – Yuval Noah Harari, Daniel Kahneman', Edge.org, 4 March 2015, www.edge.org/conversation/yuval_noah_harari-daniel_kahneman-death-is-optional.

56 'Hacking Humans – Yuval Noah Harari Roundtable at EPFL' [video], YouTube, uploaded by Yuval Noah Harari, 13 July 2019, www.youtube. com/watch?v=xhpXU0x5894&ab_channel=YuvalNoahHarari [retrieved 10 November 2022].

57 Sean Stevens, 'The coddling of the American mind: How good intentions and bad ideas are setting up a generation for failure', Heterodox Academy blog, 11 September 2018, heterodoxacademy.org/blog/coddling-of-the-american-mind/.

58 'Russell Brand & Jordan Peterson – Kindness VS Power | Under The Skin #46' [video], YouTube, uploaded by Russell Brand, 15 February 2018, www.youtube.com/watch?v=kL61yQgdWeM [retrieved 10 November 2022].

59 Erich Neumann, *The Great Mother: An Analysis of the Archetype*, tr. Ralph Manheim (Princeton: Princeton University Press, 1955), p. 68.

60 Miranda Bryant, '"I was risking my life": Why one in four US women return to work two weeks after childbirth', *Guardian*, 27 January 2020, www.theguardian.com/us-news/2020/jan/27/maternity-paid-leave-women-work-childbirth-us.

61 Kirsten Weir, 'Maximizing children's resilience', American Psychological Association, September 2017, www.apa.org/monitor/2017/09/cover-resilience.

62 Jay Belsky, 'Early day care and infant–mother attachment security', Encyclopedia of Early Childhood Development, May 2020, www.child-encyclopedia.com/attachment/according-experts/early-day-care-and-infant-mother-attachment-security.

63 Gerhardt, p. 27.

64 Joseph E. Beeney et al., 'Disorganized attachment and personality functioning in adults: A latent class analysis', *Personality Disorders* 8:3 (2017): 206–16.

65 Benjamin Bratton, *The Revenge of the Real: Politics for a Post-Pandemic World* (New York: Verso, 2021), Kindle edn, location 802.

66 Ibid., location 803.

67 Ibid., location 1718.

68 Lewis, p. 235.

69 Bratton, location 524.

70 Ibid., location 526.

71 Zoë Corbyn, '"Bossware is coming for almost every worker": The software you might not realize is watching you', *Guardian*, 27 April 2022, www.theguardian.com/technology/2022/apr/27/remote-work-software-home-surveillance-computer-monitoring-pandemic.

72 Sheryl Sandberg, *Lean In: Women, Work, and the Will to Lead* (London: WH Allen, 2013).

73 Caroline Bryson et al., *The Role of Informal Childcare: A Synthesis and Critical Review of the Evidence*, Nuffield Foundation, 2012, www.nuffieldfoundation.org/sites/default/files/files/The_role_of_informal_childcare_FULL_REPORT.pdf.

74 Justine Roberts, 'Three-quarters of mothers say Covid-19 has negatively impacted their mental health', Mumsnet, 1 April 2022, www.mumsnet.com/news/three-quarters-of-mothers-say-covid-has-negatively-impacted-their-mental-health; Natasha Walter, 'Guilt and fury: how Covid brought mothers to breaking point', *Guardian*, 28 February 2021, www.theguardian.com/lifeandstyle/2021/feb/28/mums-women-coronavirus-covid-home-schooling-inequality.

75 Hugo Bottemanne et al., 'Becoming a mother during COVID-19 pandemic: How to protect maternal mental health against stress factors', *Frontiers in Psychiatry* 12:764207 (2022), doi.org/10.3389/fpsyt.2021.764207.

76 Tucker, p. 145.

77 Lauren C. Shuffrey et al., 'Association of birth during the COVID-19 pandemic with neurodevelopmental status at 6 months in infants with and without in utero exposure to maternal SARS-COV-2 infection', *JAMA Pediatriatrics* 176:6 (2022), doi.org/10.1001/jamapediatrics.2021.5563.

78 Sean C. L. Deoni et al., 'The COVID-19 pandemic and early child cognitive development: A comparison of development in children born during the pandemic and historical references', doi.org/10.1101/2021.08.10.21261846.

79 Donna Ferguson, 'Life in lockdown held back progress of under-fives', *Guardian*, 24 April 2022, www.theguardian.com/lifeandstyle/2022/apr/24/life-in-lockdown-held-back-progress-of-under-fives.

80 Branwen Jeffreys, 'Lockdowns hurt child speech and language skills – report', BBC News, 27 April 2021, www.bbc.co.uk/news/education-56889035.

81 Deoni et al.

6. MEAT LEGO GNOSTICISM

1 n1x, 'Gender acceleration: A blackpaper', Vast Abrupt, 31 October 2018, vastabrupt.com/2018/10/31/gender-acceleration/.

2 Helena, 'By any other name', Prude Posting, 19 February 2022, lacroicsz. substack.com/p/by-any-other-name.

3 Steven A. Richards, 'Purification rites: An autobiographical essay', Cut Down Tree, 26 April 2022, cutdowntree.substack.com/p/purification-rites.

4 Rudolph M. Bell, *Holy Anorexia* (Chicago: University of Chicago Press, 1987).

5 Emma Boyes, 'Second Life realtor makes $1 million', GameSpot, 27 November 2006, www.gamespot.com/articles/second-life-realtor-makes-1-million/1100-6162315/.

6 See, for example, Matthew Ball, *The Metaverse: And How It Will Revolutionize Everything* (New York: Liveright, 2022).

7 Elizabeth Anderson, 'Teenagers spend 27 hours a week online: How internet use has ballooned in the last decade', *Daily Telegraph*, 11 May 2015.

8 Kurt Schlosser, 'New research finds 95% of teens have access to a smartphone; 45% online "almost constantly"', GeekWire, 1 June 2018, www.geekwire. com/2018/new-research-finds-95-teens-access-to-a-smartphone-45-online-almost-constantly.

9 Jonathan Haidt and Jean M. Twenge, 'This is our chance to pull teenagers out of the smartphone trap', *The New York Times*, 31 July 2021, www.nytimes. com/2021/07/31/opinion/smartphone-iphone-social-media-isolation.html.

10 Jonathan Haidt, 'The dangerous experiment on teen girls', *Atlantic*, 21 November 2021, www.theatlantic.com/ideas/archive/2021/11/facebooks-dangerous-experiment-teen-girls/620767/.

11 'What Instagram does to teens', What Next: TBD podcast, Slate, 1 October 2021, slate.com/podcasts/what-next-tbd/2021/10/how-instagram-hurts-teens-leaked-report.

12 Melissa C. Mercado et al., 'Trends in emergency department visits for nonfatal self-inflicted injuries among youth aged 10 to 24 years in the United States, 2001–2015', *JAMA* 318:19 (2017): 1931–3, doi.org/10.1001/jama.2017.13317.

13 Denis Campbell, 'Stress and social media fuel mental health crisis among girls', *Guardian*, 23 September 2017, www.theguardian.com/society/2017/sep/23/stress-anxiety-fuel-mental-health-crisis-girls-young-women.

14 'Referrals to GIDS, financial years 2010–11 to 2021–22', Gender Identity Development Service, 2021, gids.nhs.uk/about-us/number-of-referrals/.

15 John W. Delahunt et al., 'Increasing rates of people identifying as transgender presenting to Endocrine Services in the Wellington region', *New Zealand Medical Journal* 131:1468 (2018): 33–42, assets-global.website-files.com/5e332a62c703f653182faf47/5e332a62c703f632472fd421_Delahunt-FINAL.pdf.

16 Madison Aitken et al., 'Evidence for an altered sex ratio in clinic-referred adolescents with gender dysphoria', *Journal of Sexual Medicine* 12:3 (2015): 756–63.

17 Jody L. Herman, Andrew R. Flores and Kathryn K. O'Neill, 'How many adults and youth identify as transgender in the United States?', Williams Institute, UCLA School of Law, June 2022, williamsinstitute.law.ucla.edu/publications/trans-adults-united-states/.

18 Robin Respaut and Chad Terhune, 'Putting numbers on the rise of children seeking gender care', Reuters, 6 October 2022, www.reuters.com/investigates/special-report/usa-transyouth-data/.

19 Abigail Shrier, *Irreversible Damage: Teenage Girls and the Transgender Craze* (London: Swift Press, 2020), Kindle edn, location 754.

20 'Referrals to GIDS, financial years 2010–11 to 2021–22'.

21 'Grimes: Music, AI, and the Future of Humanity | Lex Fridman Podcast #281' [video], YouTube, uploaded by Lex Fridman, 29 April 2022, www.youtube.com/watch?v=KOwm7GUjcg8 [retrieved 11 November 2022].

22 Martine Rothblatt, *From Transgender to Transhuman: A Manifesto On the Freedom of Form* (self-published, 2011), Kindle edn, location 624.

23 Ibid., location 742.

24 Ibid., location 849.

25 Ibid., location 844.

26 Ibid., location 860.

27 Ibid., location 861.

28 Ibid., location 438.

29 See, for example, Pope Francis, 'Address to the Leadership of the Episcopal Conferences of Latin America during the General Coordination Meeting', speech given at Sumaré Study Center, Rio de Janeiro, 28 July 2013. Transcript available at www.vatican.va/content/francesco/en/speeches/2013/july/documents/papa-francesco_20130728_gmg-celam-rio.html.

30 Rebecca Denova, 'Gnosticism: Definition', World History Encyclopedia, 9 April 2021, www.worldhistory.org/Gnosticism/.

31 'International Bill of Gender Rights (4 July 1996)', Digital Transgender Archive, www.digitaltransgenderarchive.net/files/2z10wq28m.

32 'Yogyakarta Principles plus 10', yogyakartaprinciples.org/principles-en/yp10/.

33 Helen Joyce, *Trans: When Ideology Meets Reality* (London: Oneworld, 2021), chapter 11.

34 *Only Adults? Good Practices in Legal Gender Recognition for Youth*, IGLYO/Thomson Reuters Foundation/Dentons, November 2019, www.iglyo.com/wp-content/uploads/2019/11/IGLYO_v3-1.pdf.

35 Abigail Shrier, 'Child custody's gender gauntlet', *City Journal*, 7 February 2022, www.city-journal.org/child-custody-gender-gauntlet.

36 Abigail Shrier, 'When the state comes for your kids', *City Journal*, 8 June 2021, www.city-journal.org/transgender-identifying-adolescents-threats-to-parental-rights.

37 'Canadian man jailed for calling his biologically female child as "daughter"', OpIndia, 18 March 2021, www.opindia.com/2021/03/canadian-man-jailed-for-calling-his-biologically-female-child-as-daughter/.

38 @ZJemptv on Twitter, 2 December 2020, twitter.com/ZJemptv/status/1334159646362382340?s=20&t=vQjqb_01elPJQT2WTDeixA [retrieved 5 June 2022].

39 Thomas Ross, '"We are talking about masturbation now": Duke hosts panel on transgender surgeries for teens', Campus Reform, 5 April 2022, campusreform.org/article?id=19295.

40 This, too, has taproots into the contraceptive revolution, where legal precedent governing the tension between reproductive interventions, parental authority and youth 'consent' was first set in *Gillick v West Norfolk*, a 1985 court case brought by mother-of-ten Victoria Gillick against health authorities, in an attempt to prevent doctors prescribing contraceptives to girls under 16 without their parents' consent. Her attempt was refused, and the legal test of 'Gillick competency' is now applied to evaluate whether under-16s may reasonably be deemed able to consent to medical treatment without their parents' involvement. Source: www.e-lawresources.co.uk/cases/Gillick-v-West-Norfolk.php.

41 Rothblatt, location 769.

42 Katie Muldowney, Ignacio Torres and Alexa Valiente, 'Transgender teen and "I Am Jazz" star Jazz Jennings on sharing the final steps of her transition journey: her gender confirmation surgery', ABC News, 15 October 2018, abcnews.go.com/Health/transgender-teen-jazz-star-jazz-jennings-sharing-final/story?id=58513271.

43 Corinne Segal, 'Trans patients, looking for fertility options, turn to cancer research', PBS, 22 January 2017, www.pbs.org/newshour/health/trans-patients-looking-fertility-options-turn-cancer-research.

44 Kristin Samuelson, 'Transgender youth faced with tough decision to freeze sperm or eggs', Northwestern Now, 15 April 2019, news.northwestern.edu/stories/2019/04/transgender-fertility-preservation/.

45 'Age is the key factor for egg freezing success says new HFEA report, as overall treatment numbers remain low', Human Fertilisation & Embryology Authority press release, 20 December 2018, www.hfea.gov.uk/about-us/news-and-press-releases/2018-news-and-press-releases/press-release-age-is-the-key-factor-for-egg-freezing-success-says-new-hfea-report-as-overall-treatment-numbers-remain-low.

46 'How Does Jazz Feel About Having An Orgasm? | I Am Jazz' [video], YouTube, uploaded by TLC, 7 February 2018, www.youtube.com/watch?v=SsBczOiOq9M&ab_channel=TLC [retrieved 22 November 2022]; Natalie Stone, 'Jazz Jennings discusses "the sexual stuff" with her doctor ahead of gender confirmation surgery', People, 1 January 2019, people.com/tv/jazz-jennings-talks-sexual-stuff-orgasm-libido-doctor-before-gender-confirmation-surgery/.

47 Abigail Shrier, 'Why Marci matters', The Truth Fairy, 6 October 2021, abigailshrier.substack.com/p/why-marci-matters.

48 Korin Miller and Jennifer Nied, 'Jazz Jennings says she is "super happy with the results" of her 3rd gender confirmation surgery', Women's Health, 5 February 2020, www.womenshealthmag.com/health/a23828566/jazz-jennings-gender-confirmation-surgery-complication/.

49 Maya Kailas, 'Prevalence and types of gender-affirming surgery among a sample of transgender endocrinology patients prior to state expansion of insurance coverage', Endocrine Practice 23:7 (2017): 780–6.

50 Respaut and Terhune.

51 'Masculinizing hormone therapy', Mayo Clinic, 18 October 2022, www.mayoclinic.org/tests-procedures/masculinizing-hormone-therapy/about/pac-20385099.

52 Mamoon Rashid and Muhammad Sarmad Tamimy, 'Phalloplasty: The dream and the reality', Indian Journal of Plastic Surgery 46:2 (2013): 283–93.

53 Joyce, pp. 223–43.

54 Andrew R. Flores, Taylor N. T. Brown and Andrew S. Park, Public Support for Transgender Rights: A Twenty-three Country Survey, Williams Institute, UCLA School of Law/Buzzfeed/IPSOS, December 2016, williamsinstitute.law.ucla.edu/wp-content/uploads/Public-Opinion-Trans-23-Countries-Dec-2016.pdf.

55 See, for example, Cinzia Arruzza, Tithi Bhattacharya and Nancy Fraser, Feminism for the 99%: A Manifesto (London: Verso, 2019).

56 Samuel Goldman, 'The American elite will be female', The Week, 8 September 2021, theweek.com/us/opinion/1004595/the-college-future-is-female.

57 Douglas Belkin, 'A generation of American men give up on college: "I just feel lost"', Wall Street Journal, 6 September 2021, www.wsj.com/articles/college-university-fall-higher-education-men-women-enrollment-admissions-back-to-school-11630948233.

58 David Brown, 'How women took over the military–industrial complex', Politico, 1 February 2019, www.politico.com/story/2019/01/02/how-women-took-over-the-military-industrial-complex-1049860.

59 Katie King, 'New female law students outnumber males two to one for first
    time ever', Legal Cheek, 12 January 2018, www.legalcheek.com/2018/01/
    new-female-law-students-outnumber-males-two-to-one-for-first-time-ever.

60 Charlotte Tobitt, 'Survey finds growing UK journalism workforce of nearly
    100,000 still lacks ethnic diversity', *Press Gazette*, 13 May 2021, pressgazette.
    co.uk/nctj-diversity-journalism-number-journalists/.

61 'Broken ladders: Barriers to women's representation in nonprofit leadership',
    American Association of University Women, May 2018, www.aauw.org/app/
    uploads/2020/03/women-in-leadership.pdf.

62 'Does the charity sector have a problem with women?', Charity Finance Group
    blog, 9 November 2015, cfg.org.uk/news/blog/does-the-charity-sector-have-
    a-problem-with-women.

63 David Ainsworth, 'Why is the charity sector so white?', Civil Society, 2 July
    2018, www.civilsociety.co.uk/voices/david-ainsworth-why-is-the-charity-
    sector-so-white.html.

64 'Higher education student statistics: UK, 2016/17 – Subjects studied', Higher
    Education Statistics Agency, 11 January 2018, www.hesa.ac.uk/news/11-01-
    2018/sfr247-higher-education-student-statistics/subjects.

65 Mitchell Langbert, 'Homogenous: The political affiliations of elite liberal arts
    college faculty', National Association of Scholars, Summer 2018, www.nas.
    org/academic-questions/31/2/homogenous_the_political_affiliations_of_elite_
    liberal_arts_college_faculty.

66 'The UK people profession in numbers', Chartered Institute of Personnel and
    Development, 10 October 2022, www.cipd.co.uk/knowledge/strategy/hr/
    uk-people-profession-numbers#gref.

67 Lisa Burden, 'HR is overwhelmingly white and female, data indicates', HR
    Dive, 20 February 2019, www.hrdive.com/news/hr-is-overwhelmingly-white-
    and-female-data-indicates/548600.

68 'School workforce in England: Reporting year 2021', Department for Education,
    9 June 2022, explore-education-statistics.service.gov.uk/find-statistics/school-
    workforce-in-england.

69 'Who are the nation's 4 million teachers?', USA Facts, 14 December 2020,
    usafacts.org/articles/who-are-the-nations-4m-teachers/.

70 'How to earn your teacher certification', All Educational Schools, www.
    alleducationalschools.com/teacher-certification/.

71 Lawrence A. Greenfeld and Tracy L. Snell, 'Bureau of Justice statistics special
    report: Women offenders', US Department of Justice, December 1999, bjs.
    ojp.gov/content/pub/pdf/wo.pdf.

72 Rosa Freedman, Kathleen Stock and Alice Sullivan, 'Evidence and data on
    trans women's offending rates', UK Parliament, November 2020, committees.
    parliament.uk/writtenevidence/18973/pdf/.

73 Martin Evans, 'Transgender prisoner born a male who sexually assaulted female
    inmates after being jailed for rape is sentenced to life', *Daily Telegraph*, 11 October
    2018, www.telegraph.co.uk/news/2018/10/11/transgender-prisoner-born-

male-sexually-assaulted-female-inmates/.

74 Nazia Parveen, 'Karen White: how "manipulative" transgender inmate attacked again', *Guardian*, 11 October 2018, www.theguardian.com/society/2018/oct/11/karen-white-how-manipulative-and-controlling-offender-attacked-again-transgender-prison.

75 Matt Masterson, 'Lawsuit: Female prisoner says she was raped by transgender inmate', WTTW News, 19 February 2020, news.wttw.com/2020/02/19/lawsuit-female-prisoner-says-she-was-raped-transgender-inmate.

76 Andrea Blanco, 'Two inmates at all-women's New Jersey jail are PREGNANT after both had sex with transgender prisoners: ACLU won battle to house 27 trans inmates there', *Daily Mail*, 13 April 2022, www.dailymail.co.uk/news/article-10716417/Two-women-female-New-Jersey-prison-PREGNANT-trans-inmates.html.

77 Susan N. Herman, 'The women of the ACLU', American Civil Liberties Union, 13 April 2011, www.aclu.org/blog/smart-justice/mass-incarceration/women-aclu.

78 Douglas H. Russell et al., 'Prevalence of mental health problems in transgender children aged 9 to 10 years in the US, 2018', *JAMA Network Open* 5:7 (2022), doi.org/10.1001/jamanetworkopen.2022.23389.

79 'Correction to Bränström and Pachankis', *American Journal of Psychiatry*, 1 August 2020, ajp.psychiatryonline.org/doi/10.1176/appi.ajp.2020.1778correction.

80 Janice Raymond, *The Transsexual Empire: The Making of the She-Male* (Boston: Beacon Press, 1979), p. 150. Available online at janiceraymond.com/wp-content/uploads/2017/08/The%20Transsexual%20Empire.pdf.

81 Alyssa Wright, 'Trans-tech is a budding industry: So why is no one investing in it?', *Forbes*, 8 December 2020, www.forbes.com/sites/alyssawright/2020/12/08/trans-tech-is-a-budding-industry-so-why-is-no-one-investing/?sh=7cb2b774e3c3.

82 Emma Kinery and Alex Tanzi, 'Biden's $1.75 trillion student debt problem by the numbers', *Time*, 30 April 2022, time.com/6172402/biden-student-debt-problem/.

83 Melissa Korn and Andrea Fuller, 'NYU is top-ranked – in loans that alumni and parents struggle to repay', *Wall Street Journal*, 19 December 2021, www.wsj.com/articles/nyu-college-graduate-parent-student-loans-11639618241?mod=e2tw.

84 'Milk stork introduces the stash surrogacy bundle', PR Newswire, 14 April 2022, www.prnewswire.com/news-releases/milk-stork-introduces-the-stash-surrogacy-bundle-301525614.html.

85 Adrian Addison and Rosaleen Fenton, 'Doctor planning risky womb transplant to allow transgender woman to carry a baby', *Mirror*, 5 May 2022, www.mirror.co.uk/news/world-news/doctor-planning-risky-womb-transplant-26882914.

86 Devyani Nighoskar, 'Indian female farmers going "womb-less" to boost productivity', Al Jazeera, 24 July 2019, www.aljazeera.com/features/2019/7/24/indian-female-farmers-going-womb-less-to-boost-productivity.

87 Victoria Allen, 'Women being "bribed" by IVF clinics with free egg-freezing service worth almost £10,000 if they give away half of their eggs to someone

else', *Daily Mail*, 24 March 2019, www.dailymail.co.uk/news/article-6845673/
Women-bribed-IVF-clinics-free-egg-freezing-service-worth-10-000.html.

88 Laura Cancherini et al., 'What's ahead for biotech: Another wave or low tide?',
McKinsey & Company, 30 April 2021, www.mckinsey.com/industries/life-
sciences/our-insights/whats-ahead-for-biotech-another-wave-or-low-tide.

89 Carina Storrs, 'Are there unintended consequences to calling breast-feeding
"natural"?', CNN, 4 March 2016, edition.cnn.com/2016/03/04/health/breast-
feeding-natural-vaccine-fears/index.html.

90 Marci Bowers, 'Tilapia fish skin for vagina?', marcibowers.com/transfem/tilapia/.

91 Tao Tan et al., 'Chimeric contribution of human extended pluripotent stem
cells to monkey embryos *ex vivo*', *Cell* 184:8 (2021): 2020–32, www.cell.com/
cell/pdf/S0092-8674(21)00305-6.pdf.

92 Michael Irving, 'Human–monkey chimera embryos created in lab for first time',
New Atlas, 15 April 2021, newatlas.com/science/human-monkey-chimera-
embryos/.

93 Tony Katz, 'Bioethicist suggests re-engineering humans to become allergic
to meat', WIBC, 22 June 2021, wibc.com/111353/bioethicist-suggests-re-
engineering-humans-to-become-allergic-to-meat/.

94 Robert Epstein, 'The empty brain', *Aeon*, 18 May 2016, aeon.co/essays/your-
brain-does-not-process-information-and-it-is-not-a-computer.

95 Charlotte Bateman, 'China's organ harvesting trade unveiled by study which
claims living prisoners used for transplants', Sky News, 5 April 2022, news.sky.
com/story/chinas-organ-harvesting-trade-unveiled-by-study-which-claims-
living-prisoners-used-for-transplants-12583209.

INTERLUDE: DETRANSITION

1 Lisa Littman, 'Individuals treated for gender dysphoria with medical and/
or surgical transition who subsequently detransitioned: A survey of 100
detransitioners', *Archives of Sexual Behavior* 50 (2021): 3353–69, doi.org/10.1007/
s10508-021-02163-w.

2 Elie Vandenbussche, 'Detransition-related needs and support: A cross-sectional
online survey', *Journal of Homosexuality* 69:9 (2022): 1602–20, doi.org/10.108
0/00918369.2021.1919479.

3 At the time of writing, these are Alaska, Colorado, New Jersey, New Mexico,
Oregon and Vermont, plus Washington, DC. Megan Messerly, 'Abortion laws
by state: Where abortions are illegal after Roe v. Wade overturned', *Politico*,
24 June 2022, www.politico.com/news/2022/06/24/abortion-laws-by-state-
roe-v-wade-00037695.

4 'What are the abortion time limits in EU countries?', Right To Life, righttolife.
org.uk/what-are-the-abortion-time-limits-in-eu-countries.

5 Anthony Wells, 'Polling on abortion', UK Polling Report, 6 October 2012,
ukpollingreport.co.uk/blog/archives/6253.

6   Martin Robbins, 'Why are women more opposed to abortion?', *Guardian*, 30 April 2014, www.theguardian.com/science/the-lay-scientist/2014/apr/30/ why-are-women-more-opposed-to-abortion.

7   'Majority of women oppose radical abortion law change', Christian Action Research and Education (CARE), 22 October 2018, care.org.uk/news/2018/10/ majority-of-women-oppose-radical-abortion-law-change.

7. Abolish Big Romance

1   Leo Strauss, 'Restatement on Xenophon's Hiero', in Victor Gourevitch and Michael S. Roth (eds), *On Tyranny: Corrected and Expanded Edition, Including the Strauss–Kojève Correspondence* (1948; Chicago: University of Chicago Press, 2013), p. 210.

2   Tucker, pp. 209–39.

3   Richard Fry, 'Young women are out-earning young men in several U.S. cities', Pew Research Center, 28 March 2022, www.pewresearch.org/fact-tank/2022/03/28/ young-women-are-out-earning-young-men-in-several-u-s-cities/.

4   Marie Solis, 'We can't have a feminist future without abolishing the family', *Vice*, 21 February 2020, www.vice.com/en/article/qjdzwb/sophie-lewis-feminist-abolishing-the-family-full-surrogacy-now.

5   @jmrphy on Twitter, 11 October 2020, twitter.com/jmrphy/status/1315 064925144838145?s=21&t=-bFNo7EAymDfXzYk0WFB0w [retrieved 11 November 2022].

6   'Most marriages and divorces are low conflict', Divorce Source, Inc., www. divorcesource.com/ds/considering/most-marriages-and-divorces-are-low-conflict-483.shtml.

7   @jmrphy on Twitter, 11 October 2020, twitter.com/jmrphy/status/1315 062850600095744?s=21&t=-bFNo7EAymDfXzYk0WFB0w [retrieved 11 November 2022].

8   '2016 annual relationship, marriage, and divorce survey: Final report', Avvo. com, marketing-assets.avvo.com/media-resources/avvo-research/2016/avvo_ relationship_study_2016_final_report.pdf.

8. Let Men Be

1   Bronze Age Pervert, *Bronze Age Mindset* (self-published, 2018), p. 168.

2   Ewan Somerville, 'Campus feminists censured for excluding trans students', *Daily Telegraph*, 13 March 2021.

3   'Informal networks and corporate board appointments', Centre for Market and Public Organisation, University of Bristol, 2012, www.bristol.ac.uk/media-library/sites/cmpo/migrated/documents/informalnetworks.pdf.

4   Amelia Gentleman, 'Cherie Blair backs campaign for Garrick club to admit

women', *Guardian*, 16 August 2021, www.theguardian.com/politics/2021/aug/16/cherie-blair-backs-campaign-for-garrick-club-to-admit-women.

5 Rob Walker, 'Scouting for girls gives group its biggest boost in years', *Guardian*, 16 June 2019, www.theguardian.com/society/2019/jun/16/girls-join-scouts-in-record-numbers-beavers-cubs.

6 David Oakley, 'Women take chunk out of "glass ceiling"', *Financial Times*, 29 October 2012, www.ft.com/content/999ec8fc-1f7c-11e2-841c-00144feabdc0.

7 Mike Allen, 'Sen. Josh Hawley defends speech on porn and video games', Axios, 8 November 2021, www.axios.com/2021/11/07/josh-hawley-masculinity-porn-video-games.

8 Jonathan Capehart, 'Josh Hawley's problem with masculinity', *Washington Post*, 3 August 2022, www.washingtonpost.com/opinions/2022/08/03/josh-hawley-masculinity-problem/.

9 Ryan Bort, 'Josh Hawley's bizarre obsession with masculinity is the most pathetic front yet in the GOP's culture war', *Rolling Stone*, 8 November 2021, www.rollingstone.com/politics/politics-news/josh-hawley-masculinity-obsession-1254776/.

10 Andy Dolan, 'Time gentleman please: After 146 years, our oldest working men's club closes rather than admit women', *Daily Mail*, 20 February 2014, www.dailymail.co.uk/news/article-2563647/Hanging-flat-caps-time-Britains-oldest-working-mens-club-forced-close-members-refuse-admit-women.html.

11 Joyce F. Benenson and Henry Markovitz, *Warriors and Worriers: The Survival of the Sexes* (Oxford and New York: Oxford University Press, 2014).

12 Ibid., p. 45.

13 Helen Chandler-Wilde and Will Bolton, 'Sexism row erupts as men-only farmers' group refuses to admit women', *Daily Telegraph*, 16 April 2022.

14 Angus Deaton and Anne Case, *Deaths of Despair and the Future of Capitalism* (Princeton: Princeton University Press, 2020).

15 Daniel A. Cox, 'Men's social circles are shrinking', Survey Center on American Life, 29 June 2021, www.americansurveycenter.org/why-mens-social-circles-are-shrinking/.

16 'The facts: why we need to talk about suicide', Campaign Against Living Miserably (CALM), www.thecalmzone.net/thelastphoto/the-facts. Quoted in Power, *What Do Men Want?*, p. 74.

17 'Who is most at risk of suicide?', ONS, 7 September 2017, www.ons.gov.uk/peoplepopulationandcommunity/birthsdeathsandmarriages/deaths/articles/whoismostatriskofsuicide/2017-09-07.

18 Augustine J. Kposowa, 'Marital status and suicide in the National Longitudinal Mortality Study', *Journal of Epidemiology and Community Health* 54:4 (2000): 254–61, doi.org/10.1136/jech.54.4.254.

19 Helen Watts, 'Girlguiding: campfires, crafts and compelled belief', Woman's Place UK, 8 July 2020, womansplaceuk.org/2020/07/08/girlguiding-campfires-crafts-compelled-belief/.

20 Laurie Essig, 'The men are not alright', *Ms.*, 8 August 2019, msmagazine.

com/2019/08/08/the-men-are-not-alright/.

21 Robert D. Francis, 'Him, not her: Why working-class white men reluctant about Trump still made him President of the United States', *Socius* 4 (2018): 1–11, doi.org/10.1177/2378023117736486.

22 Genevieve Gluck, 'Trans killer with a "blood fetish" married female inmate while incarcerated in a women's prison', Reduxx, 2 August 2022, reduxx. info/exclusive-trans-killer-with-a-blood-fetish-married-female-inmate-while-incarcerated-in-a-womens-prison/.

23 'Sexual orientation, UK: 2020', ONS, 25 May 2022, www.ons.gov.uk/ peoplepopulationandcommunity/culturalidentity/sexuality/bulletins/ sexualidentityuk/2020.

24 See Gluck, for example.

25 Joyce, p. 163.

26 Lolita C. Baldor, 'Army eases fitness test standards for women, older troops', *U.S. News & World Report*, 23 March 2022, www.usnews.com/news/politics/ articles/2022-03-23/army-eases-fitness-test-standards-for-women-older-troops.

27 @HairyMonkeyGor1 on Twitter, 3 March 2022, twitter.com/hairymonkeygor1/ status/1499490227286691846?s=21&t=3vk7sFxk02FqqBrvnbigYw [retrieved 11 November 2022].

28 Bronze Age Pervert, p. 166.

29 @altering_egos on Twitter, 25 June 2022, twitter.com/altering_egos/status /1540816010441330689?s=21&t=0AIXn6scc-bq3nbJ1o4W1g [retrieved 10 November 2022].

30 @PonchoRebound on Twitter, 31 March 2022, twitter.com/PonchoRebound/ status/1509552415619563529?s=20&t=Ac8dwtwI_5s9JZermG870w [retrieved 10 November 2022].

31 Ibid.

9. REWILDING SEX

1 No longer available on TikTok but on Twitter: @WAPLIQUOR, 14 April 2021, twitter.com/WAPLIQUOR/status/1382152306272071681?s=20&t=m XzH6Ph4xK-4r7E93UZbrg [retrieved 11 November 2022].

2 Tucker Higgins, 'Alex Jones' 5 most disturbing and ridiculous conspiracy theories', CNBC, 14 September 2014, www.cnbc.com/2018/09/14/alex-jones-5-most-disturbing-ridiculous-conspiracy-theories.html.

3 'Unnoticed sex reversal in amphibians due to artificial estrogen from pills', Science Daily, 4 April 2016, www.sciencedaily.com/releases/2016/04/160404090836. htm.

4 'Hormone disruptors linked to genital changes and sexual preference', Living on Earth, 7 January 2011, www.loe.org/shows/segments.html?programID=11-P13-00001&segmentID=7.

5   Katherine Dee, personal communication, 25 August 2022.

6   @ch1efqueef on Twitter, 15 July 2022, twitter.com/ch1efqueef/
     status/1547983552695832576?s=20&t=hMGnDndRW8VmmQAMV1DfLQ
     [retrieved 11 November 2022].

7   @mimzyselfhood on Twitter, 15 July 2022, twitter.com/mimzyselfhood/sta
     tus/1548002003627847681?s=20&t=SPgzT2DGbNaiIIHamfb-iA [retrieved
     11 November 2022].

8   @eigenrobot on Twitter, 29 June 2022, twitter.com/eigenrobot/status/154
     1942951617740803?s=20&t=SH9mZWu7Uq-92bIXSYWFfw [retrieved 11
     November 2022].

9   Anya Zoledziowski, '"Holistic healers" on TikTok want you to quit birth
     control', *Vice*, 22 July 2022, www.vice.com/en/article/xgyd5a/natural-birth-
     control-tiktok.

10   Julian, 'Why are young people having so little sex?'

11   'Watching porn can harm a male's ability to have sex in real life', Fight the New
     Drug, 7 August 2020, fightthenewdrug.org/porn-is-taking-away-mens-ability-
     to-have-actual-sex/.

12   Gigi Engle, 'Are you using a "death grip" during masturbation? It could be
     messing with your sex life', *Men's Health*, 4 April 2019, www.menshealth.com/
     sex-women/a27044367/death-grip-masturbation/.

13   Louise Perry, 'The sex recession: How our love lives are stunted by hyper-
     sexualisation', 5 May 2021.

14   Bridget Phetasy, 'I regret being a slut', Beyond Parody with Bridget Phetasy,
     17 August 2022, bridgetphetasy.substack.com/p/slut-regret.

15   Melinda Tankard Reist, 'Sex before kissing: How 15-year-old girls are
     dealing with porn-obsessed boys', Fight the New Drug, 21 October 2018,
     fightthenewdrug.org/sex-before-kissing-15-year-old-girls-dealing-with-boys/.

16   Debbie White, 'Teen suffers life-changing injury trying to imitate porn', *New
     York Post*, 16 January 2019, nypost.com/2019/01/16/teen-suffers-life-changing-
     injury-trying-to-imitate-porn/.

17   George Mair, 'Sex stats: Over two-thirds of men under 40 have slapped, choked,
     gagged or spat on partner during sex, BBC Scotland doc finds', *Scottish Sun*,
     23 March 2020, www.thescottishsun.co.uk/news/5415762/rough-sex-bbc-
     scotland-partner-men/.

18   Gigi Engle, 'Consent and BDSM: What you should know', *Teen Vogue*, 1 July
     2017, www.teenvogue.com/story/bdsm-consent.

19   Jean Hannah Edelstein, 'Dating after #MeToo: I've had a lot of sex out of
     politeness. How do I say no?', *Guardian*, 25 April 2018, www.theguardian.
     com/lifeandstyle/2018/apr/25/dating-after-metoo-ive-had-a-lot-of-sex-out-
     of-politeness-how-do-i-say-no.

20   Phetasy.

21   'How Wolves Change Rivers' [video], YouTube, uploaded by Sustainable
     Human, 13 February 2014, www.youtube.com/watch?v=ysa5OBhXz-Q&ab_
     channel=SustainableHuman [retrieved 11 November 2022].